ANTISOCIAL BEHAVIOUR IN STUDENTS

DETECTION AND MANAGEMENT

SPECIAL EDUCATION SERIES

ANTISOCIAL BEHAVIOUR IN STUDENTS

DETECTION AND MANAGEMENT

Dr. G. Lokanadha Reddy
Professor
Department of Education
Alagappa University
Karaikudi–630 003

Dr. V. Shyamala
Principal
Jay Hind Silver Jubilee
Matric Hr. Sec. School
Ayanavaram
Chennai–600 023

&

Dr. A. Kusuma
Reader
Dept. of Human Development
and Family Studies
Sri Padmavathi Mahila
Visvavidhyalayam
Tirupati–517 502

Dr. P. Santhakumari
P.G. Asst. in English
Govt. Hr. Sec. School
Chatrapatti–626 102

DISCOVERY PUBLISHING HOUSE
NEW DELHI-110002

First Published – 2005

Reprinted – 2025

ISBN: 978-81-7141-931-9

Antisocial Behaviour in Students
Detection and Management

Published by:
DISCOVERY PUBLISHING HOUSE PVT. LTD.
4383/4B, Ansari Road, Darya Ganj
New Delhi-110 002 (India)
Phone: +91-11-23279245; 23253475; 43596065
Mobile: +91 9811179893 / +91 9871656464
E-mail: discoverybooksindia@gmail.com
orderdphbooks@gmail.com
namitwasan9@gmail.com
web: www.discoverypublishinggroup.com

Printed at:
Infinity Imaging Systems
Delhi

FOREWORD

The book in your hands is written to enlighten the teachers, researchers and practitioners in the field of education in general, and special education in particular. The problem that all teachers face is how to cope with the students exhibiting antisocial behaviour. It is a fact that every school constitutes at least 5 to 15 per cent of the total student population with various types of antisocial behaviour like ADHD, ODD and CD or the co-morbidity of all the three.

The authors of this book seem to have set out to offer the intellectual scaffolding and practical strategies to the teachers of today and tomorrow so as to make them to be more effective while dealing with the students of antisocial behaviour. The authors also highlight the ways and means of early identification of antisocial behavioural tendencies along with need for proper parenting practices, positive peer group associations, neighbourhood motivational factors and community participation for the development of pro-social behaviours in children and adolescents.

The printed words of this book clearly reflect the competencies of the authors gained through their intensive teaching, research and counselling activities in the area of antisocial behaviour. The comprehensive interventional strategy expounded and used by the authors is the testimony to their field expertise. The use of such strategies to overcome antisocial behaviour in students is the need of the hour in any country around the world. In this sense, the topic of this book is of international perspective. I am sure, this book will be of immense use to all those who work with students exhibiting the antisocial behaviour.

Dr. P. Kanniappan
Vice Chancellor
Alagappa University
Karaikudi–630 003

PREFACE

A child, as an individual, as a member of the family, and as a part of society, affects and is affected by the environmental factors. Irrespective of the economic status of any country, antisocial behaviour is globally ubiquitous. The concept of antisocial behaviour is slowly gaining momentum in India too. In the Western world, particularly in USA and UK, a well-defined legal framework and remedial modalities are in vogue to combat antisocial behaviours.

The present book is an endeavour to bring to limelight antisocial behaviours prevalent among the student population. As antisocial behaviour is multidimensional in nature, any intervention programme must involve parents, peers, community and school. In this respect, it is wise to generate some understanding in the target population on various aspects of antisocial behaviour in students. As such, this book is a modest attempt to delineate the concept of antisocial behaviour, factors associated with antisocial behaviour, development of antisocial behaviour in children, identification and assessment, and prevention and intervention strategies.

To tackle the problem of antisocial behaviour at home, school and community levels, parents, teachers and community educators should be aware of the nature and characteristics of antisocial behaviour in students. It is a well-known fact that different individual and environmental factors contribute to antisocial behaviour in students. An awareness of such factors enables the parents and educators to develop right thinking patterns, use proper parenting practices, tone up positive peer group associations and prevent antisocial behavioural tendencies among students. The book presents a vivid picture about the course of development of antisocial behaviour from

ADHD through ODD to CD. It also spells out various measures available for assessing antisocial behaviours. The book is an innovative attempt in the development and use of intervention strategies to overcome antisocial behaviours in students mostly based on the authors' experiences with student community. In addition, the present book highlights the need for integrated, need-based, situation-oriented and individualistic programmes so as to instil pro-social behaviour in students. To achieve this goal, the intervention strategies must be oriented towards the child, parents, peers and neighbourhood / community.

Apart from our own experiences, this book is prepared with extensive readings of works done by varied professionals in different parts of the world. We feel that this book will be of immense value to the researchers, teachers and students at school, college and university levels. We also hope that it will serve the purpose to which it is intended and we welcome suggestions, if any, for improvement.

I express my sincere gratitude to the Ministry of Social Justice and Empowerment, Government of India, New Delhi, for providing publication grant to publish this book. Without the Ministry's financial assistance, I might have not brought out this publication successfully.

Finally, we thank M/S. Discovery Publishing House, New Delhi, for the great interest and promptness they have evinced in bringing out this book at an early date inspite of their many commitments in the publishing field.

—Authors

CONTENTS

1

CONCEPT OF ANTISOCIAL BEHAVIOUR

OBJECTIVES

This chapter deals with the concept of Antisocial behaviour. After reading this chapter, the reader should be able to:

(i) List out characteristics of students with Antisocial behavioural causes of Antisocial behaviour in students

(ii) Perceive the patterns of Antisocial behaviour

(iii) Discuss the theories of Antisocial behaviour, and

(iv) Explain the need to overcome Antisocial behaviour.

"We worry about what a child will become tomorrow.

Yet, we forget that he or she is someone today".

—Stacia Tausher

Children and adolescents face a plethora of stressful problems today, including family and relationship conflict, death of close family members or friends, and academic and social pressures. These have been found to contribute to an increased risk of various emotional-social-cognitive difficulties in adolescents, including, academic failure, social misbehaviour and interpersonal problems and depression (Matheny et al., 1993).

Indian society consists of many diverse socio-cultural and economic groups. Almost two-thirds of Indian children and adolescents are economically, socially and educationally disadvantaged in some way or the other (Dash & Hariharan, 1988; Shukla, 1994). The adolescent segment of India's population is on the rise and hence India, with more resource-limited families, is the ideal place to examine factors associated with adolescent behaviour (Carson et al., 1999; Nanda & Dash, 1996).

Antisocial behaviour of the young is not acceptable to the society and the delinquent is forbidden by law. It is a multifactor phenomenon caused by genetical, physiological, psychological and sociological factors that interact in different ways (Shanmugam, 1981). Some common behavioural problems exhibited by adolescent students include disobedience and even violence towards parents, school dropout, smoking, alcoholism and other drug use, petty crime, and various other manifestations of juvenile delinquency (Chaudhari & Choudhari, 1993; Shukla, 1994; Simhadri 1989).

'Kids will be kids' is a common phrase often invoked to account for the overt aggressiveness and bullying behaviour among children. Somehow, however, over the years, this quaint adage has lost its presumption of boisterous innocence and youthful exuberance in reference to the aggressive and antisocial behaviour of some of today's youth.

There is a growing perception in our society that aggressive and antisocial behaviour among children and youth has become more confrontative, violent, and common place. Youth violence is also seen as more likely to involve weapons and gangs, to be more destructive, more virulent, and to involve more females and children of younger ages than ever before. While there is a lack of hard evidence to support an actual increase in the prevalence and severity of youth violence, there is, nonetheless, a growing sense of urgency to address the many facets related to this complex social issue. As Bala (1994) has noted, "Although one can ask how much of this increase is due to heightened sensitivity to violence and an increase in reporting rates, it is apparent that the public and professionals are increasingly concerned about youth violence". Clearly, violence among children and youth is an issue that needs to be examined, understood, and ameliorated through effective, concerted, and sustained efforts.

Growing problems of discipline in schools, and school violence in particular, seem to many educators nowadays some sort of trans-national epidemic that moves and extend from country to country completely changing the landscape of our school system. For some years now, educators and researchers have been referring to these phenomena in quite different ways: school violence, discipline problems, conflicts, and antisocial behaviour. Each of them reflects a distinct approach to the whole issue, one that in turn stems from the different academic and professional disciplines dealing with the phenomena involved. Antisocial behaviour seems to be a pervasive phenomenon in our society, including schools; violence is versatile and multi-faceted, it takes many different forms and grasps public attention in very many different ways.

In recent years the number of children and youth who have taken a path to school failure, antisocial behaviour and violence has grown significantly. Children start along this path of destructive behaviour because they are exposed to family, neighbourhood, school and/or societal risk factors at a young age. These factors include poverty, harsh parenting, family transitions, unemployment, urbanisation and industrialisation and many more. Increasingly, children are also coming from homes where antisocial behaviour is accepted. These youth at school are with the belief that violence is the solution to conflict. They are convinced that the actions of others are biased against them personally and this distorts their ability to correctly interpret any behaviour. As a defence, they tend to act aggressively, a behaviour called active aggression, in situations where they feel threatened.

Rather than dealing with the situation proactively, our society is becoming more tolerant and adjusting lifestyles to compensate for violent behaviour. We must change our direction.

The rising incidence of youth violence cannot be controlled by punishment it is essential that we take a personal and political stand that denounces all forms of violence. We must, as a society, re-examine our beliefs and reprioritise our values, turning away from aggression, competition and dominance, towards empathy, mutuality, cooperation and interdependence. This will require a reinvestment of resources into social programmes that strengthen families, reduce substance abuse, eliminate poverty and increase a spirit of community belonging in order to decrease social alienation.

CONCEPT AND MEANING OF ANTISOCIAL BEHAVIOUR

Of even more concern is the clear failure of our society to effectively cope with these problems. Instead of offering prevention, early intervention and treatment, we have built more prisons and increasingly enacted laws that treat youth as adult criminals. These developments are more frustrating in light of the existence of well-proven methods of identifying young children who are at high risk for violent and destructive behaviours as teenagers or adults.

In fact, we now know that certain specific antisocial behaviour patterns and high levels of aggression exhibited in preschool and kindergarten are not just correlated, but are highly predictive, of violent, delinquent and criminal behaviours in middle school, later adolescence and adulthood (Fagan, 1996; Walker et al., 1996).

Antisocial behaviour amongst young people has increasingly become a matter of public concern (HMIC, 1997, 1999; Home Office, 2002a, 2003). There can be no doubt of the detrimental effect that antisocial behaviour has on the quality of life of those who experience it (Budd & Sims, 2001). Antisocial behaviour may also contribute to neighbourhood decline (Wilson & Kelling, 1982) and is associated with offending (Farrington, 1996).

Persons with antisocial behaviour have an inability to control anger and suffer from mood swings. Acts of violence and abuse between family members within a household can also be antisocial behaviour that has consequences that affect others. The types of acts that can be termed as antisocial are difficult to list because of cultural variations in different countries. The socio-economic conditions also affect the definition of antisocial behaviour. Antisocial behaviour can range from inconsiderate parking of vehicles to extreme acts of harassment and violence. Often seemingly trivial things can cause major problems. Graffiti, broken windows, dumped rubbish, people forced from their homes and empty properties that are difficult to let are all results of antisocial behaviour.

In our society, the types of acts that can be considered as antisocial (Chauhan, 1983) are acquisitive tendency, forgery and aggression. The highest percentage of children has the immediate aim of gratifying acquisitive tendency. Stealing is the most common act that starts from family and if not detected at the initial stage and dealt with adequately is generalized to other situations in neighbourhood, school and shops, etc. Stealing releases tension and particularly sexual tension, and gratifies the needs of antisocial. Generally, stealing is done in adolescence by groups that develop cohesion. Lying also helps in adjustment to the social groups. Forgery is another act that is committed by students. They can forge the signature of their parents on report cards and cheques and draw money from the bank.

Aggression is found in great percentage among the adolescents. It gives relief to the antisocial. Aggression may be direct or indirect against the animate or inanimate objects of the environment. Antisocial behaviour can be broadly broken into two components: *the presence of antisocial behaviour*, i.e. angry, aggressive, or disobedience, and the *absence of prosocial behaviour*, i.e., communicative, affirming, or cooperative (Gale Research, 1998).

There is some type of antisocial behaviour that is endemic to school life, which emerges as part of school culture and has to do with the configuration of interpersonal relations therein. This violence affects every student, even those who are apparently just spectators because it is part of the context and part of the content of the socialization process in schools. In other words, it is part of what is learned by students at school.

Following categorization of violent and antisocial phenomena (Moreno, 1998a & 1998b; Moreno y Torrego, 1999a, 1999b), is quite useful, to review the current situation: Disruptive behaviour in classrooms, Discipline problems (interpersonal conflicts, specially teacher-student), Bullying, Vandalism, Physical violence, Sexual harassment and abuse, Absenteeism and drop-out and Fraud (cheating, plagiarism and influence peddling). Four of these categories- -discipline problems, vandalism, physical violence and absenteeism—share a very high public visibility, inside and outside of the school. Thus, it is no surprise that they are taken as 'everything which is there' in terms of school violence; parents, administrators, policy-makers and public opinion in general are worried primarily about these issues (Mooij & Funk, 1997).

Adolescence is a crucial time for the emergence of antisocial and criminal behaviour that, for some, persists into adulthood; at considerable cost to individuals, families and the wider community. Much research has been devoted to the identification of risk factors associated with the occurrence of criminal and antisocial behaviour, with the aim of preventing such problems. However, much of the research has been cross-sectional or covered restricted age spans, conducted in other countries, employed disadvantaged samples, and focused on males. And it's adolescents, particularly boys, who commit higher rates of crime than any other age group (Federal Bureau of Investigation, 1989). Even more disturbing is the fact that young children are increasingly involved in deadlier crime. There has been a significant increase in juvenile crime in the most serious categories: murder, rape, robbery and aggravated assault. Between 1988 and 1992, juvenile arrests for violent crime increased nearly 50% (Snyder & Sickmund, 1995), and this certainly does not bode well for the future.

DEFINITIONS OF ANTISOCIAL BEHAVIOUR

A useful starting point is to look at the changing meaning of the word 'antisocial'. According to Stuart Waiton (2004), the first use of the word was in 1802 to denounce the 'rebellious, antisocial and blasphemous books' published during the French

Revolution.' Antisocial—opposed to the principles on which society is constituted' was a political and moral term used by conservatives to denounce those perceived to be a threat to society. In 1989, the dictionary definition of the word was changed. While maintaining the above meaning there was added 'causing annoyance and disapproval in others: children's antisocial behaviour'.

Antisocial behaviour is a subjective relative concept, which can vary over time and location. The term antisocial behaviour has grown in its use and meaning over time and has been constructed as a significant social problem since the early 1990's. The use of the term antisocial behaviour has expanded throughout the 1990's and into the 21st century. The term antisocial, as well as having the meaning 'opposed to sociality'—which has not changed over time—also has another meaning. 'Antisocial'—'Opposed to the principles on which society is constituted' (Oxford English Dictionary, 1885). In the New Oxford English Dictionary (1989) the definition of antisocial has changed to, 'Contrary to the laws and customs of society: causing annoyance and disapproval in others: children's antisocial behaviour.'

The changing definition of the word antisocial at one level simply tells us how a word is used differently. However the change also suggests changes to societies' outlook, concerns and preoccupations. That children are now used as significant to the term antisocial gives us a sense of the concern about the behaviour of young people.

Today it is the misbehaviour of children that is so defined. In this respect the term is now less about 'social' norms and values and very little to do with politics and morals but much more to do with the annoyance caused by the individual behaviour of one person to another. The term therefore has less of a social and more of an individual meaning, while also, adding a new focus upon the feelings of those suffering from the antisocial act—i.e. the causing of annoyance and disapproval in others.

To elaborate on the above, the definition of antisocial as, 'Contrary to the laws and customs of society; causing annoyance and disapproval in others: children's antisocial behaviour', does not mean that there are now two meanings presented here for the word antisocial, but rather the semicolon links the original meaning of contrary to the laws and customs of society with the acts that cause disapproval in others. This is then directly linked to the example of children. In other words, the word antisocial is equating the mischievous behaviour of children with a threat, challenge or opposition to the laws and customs of society. There is thus a certain significance being given to those who are deemed to act in an antisocial manner i.e. in a manner against society.

The growing use of the term antisocial behaviour suggests a few things. Firstly the age range within the discussion of juveniles has been lost and antisocial behaviour attributed to teenagers no longer has a shelf life that the term juvenile antisocial behaviour suggested. Therefore antisocial acts can be attributed to children, teenagers and adults—with no distinction made in the term used. Here, we see both the infantalisation of adult behaviour (which is now equated through the use of the term antisocial behaviour with that of children), and the criminalisation of children whose actions can now be linked through the same term to actions of adults. The distinction between criminal and non-criminal acts is also lost in the use of the term antisocial. With violent crime, petty crime, nuisance, noise, tantrums, begging, road rage etc. all being described as a package through the use of the term antisocial. These examples, of the use of the term antisocial behaviour, as a whole imply a possible continuum of a type of behaviour both in time and in the nature of the offence.

A juvenile delinquent was defined in a certain age bracket that suggests that the juvenile would perhaps grow up and out of his/her antisocial behaviour, thus distinguishing the teenager from the child and adult. The new use of the term antisocial behaviour suggests a possible continuum of the behaviour of juvenile delinquents with that of children and adults. It also brings together within the one term a range of types of behaviour from the most petty and childish acts (once described perhaps as mischievous) to the more serious violent and or criminal acts. At the same time the very use of the term 'antisocial' behaviour links the annoying acts of individuals—often adolescents and children—with a challenge, threat or disruption to society—the social.

Mental Health clinicians, criminologists and personality psychologists conceptualise and measure antisocial behaviour somewhat differently. Mental health clinicians interested in pathological behaviour conceptualise antisocial behaviour as a mental disorder. As a result, their definitions require that the behaviour is seriously harmful to others, involves a number of different types of antisocial acts, or has persisted over a long time period. Criminologists conceptualise antisocial behaviour as behaviour that is against law. Personality psychologists conceptualise antisocial traits in terms of attitudes, beliefs, interests and preferences that indicate an inclination to take advantage of or harm others, or a willingness to break the law. As a result, their definitions do not require that any antisocial act has occurred. All three fields share in common the underlying assumption that antisocial behaviour is the behaviour that violates the rights and safety of others.

Defining behaviour as antisocial depends on a number of factors including context, location, community tolerance and quality of life expectations (Nixon et al., 2003). Quite often in practice there is no single definition of antisocial behaviour at all. It is also very common for a list of behaviours that are considered to be antisocial to be presented (Moore & Lawrence, 2000). Bland and Read (2000) noted that police services rarely have a specific definition and officers generally took a 'common sense' view of what constituted antisocial behaviour, drawing on day-to-day operational experiences.

Similarly a review of definitions used in 1998 Community Safety Strategies showed that Crime and Disorder Reduction Partnerships rarely had a formal definition: it being more common to cite examples of the types of behaviour that might be construed as antisocial (Bullock & Loxley, 1999). Thus, in practice, actions defined as antisocial cover a broad spectrum of behaviours (Crime Reduction Toolkit, 2000) such as Using and selling drugs, Unkempt gardens (e.g. those which attract dumping of goods, creating 'eyesores'), Alcohol and solvent abuse, Prostitution, Verbal abuse, Uncontrolled pets and animals, Intimidating gatherings of young people in public places, Harassment (including racist and homophobic incidents), Damage to property (including graffiti and vandalism), Intimidation, Nuisance from vehicles (including parking and abandonment), Nuisance from business use, Rubbish dumping and misuse of communal areas, Riding/cycling on footpaths, Aggressive begging, Dropping litter, Racial harassment, Noisy parties/neighbours, Substance misuse and Public drunkenness.

The Microsoft Encarta Reference Library (2002) defines Behaviour as 'the way in which a person, organism or group responds to a certain set of conditions'. Social behaviour confirms to the morals, standards or community-held values of society. Behaviour, which results in social disapproval, is referred to as antisocial because it is harmful to maintaining social order. Antisocial connotes actions that harm specific individuals or social groups, either when such harm is intended or when the harm is foreseen but judged irrelevant (Loeber, 1985).

Antisocial behaviour involves ".... Recurring violations of socially prescribed patterns of behaviour" such as aggression, hostility, defiance, and destructiveness (Walker, Colvin, & Ramsey, 1995), vandalism, rule infractions, defiance of adult authority, and violation of the social norms and mores of society (Simcha-Fagen et al., 1975). Antisocial behaviour is the behaviour that causes or is likely to cause harassment, alarm or distress to one or more persons.

Antisocial behaviours reflect a failure of the individual to conform his or her behaviour to the expectations of some authority figure, to societal norms, or to respecting the rights of other people. The behaviours can range from mild conflict with authority figures, through major violation of societal norms, to serious violations of the rights of others (Frick, 1998).

Antisocial behaviour refers to any acts that are violations of social rules including against people or property e.g. cheating, stealing, truanting, and fighting (Rutter, Giller, & Hagell, 1998). As far as this book is concerned, *Antisocial behaviour refers to the behaviour exhibited by troublesome children. Attention deficit hyperactivity disorder (ADHD), Oppositional defiant disorder (ODD), and Conduct disorder (CD) are the characteristic behaviours of troublesome children.* Troublesome behaviours are more disturbing to others than to themselves. They hamper individual development as well as the development of others.

BEHAVIOURS EXHIBITED BY TROUBLESOME CHILDREN

There is much heterogeneity in antisocial behaviour (Rutter, Giller, & Hagell, 1998). Children with antisocial behaviour can vary widely in terms of the specific symptoms as well as the associated features (e.g., academic deficiencies, parent dysfunctions). These group around inborn traits and characteristics related to personality, temperament, and cognitive ability, community and social characteristics and school-related issues.

Problems such as Attention Deficit Hyperactivity Disorder, impulsivity and restlessness, depression, attachment disorder, and exposure to traumatic or stressful life events affect the ways children interact with peers, teachers, parents, and others. Biologically related conditions, including many mental disorders may lead to the development of serious social and Behaviour problems (Farrington, 1989; Klinteberg et al., 1993; Loeber, 1990,1996; Thornberry, 1998; Williams et al., 1997). These problems often manifest themselves in sensation seeking activities and low harm-avoidance behaviours, which are linked to delinquency (Farrington, 1989). Other mental health problems, defined by specific behavioural indicators, including oppositional and defiant disorder and conduct disorder, often correlate highly with continued antisocial behaviour (Loeber & Hay, 1996).

As it is, there is no specific survey conducted in India to identify Antisocial behaviour, but in any school, one can find children with antisocial behaviours of varied types (Attention Deficit Hyperactivity Disorder, Oppositional Defiant Disorder and Conduct Disorder).

Attention Deficit Hyperactivity Disorder

Prior to entering the school system, some children are unable to concentrate and stay on track. They are impulsive and hyperactive. Most parents cope up with the symptoms, believing that the child is just more active than others. These symptoms, however, come to the forefront in the classroom and often lead to referral to a professional. Attention deficit hyperactivity disorder is a complex condition, which, in the most serious cases, leaves personal, academic and social scars well into adulthood. Cognitive impairments cause serious academic problems—low reading scores, language impairment, and poor grades. If unaddressed, these impairments increase the risk of school failure, amplifying any innate risks for developing antisocial or delinquent behaviour (Garnett, 1994; Gottfredson, 1987; Hawkins, 1995; Keilitz & Dunivant, 1986; Thornberry, 1994). This means that some children with ADHD and reading disabilities may also be predisposed to aggression (Cornwall & Bauden, 1992; Dykman, Ackerman, & Raney, 1993). These traits may be physiologically and biologically based and therefore resistant to change. Young children may exhibit hostility towards authority, and be diagnosed as oppositional defiant disorder. Older children may engage in violent behaviours, and be diagnosed as conduct disorders. A small percentage of children with antisocial behaviour grow up to become adults with antisocial personality disorder, and a greater proportion suffer from the social, academic, and occupational failures resulting from their antisocial behaviour.

Incidence

ADHD, characterised by inattention, impulsivity, and hyperactivity, is among the most common disorders of childhood, affecting between 4% and 6% of the school-age population. Remarkably, ADHD is seven times more common in boys than girls (Garfinkel & Wener, 1989). Girls with ADHD seldom develop antoisocial and violent behaviour (Herrrero, Hechtman,

& Weiss, 1994). Mantzicopoulos and Morrison (1994) also noted that as boys progressed from kindergarten to second grade, they were perceived as more defiant, inattentive, and hyperactive than girls. Boys appear more vulnerable than girls to several neuro-developmental disorders such as mental retardation, autism, learning disabilities, and ADHD (American Psychiatric Association, 1987). Cognitively, girls appear to have greater skills in language development (Huttenlocher et al., 1991), and greater ability to maintain motivation in the face of disruption (Gold, Crombie, & Noble, 1987).

Causes

ADHD is primarily considered to be a genetic disorder. There is strong evidence that children with this disorder are born with a gene which makes them more likely to develop ADHD. Thus there is usually a history that some members of the family have also suffered from the disorder. A linkage between ADHD and a specific genetic abnormality has been found (Hauser et al., 1993). According to them, the genetic abnormality results in generalised resistance to thyroid hormone, and the presence of this resistance is strongly associated with the existence of ADHD. Thus, this study implies that routine evaluation of children with ADHD should include an assessment of thyroid function. A chemical called Dopamine is involved in ADHD. Researchers think that changes in the genes that make the chemicals that transport Dopamine and bind it in the brain may be what is inherited (Cook, 1999).

The genetic influence is the strongest in the case of hyperactivity, whether considered as a continuously distributed dimension or as a disorder applying only to a small proportion of the population (Goodman & Stevenson 1989; Levy et al., 1997; Sherman, Iacono, & McGue, 1997). It is apparent that the genetic liability to hyperactivity overlaps with that for antisocial behaviour when the two are associated (Silberg et al., 1996a, 1996b). By sharp contrast, the genetic component is very weak, and environmental influences are preponderant, in the case of antisocial behaviour which is unassociated with hyperactivity or problems in peer relationships and which is reported only by youths themselves (Eaves et al., 1977) and not associated with social behavioural malfunction that is evident to parents (Silberg et al., 1996a). It has been suggested that impulsivity, inattention, and overactivity in children with ADHD is due to impairment of high level cognitive functions. These functions include the ability to initiate, inhibit, and alter actions according to circumstances. Children with pervasive ADHD symptoms (both in school and home) had greater deficits than those who had symptoms only in school (Schachar et al., 1995).

The study by Sherman, William and McGue (1997) on identical and fraternal twins suggested the presence of two genetically determined subtypes of ADHD identified in DSM III and DSM III-R: predominantly inattentive and (2) predominantly hyperactive-impulsive. ADHD should be viewed on a continuum rather than as a disorder which is diagnosed by the presence of a certain number of symptoms. Impulsivity, inattention, and hyperactivity are present in all people (Levy et al., 1997). However, when the manifestation of these traits becomes extreme and deviate from the acceptable norm, intervention is required.

Very low birth weight or at times, even an unduly short gestation can be associated with brain damage leading to mental retardation (Casaer et al.,1991). Often, obstetric damage is relevant to hyperactive or impulsive behaviour (Neligan et al., 1976; Nichols & Chen, 1981; Taylor et al., 1991) or with violent crime (Lewis et al., 1979; Raine et al., 1994,1996,1997).

Babies exposed in the womb to high levels of alcohol show increased levels of problems, including inattention and hyperactivity (Steissguth, 1993; Steissguth et al., 1984). Familial and psychosocial risk factors for ADHD were examined (Biederman et al., 1992). Participants were 140 children who suffered from ADHD, 120 children without ADHD and close biological controls of both groups. Relatives of ADHD children had a higher risk for ADHD, other antisocial disorders, major depressive and anxiety disorders, and substance dependence than relatives of normal controls.

Alcoholism in parents is also associated with an increased risk of ADHD. If a parent has alcoholism, their child is about twice ask likely to have ADHD. If both parents have alcoholism, the risk is three times as high. It is unclear whether this is from being related to an alcoholic parent or from living with them (Kuperman et al., 1999).

Characteristics

The major characteristics of ADHD include

(i) being easily distracted by irrelevant stimuli

(ii) appearing not to listen to others

(iii) difficulty maintaining prolonged concentration on a task, especially if it is boring and repetitive

(iv) fidgeting frequently

(v) having difficulty remaining seated

(vi) talking excessively

(vii) frequently interrupting others

(viii) answering questions before they have been completed, and

(ix) engaging in dangerous activities without considering their potential consequences.

To determine the specificity of the symptoms of inattention, impulsivity, and hyperactivity to the diagnosis of ADHD, 102 children between 6.5 and 13 years of age were studied (Halperin et al.,1992). Three groups were compared: 31 children with ADHD, 53 children with disorders other than ADHD. And 18 children with no disorder (control group). Performance tests and activity level measures were used to measure inattention, impulsivity and hyperactivity levels. The results showed that both ADHD and non-ADHD children were more inattentive than normal controls. There was no difference in inattention between ADHD and non-ADHD children. ADHD children were more impulsive than the normal controls.

They were not more impulsive than non-ADHD patients. ADHD students were more active than both the non-ADHD children and the normal controls. There was no difference in the activity level of non-ADHD patients and normal controls. fhe findings indicate that inattention is not a symptom that is unique to ADHD. Rather, hyperactivity is the symptom by which ADHD is uniquely characterised.

ADHD plays a main role as children with (or showing signs of) ADHD exhibit problems 'fitting in'. This is possibly due to the fact that with less attention combined with hyperactivity leads to greater chances of 'wandering off' or 'tuning out' neccesary information. According to Children with ADHD have great difficulties discontinuing unwanted or inappropriate behaviours, making them a candidate for rejection. They are also more prone to aggressive action as an outlet for frustration Matthys et al., 1998).

Clark, Prior, and Kinsella (2000) administered two neuropsychological measures of executive functions—Six Elements Tests (SET) and also Hayling Sentence Completion Test (HSCT) to 110 adolescents, aged 12-15 years. Participants comprised of four groups: ADHD only (n = 35), ADHD and ODD/ CD (n = 38), ODD/CD only (n = 11), and a normal community control group (n = 26). Results indicated that adolescents with ADHD performed significantly worse on both the SET and HSCT than those without ADHD, whether or not they also had ODD/ CD.

The adolescents with ADHD and with co-morbid ADHD and ODD/CD were significantly more impaired in their ability to generate strategies and to monitor their ongoing behaviour compared with age-matched controls and adolescents with ODD/ CD only. It is argued that among adolescents with clinically significant levels cf externalising behaviour problems, executive function deficits are specific to those with ADHD.

Course

Many ADHD children develop violent behaviour. The study by Satterfield, Hoppe and Schell (1982) showed that 45% were convicted of at least one serious offence in adolescence (58% of lower class, 36% of middle class and 52% of upper class). 45% were convicted of at least one serious offence in adolescence

(58% of lower class, 36% of middle class and 52% of upper class). Around 66% of the children with ADHD were found to continue to have symptoms of the disorder in adulthood and 23% developed antisocial personality disorder (Weiss et al., 1985). Children with attention deficit hyperactivity disorder (ADHD) are at higher risk of developing antisocial behaviour or substance abuse as adults. Children with ADHD are prone to develop Oppositional defiance disorder. 20% of children had both disorders (Biederman et al., 1991). A substantial literature validates a relationship between ADHD and increased risk for subsequent involvement in antisocial behaviour (Biederman et al., 1996; Hechtman, 1996; MacDonald & Achenbach, 1996; Shamsie et al.,1999; Taylor et al., 1996). Although behaviours in ADHD children show signs of normalization (Fischer, Barkley, Fletcher & Smallish, 1993), they continue to have difficulties right through to adulthood in behavioural, social and emotional aspects. It is possible that these difficulties pertain to their peer status and lack of social skills due to being stably rejected from an early age. Of all the behavioural features that predispose to antisocial behaviour, hyperactivity or inattention has the most robust association (Hinshaw, 1987; Hinshaw et al., 1993).

The Cambridge study of inner London boys (Farrington, 1992; Farrington et al., 1990b), the Christchurch longitudinal study (Fergusson, Horwood, & Lloyd, 1991; Fergusson et al., 1993), the Pittsbrgh study (Loeber et al., 1993), Magnusson's Swedish longitudinal study (Magnusson et al., 1993), the Dunedin study (McGee et al., 1984; Moffit, 1990b), Taylor's follow-up of intensively studied subgroups from his epidemiological sample (Taylor et al., 1996), and long-term follow-ups of clinical samples (Satterfield & Schell, 1997) all document the association.

Lynam (1996) has argued that this combined pattern of hyperactivity and antisocial behaviour constitutes the early manifestations of psychopathy. The 15 years follow-up study of a group of hyperactive children by Herrero et al. (1994) suggested that children with ADHD who behave aggressively are more likely to become antisocial adults and therefore require more intensive follow-up. ADHD predicted cigarette-smoking in mid-adolescence (19% of children with ADHD were smokers compared to 10% of children without ADHD) and cigarette smoking in children with ADHD was often a first step towards substance abuse (Milberger et al., 1997).

Horner and Scheibe (1997) found that children with ADHD reported lower self-esteem than children without ADHD and felt better about themselves with drug use. Recent epidemiological studies suggest that both social anxiety and attention deficit hyperactivity disorder (ADHD) in childhood might predict levels of delinquent behaviour in adolescence. Another study (Pine et al., 2000) prospectively examined the influence of social phobia and ADHD symptom scale scores on the correlation in conduct disorder symptom scale scores over time. An epidemiologically selected sample of 776 young people living in Upstate New York received DSM-based psychiatric assessments in 1983, 1985, and 1992 using structured interviews. Correlations among conduct disorder scales over time were examined as a function of social phobia and ADHD ratings. Individuals with low scores on social phobia scales or high scores on ADHD scales exhibited the highest correlation in conduct disorder symptom scales over time.

There was also a suggestion that low scores on social phobia scales predicted later risk for conduct disorder. Low scores on social phobia symptom scales or high scores on ADHD scales predict stronger across-time correlations in conduct disorder symptom scales. Various cognitive or biological factors might account for these moderating effects on conduct problems.

Hyperactivity, limited attention span, restlessness, risk-taking, poor social skills and certain beliefs and attitudes (e.g., the necessity of retaliation), appear to favour the development of delinquent behaviour. In addition, students with certain disabilities (e.g., emotional disturbance, attention deficit-hyperactivity disorders, specific learning disabilities) are more likely to display antisocial behaviour, suggesting that these conditions may be risk factors for later aggressive and violent actions (Leone et al., 2000).

Oppositional Defiant Disorder

Oppositional defiant disorder is a pattern of disobedient, hostile, and defiant behaviour towards authority figures. The pattern must persist for at least six months and must go beyond the bounds of normal childhood misbehaviour. This disorder is defined in terms of socially disapproved behaviours that do not involve illegal activities as such (e.g., 'deliberately annoys people', or 'is often angry or resentful').

Incidence

One third of all children, with any disorder, are diagnosed to be having Oppositional defiance disorder. Estimates suggest that 2%-16% of children and teens have ODD. It is one of the most common disorders of children in the preadolescent age group. It typically begins by age 8. In younger children, ODD is more common in boys than in girls (Rey, 1993). In older children, there is very little gender difference in rates.

A rate of 29 per thousand in boys and 24 per thousand in girls was found in the Virginia Twin study of Adolescent Behaviour and Development (VTSABD) sample of 1,412 twin pairs aged 8 to 16 (Simonoff et al., 1997). There was however, a difference in frequency in boys and girls in the age trend. The order increased in frequency in boys but not in girls, so that ODD was more frequent in the younger girls (as compared with boys) but more frequent in the older boys (as compared with girls).

Only a small gender difference was found for ODD in (American) Great Smoky Mountains study using the same diagnostic instrument (Costello et al., 1996). Their sex ratio was 1.4 (i.e., 1.4:1). The findings are in good agreement with the self-report data and also with other findings with respect to gender differences in patterns of aggression. It may be concluded that there is very little difference between boys and girls in the frequency with which they show oppositional, defiant, and spiteful behaviour.

Causes

The cause of this disorder is unknown. Theories suggest that it may be related to a child's temperament and the family's reaction to that temperament; a genetic predisposition; brain chemical imbalances; or neurological disorders.

Most children by the age of 4-6, learn to comply, to respect, and to co-operate. At times, there may be problems in the brain that cause ODD. Defects in or injuries to certain areas of the brain can lead to serious behavioural problems in children. It may also be caused by a chemical imbalance in the brain. If a child comes to a clinic and is diagnosed with ADHD, about 30-40% of the time the child will also have ODD (Kuhne et al., 1997). In addition, ODD has been linked to abnormal amounts of special chemicals in the brain called neurotransmitters. Neurotransmitters help nerve cells in the brain communicate with each other. If these chemicals are out of balance or not working properly, messages may not make it through the brain correctly, leading to symptoms of ODD, and other mental illnesses. Further, many children and teens with ODD also have other mental illnesses, such as ADHD, learning disorders, depression or an anxiety disorder, which may contribute to their behaviour problems.

However, some children do not become socialized and develop the disorder due to reasons such as absence of a caring adult, inconsistent parental discipline practices, ignorance of correct use reward and punishment techniques, uncared ADHD in children, parental psychopathy such as anxiety, depression, and medical disorders (Shamsie, 1999).

If a parent is alcoholic and has been in trouble with the law, their children are almost three times likely to have ODD. That is, 18% of children will have ODD if the parents are alcoholic and the father has been in trouble with the law (Kuperman et al., 1999). Many children and teens with ODD have close family members with mental illnesses, including mood disorders, anxiety disorders and personality disorders. This suggests that a vulnerability to develop ODD may be inherited.

Characteristics

It's not unusual for children—especially those in their "terrible twos" and early teens—to defy authority every now and then. They may express their defiance by arguing, disobeying or talking back to their parents, teachers or other adults. When this behaviour lasts longer than six months and is excessive compared to what is usual for the child's age, it may mean that the child has a type of behaviour disorder called oppositional defiant disorder (ODD). They are commonly described as being hostile, negative, defiant, oppositional, pessimistic, aggressive, argumentative, angry, resentful, frustrated, accusatory, unreasonable, blaming, spiteful, vindictive, bad temper, or foul-mouthed.

The criteria for ODD are: A pattern of negativistic, hostile, and defiant Behaviour lasting at least six months during which four or more of the following are present:

(i) Often loses temper

(ii) often argues with adults

(iii) often actively defies or refuses to comply with adults' requests or rules

(iv) often deliberately annoys people, and

(v) often blames others for his or her mistakes or misbehaviour.

Based on DSM-IV, students with ODD are characterised by throwing repeated temper tantrums, excessively arguing with adults, actively refusing to comply with requests and rules, deliberately trying to annoy or upset others, or being easily annoyed by others, blaming others for your mistakes, having frequent outbursts of anger and resentment, being spiteful and seeking revenge, swearing or using obscene language and saying mean and hateful things when upset. In addition, many children with ODD are moody, easily frustrated and have a low self-esteem. They also may abuse drugs and alcohol.

Oppositional defiant disorder is a persistent pattern (lasting for at least six months) of negativistic, hostile, disobedient, and defiant behaviour in a child or teen without serious violation of the basic rights of others. This disorder is characterized by two different sets of problems. These are aggressiveness and a tendency to purposefully bother and irritate others.

Children and adolescents with ADHD alone do things without thinking, but not those with ODD. An ADHD child may impulsively push someone too hard on a swing and knock the child down on the ground. She would likely be sorry she did this afterward. A child with ODD plus ADHD might push the kid out of the swing and say she didn't do it.

Children and adolescents with ODD produce strong feelings in people. They try to get a reaction out of people, and they are often successful. Common ones are: inciting spouses to fight with each other and not focus on the child, making outsiders believe that all the fault lies with the parents, making certain susceptible people believe that they can "save" the child by doing everything the child wants, setting parents against grandparents, setting teachers against parents, and inciting the parents to abuse the child.

ODD is characterized by aggressiveness, but not impulsiveness. In ODD people annoy others purposefully, while it is usually not so purposeful in ADHD. ODD signs and symptoms are much more difficult to live with than ADHD. Children with ODD can sit still. Children and adolescents with ADHD alone do things without thinking, but not necessarily oppositional things. In comparison to ADHD alone, children and adolescents with ODD plus ADHD or just ODD are much more difficult to be with. The destructiveness and disagreeableness are purposeful. Lying becomes a way of life, and getting a reaction out of others is the chief hobby. Perhaps hardest of all to bear, they rarely are truly sorry and often believe nothing is their fault. An ADHD child may impulsively push someone too hard on a swing and knock the child down on the ground. She would likely be sorry she did this afterward. A child with ODD plus ADHD might push the kid out of the swing and say she didn't do it.

Course

The oppositional defiance disorder becomes serious with age. As a child grows in size, and strength, aggressive behaviour has more serious consequences. As they grow older, many of these children develop bchaviours which are the symptoms of conduct behaviour. These behaviours include hitting, stealing and destruction of property. Recent research suggests that all things being equal, girls with ODD plus ADHD have significantly worse social problems than boys with ODD plus ADHD (Carlson et al., 1997). Probably, 15-20% will have problems with their mood and even more are anxious (Kuhne et al, 1997). ODD may turn into something else. About 5-10 % of preschoolers with ODD will eventually end up with ADHD and no signs of ODD at all (Lavigne et al., 2001). By the time these children are in the end of elementary school, about 25% will have mood or anxiety problems which are disabling (Speltz et al., 1999). Therefore, oppositional defiant disordered children grow up to become conduct disordered youth (Shamsie, 1999). That means that it is very important to watch for signs of mood disorder and anxiety as children with ODD grow older.

Conduct Disorder

Conduct Disorder is one of the most common disorders in children and adolescents between the ages of four and sixteen. DSM-III-R identifies it as "behaviour that is socially disruptive and is often more distressing to others than to the people with the disorders". It is distinguished by a persistent pattern of behaviour in which the basic rights of others and major age-appropriate societal norms are violated. Children with this disorder have great difficulty following rules and behaving in a socially acceptable way. They are often viewed by other children, teachers, and parents as 'bad' or delinquent, rather than mentally ill. They are 'troublesome' children, more often than 'troubled" children.

Incidence

Research has shown that CD is more common among boys than among girls (Harvards Medical School, 1989; Kazdin,

1987). The study of Conduct Disorder (CD) has primarily been limited to boys. The lack of research resulted from a premise that CD in girls was rare. However CD in girls is a relatively common psychiatric diagnosis, and appears to be associated with several serious outcomes, such as Antisocial Personality Disorder and early pregnancy. Understanding gender differences in the course and severity of CD may lead to important information about etiology.

Keenan, Loeber and Green (1999) reviewed empirical studies on precursors, developmental course, risk factors and treatment for CD in girls, while highlighting similarities and differences between girls and boys. Generally, CD symptoms in girls are stable. Precursors to CD in girls probably include Oppositional Defiant Disorder and temperamental factors, but also may include certain negative cognitions. What distinguishes CD in girls is the high risk they have to develop comorbid conditions, especially internalising disorders. Risk factors for CD in girls partly overlap with those known for boys, but some factors appear to be highly salient for girls.

Causes

Children of today are future generations of any nation. Their growth would determine tomorrow's prospect. Children who get into problems at an early stage of life and adapt deviant means to achieve certain aspirations or goals, graduate into adult criminality in later years. The factors that predispose children and adolescents to conduct disorder have been studied extensively in the context of clinical referrals and adjudicated delinquents (Henggler, 1989; Patterson, Reid, & Dishion, 1992).

Neurological deficits and difficulties early in life place a youth at risk for subsequent conduct problems and delinquency (Moffit, 1993a, 1993b). Age of onset, number of different types of antisocial behaviours, and number of situations in which the antisocial behaviours are eveident (e.g., at home, school, the community) are relevant as well (Loeber, 1990). Children with earlier onset and greater diversity of problems are at great risk.

It is also evident that the association between either IQ or reading difficulties and conduct disturbance or antisocial behaviour largely applies to early onset varieties and not to those beginning in adolescence (Robins & Hill 1966; Rutter 1979; Werner & Smith, 1977). Academic deficiencies and lower IQ often predict subsequent conduct disorder (Farrington, 1991; Moffit, 1993a). Conduct disorder predicts subsequent failure at school and lower level of educational attainment (Bachman et al., 1978).

Conduct disorder and criminality in offspring are more likely when the biological relative has shown these behaviours (Cadoret, 1978). The influencing environmental factors are: adverse conditions in the home (e.g. marital discord, psychiatric dysfunction), exposure to discontinuous mothering before being placed in the final adoptive setting, and the age at which the child has been adopted.

The dual contribution of genetic and environmental influences can be seen in studies showing that conduct disorder in both the biological and the adoptive parent increases the risk of conduct disorder in the child (Brennan, Mednick, & Kandel, 1991), although the impact of the biological parent is much greater. Yet, the risk is greatly increased when both genetic and environmental influences are present (Cadoret, Cain, & Crowe, 1983).

Offord et al. (1988) found that conduct disordered children tended to be male and the eldest sibling. Large families (with four or more siblings) and family dysfunction (misunderstandings, difficulties in solving problems) were also found to predispose to conduct disorder. The fact that a parent has been arrested was a significant factor for conduct disorder in a child. Low income families tended to produce conduct disordered children only in the 4-11 year old age group. Urban or rural geography seemed to have no significant influence on conduct disorder formation.

Several researchers have attempted to identify parental characteristics related to the development of children's antisocial behaviour. For example, the occurrence of conduct disorder and delinquency in school-age and adolescent children is associated with antisocial personality characteristics in both mothers and fathers (Robins, West, & Herjanic, 1975). Although relations between parental antisocial personality and behaviour problems in younger children rarely have been examined, parents' antisocial behaviour has been shown to precede older children's behaviour problems (Robins et al., 1975).

Marital conflict has emerged across studies as a strong correlate and predictor of child behaviour problems, particularly when disagreements over childrearing practices have been examined (Dadds & Powell, 1991; Jouriles, Murphy, & O'Leary 1989; Shaw, Emery, & Tuer, 1993). Rutter and his colleagues (1975) have suggested that the presence of multiple familial stressors may be a better predictor of child behaviour problems than any specific factor alone. Consistent with this hypothesis, several investigators have found that the likelihood of behaviour problems increases with the number of stressors present (Sanson et al., 1991; Shaw, Vondra et al., 1994).

The Youth Prevention Project (Signals for future criminal behaviour) points out the following as factors related to the family. Teenage pregnancy of the mother (under the age of 18), Parents with a child abuse or child welfare history, Alcohol or drug misuse by the mother, Absence of a biological father, Divorced parents and/or stepparents, Inadequate pedagogical skills of parents, Symbiotic mother-child relationship, Socio-economic deprivation (low income, disadvantaged neighbourhood and poor housing), Neglect or abuse (mental, physical, sexual) of the child, High frequency of child care contacts, Large family (more than four children), Low educational level of parents, Child frequently witnesses violence (in the family or neighbourhood), Delinquent or convicted parents, Delinquent brother or sister, Brother and sister showing behavioural problems, Poor supervision of the child by the parents, Growing up in a foster-home or in the homes of relatives or friends, and Children from different fathers in one family.

In some families children are unable to learn societal norms, despite the fact that the parents practice them, because they do not have a warm, meaningful and confiding relationship with either parent (Rutter, 1979). In other families, children learn what a family has to teach them, but what is taught is socially undesirable. In these families, there is constant fighting, verbal abuse and abuse of power. A child growing up in such a family learns to use aggression as a means to achieve goals (Easson & Steinhilber, 1961; Sendi & Blomgren, 1975).

Characteristics

Conduct disordered children threaten, and/or are physically aggressive to others. They damage and/or steal the property of others. They stay out late at night, against the wishes of their parents and are truant from school (Shamsie, 1999). These youth violate basic rights of others, and deviate from major social norms. Behaviours which violate basic rights include all acts of threatening to hurt and actually hurting another person. It also includes the use of or damage to the property of another person. Many of these acts if committed by an adult would be considered criminal. Examples of deviating from social norms include not attending school and running away from home. Stealing is the most common act that starts from family and if not detected at the initial stage and dealt with adequately is generalised to other situations in neighbourhood, school, and shops, etc. Stealing and lying also help in adjustment to the social groups. Forging the signature of their parents on result cards and cheques are acts committed by the young offenders.

Chauhan (1983) states that aggression is found in a great per cent of adolescents expressed as bullying, mockery and abusing, torturing of animals and sexual perversion, damaging school or public property and gambling. Tendency to escape due to inability to face the reality is expressed as running away from school and home, gang membership and drinking. Children with CD are 5.5 times more likely to be addicted to cigarettes, six times more likely to be alcoholics, 7 times more likely to be addicted to pot (Disney et al., 1999). Major symptoms of conduct disorders include: expression of anger, verbal and physical aggression with other children, adults and animals, destruction of property, deceitfulness or theft and serious violation of rules. Conduct disorder probably shows the following progression. Non-compliance in pre-school leads to a coercive parent/child relationship. This then leads to rejection by peers and teachers, coercive peer and teacher relationships, association with delinquent peers and poor school performance. Ultimately this leads to delinquent and antisocial behaviours.

Aggressive types engage in fighting, property destruction, and cruelty to other people or to animals. Delinquents are likely to engage in theft, running away, lying, setting fires, and truancy from school. Aggressive children engage in significantly more aversive and coercive behaviours in their interactions in the home and are less compliant with parents' requests than are children who steal (Patterson, 1982).

The major types of aggression met within the Indian set-up (Chauhan, 1983) are:

(i) Bullying, mockery and abusing,

(ii) Torturing of animals and sexual perversion,

(iii) Damaging School or public property,

(iv) Committing suicide and gambling,

(v) Sexual acts: Abducting and raping,

(vi) Making sexual suggestions (Obscenity),

(vii) Homosexuality and heterosexuality,

(viii) Masturbation (in excess), and Prostitution,

(ix) Tendency to escape: This tendency indicates the inability of the individual to face the reality,

(x) Truancy from school and home

(xi) Gang membership, and

(xii) Drinking and Drug Addiction.

Course

The course of conduct disorder from early childhood onward reveals that aggressiveness is the most stable of all early detectable personality characteristics. Many researchers have noted the continuity in antisocial behaviour from early aggression to violent crime (Loeber, 1990,1996; Loeber & Hay, 1996; Olweus, 1979). There is the possibility that a child with difficult temperament or ADHD could develop aggressive behaviour in the preadolescent years and have the symptoms of ODD. The aggressive behaviour could continue in adolescence and the youth could be diagnosed as having conduct disorder in adolescence. The diagnosis would become Antisocial personality disorder (Shamsie, 1990).

In some ways, conduct disorder is just a worse version of ODD. However recent research suggests that there are some differences. Children with ODD seem to have worse social skills than those with CD. Children with ODD seem to do better in school (Kuhne et al., 1997). CD is a more severe form of ODD. Severe ODD can lead to CD. Milder ODD usually does not. The common thread that separates CD and ODD is safety. If a child has CD there are safety concerns. Sometimes it is the personal safety of others in the school, family, or community. Sometimes it is the safety of the possessions of other people in the school, family or community. Often the safety of the child with CD is a great concern. Children with ODD are an annoyance, but not especially dangerous. Between 30-50% of children with CD will also have ADHD (Kuhne et al., 1997).

Many conduct disordered youth have additional disorders and disabilities. It is estimated that 35% of conduct disordered youth also have ADHD (Offord & Bennett, 1994). Learning difficulties, such as reading disability, are common in conduct disordered children. Therefore, comorbidity (having more than one disorder) is common among conduct disordered youth. Conduct disordered children come from families characterised by alcoholism and criminal behaviour, harsh, lax or inconsistent discipline, less warmth, affection, and support; and unhappy marital relations. They tend to have large families, financial hardship, and live in poor and dangerous neighbourhoods (Kazdin, 1997).

PREVALENCE OF ANTISOCIAL BEHAVIOURS

The prevalence of antisocial behaviour reveals some alarming numbers. The proportion of the population with the dysfunction has been examined in several studies using standardised diagnostic criteria and assessment methods. It was detected that over three per cent of ten-year-olds had conduct disorder and almost three-quarters of all boys and one-third of all girls considered to be psychiatrically disturbed were diagnosed as having the disorder (Rutter et al., 1970).

Estimates of the rate of conduct disorder among children from ages 4 to 18 ranged approximately 2 per cent to six per cent. In the United States, this means that about 1.3 to 3.8 million children show the disorder. In Australia, 6.7 per cent of ten-year-olds (Connell et al., 1982) and in New Zealand, 6.9 per cent of seven-year-olds (McGee et al., 1984) were found to have conduct disorder. A study in Delhi (Datta Banik et al., 1972) found that among children going to primary schools, the prevalence of antisocial behaviour was 6 %.

Muralidharan (1973) found behaviour problems of children decreased as chronological age increased. The same trend was present in specific types of problems like habit disorders, aggression, delinquent behaviour, etc. When specific behaviours that comprise conduct disorder are examined and youths themselves report on their activities, the prevalence rates are extraordinarily high. For example, among youths (ages 13 to 18) more than 50 per cent admit to theft, 35 per cent to assault, 45 per cent admit to property destruction, and 60 per cent admit to engaging in more than one type of antisocial behaviour, such as aggressive acts, substance use, arson and vandalism (Feldman, Caplinger, & Wodarsk, 1983; Williams & Gold, 1972). Parents perceived the problem of disobedience shown, frequent quarrelling and running away from home by children (Murthy et al., 1974).

Behaviour problems were seen preponderantly among the boys (Boys: Girls = 10: 1). Even though it is difficult to pinpoint how many children may be identified as having antisocial behaviour at a particular age, data consistently suggest that the problem is great by most definitions. Aggressiveness, conduct problems, and antisocial behaviours encompass from one third to one half of all child and adolescent clinic referrals (Kazdin, Siegem & Bass, 1990; Robins, 1981).

The prevalence rate of conduct disorder among those four to sixteen years of age was 5.5 per cent (Offord et al., 1988). This meant that there were approximately, 100,000 cases of conduct disorder in the province of Ontario at the time of the study. Among the many noteworthy findings was the relatively high prevalence of specific antisocial behaviours. At age 6, lying was reported as a problem for the majority (53%) boys. Yet by age 12, the percentage had dropped considerably (to about 10%). For girls, the pattern was more dramatic, with a high rate of lying reported as a problem at age 6 (appropriately 48%) and none reported as a problem after age 11.

Similarly, a cross-sectional study of children from 4 to 16 years showed high rates of specific antisocial behaviours (Achenbach, 1991). Disobedience at home and destroying other people's things were reported as problems by the parents of approximately 50% and 20% of normal 4- and 5-year old children. For 16 to18 years-old adolescents, the rates for these behaviours decreased approximately 35% and 0%, respectively.

The specific rates of antisocial behaviour in these illustrative studies are not to be taken as precise estimates because definitions of antisocial behaviour and various measurement methods vary. Nevertheless, it can be clearly said that antisocial behaviour exacts a heavy toll on society. The disorder translates into impaired functioning in the classroom, in the home and with peers. Violating basic rights of others is both a key diagnostic criterion for antisocial behaviour disorder and the basis for many actions which society considers criminal. Besides the economic cost, there is also suffering of the families and the victims. There is also the waste of a young person's life who instead of realising his or her potential, spends most of the time in antisocial acts.

As it is, there is no specific survey conducted in India to identify Antisocial behaviour, but in any school, one can find children with antisocial behaviours of varied types.

CHARACTERISTICS OF STUDENTS WITH ANTISOCIAL BEHAVIOUR

Though it is very difficult to pinpoint the characteristics of students with antisocial behaviour, they may exhibit some or most of these.

(i) Physically, they are muscular and bold.

(ii) By temperament, they are aggressive, destructive, energetic, impulsive and extraverted.

(iii) In their attitudes, they are hostile, defiant, resentful, suspicious, unconventional and non submissive to authority.

(iv) Their behaviour mostly operates on concrete level rather on symbolic intellectual expression. They are less methodical to the problem.

(v) They lack affection, instability, and violate social norms.

Persistent antisocial youth exhibit a clear profile. During adolescence, they are more aggressive, more disinhibited, and more temperamentally reactive from mid-childhood onwards than individuals who later engage in little or no antisocial behaviour. Furthermore, from late childhood, this group exhibit lower social competence, and associated more frequently with antisocial peers. Given the consistency of these findings, it may be possible to identify children who are at risk of developing persistent antisocial behaviour at quite a young age, for whom targeted interventions may be beneficial.

The Oregon Social Learning Centre and the Lane County Department of Youth Services (DYS) have developed a profile of the typical severely at-risk adolescent referred to the Lane County Department of Corrections. The risk factors these students manifest are 1) parental arrest, 2) involvement of child protective services, 3) incidence of family transition (death, divorce, trauma, family upheaval), 4) involvement of special education services and 5) a history of early and/or severe antisocial behaviour. Three or more of these factors significantly increase the child's risk for long term delinquency and other problems. Many of the youth referred to DYS exhibit all five of these factors (Walker & Sprague, 1999). Furthermore, the length of time and the number of risks to which a child is exposed increases the likelihood of an aggressive, self centred and dysfunctional behavioural style.

A number of factors clearly and consistently characterised individuals who engaged in persistent antisocial behaviour. These were: more 'difficult' temperamental characteristics, such as a more intense, moody, irritable style, as well as difficulties remaining focused on tasks or activities (from early primary school on); consistent behaviour problems, particularly aggression, hyperactivity, oppositional/defiant behaviour, (from primary school on) and depression from late childhood on; lower self-control and persisting uncooperativeness (from late primary school on); consistent school difficulties and a negative attitude to school (from early secondary school on); association with antisocial peers (from late primary school on); a tendency to use drugs or to ventilate feelings to cope with life difficulties (during mid adolescence); and an attraction to risk-taking activities (during mid adolescence). Other less powerful predictors of persistent antisocial behaviour included: individual characteristics, such as higher activity levels, higher thrill and adventure seeking, lower civic-mindedness, less optimism about the future, and lower identity clarity; problematic eating patterns (a tendency to 'binge' and 'purge'); family factors, such as disruptions caused by the death of a parent or a breakdown in the parental relationship, higher family stress, and more marital conflict; less optimal parenting practices (such as lower parental monitoring, lower warmth, higher punishment); parental substance use; more problematic parent-child relationship, higher levels of alienation from parents, and lower family cohesion; and lower rates of participation in organised group activities and low attachment to peers.

PATTERNS OF ANTISOCIAL BEHAVIOURS

Each child is unique. Every child needs a strong, loving, relationship with a parent or other adult to feel safe and secure and to develop a sense of trust. Without a steady bond of a caring adult, children are at risk for becoming hostile, difficult, and hard to manage and as a result, behaviour problems are likely to occur. They may succumb to multifactor influences of genetic, physiological, psychological and sociological factors and, unable to confront the social milieu, act against the society.

Antisocial behaviour is common in adolescence. It ranges from relatively minor to quite serious acts, typically peaks during mid-to-late adolescence, and is more common among males than females. It has potentially serious consequences for adolescents both in the present and the future (Moffitt, Caspi, Harrington, & Milne, 2002), and impacts on their families and wider society (Homel et al., 1999). Persons with antisocial behaviour have an inability to control anger and suffer from mood swings. Acts of violence and abuse between family members within a household can also be antisocial behaviour that has consequences that affect others. The types of acts that can be termed as antisocial are difficult to list because of cultural variations in different countries. The socio-economic conditions also affect the definition of antisocial behaviour.

Antisocial behaviour can range from inconsiderate parking of vehicles to extreme acts of harassment and violence. Often seemingly trivial things can cause major problems. Graffiti, broken windows, dumped rubbish, people forced from their homes and empty properties that are difficult to let are all results of antisocial behaviour.

Most children exhibit antisocial behaviour during their development, and different children demonstrate varying levels of prosocial and antisocial behaviour. For example, the popular but rebellious child. Some, however, may exhibit low levels of both types of behaviours. For example, the withdrawn, thoughtful child. High levels of antisocial behaviour are considered a clinical disorder. Antisocial personality disorder is characterized by a lack of conscience. People with this disorder are prone to criminal behaviour, believing that their victims are weak and deserving of being taken advantage of. They tend to lie and steal. Often, they are careless with money and take action without thinking about consequences. They are often aggressive and are much more concerned with their own needs than the needs of others. Considerable research has focused on differentiating between young people who exhibit distinct patterns of antisocial behaviour.

Violent and Non-violent Antisocial Behaviour

Considerable research supports the notion that violent offenders are a small but distinct group from those who engage in non-violent antisocial or criminal behaviour (Farrington & Loeber, 2000; Loeber, Farrington, Rumsey, Ker, & Allen-Hagan, 1998; Maughan, Pickles, Rowe, Costello, & Angold, 2000; Nagin & Tremblay, 1999).

A comprehensive literature review undertaken by the United States Office of Juvenile Justice and Antisocial Behaviour Prevention's Study Group on Serious and Violent Juvenile Offenders (Loeber et al., 1998) revealed a number of key differences between violent and non-violent offenders. These included the findings that: violent offenders are typically male; the majority of violent offenders tend to start offending earlier, and continue offending longer, than non-violent offenders; violent offenders tend to exhibit multiple problem behaviours (for example, substance use, mental health difficulties, authority conflict problems, aggression etc); and violent offenders tend to commit a range of aggressive and non-aggressive offences.

Further support for a differentiation between violent and non-violent offenders can be found in research that has attempted to chart developmental pathways to antisocial behaviour. For example, Maughan and colleagues (2000) examined the development of aggressive and non-aggressive conduct problems in a sample of 1419 American boys and girls. These authors found only a small degree of overlap between the developmental pathways for the aggressive and non-aggressive children.. Piquero (2000), for example, claims that the difference between violent and non-violent offenders is quantitative not qualitative. Violent offenders tend to commit more offences than non-violent offenders. Based on this observation, he suggests that the difference between these groups is more a matter of degree than type, in ch case the correlates of one type of offence should be the same as another. Piquero tested this hypothesis on data from a sample of 987 American adolescents.

After controlling for frequency of offending he found that only one variable differentially predicted violent, but not non-violent offending, namely, variation in intelligence test scores. Individuals with low intelligence scores were more likely to come into police contact for a violent offence by age 18 than those who scored highly on this measure. antisocial behaviour.

Covert and Overt Antisocial Behaviour

The focus on aggressors and stealers has been expanded to consider a broader, bipolar dimension of overt and covert behaviour (Loeber et al., 1991). Overt behaviours consist of those antisocial acts that are confrontive (such as fighting, arguing, and temper tantrums). Covert behaviours, on the other hand, consist of concealed acts (such as stealing, truancy, lying, substance abuse, and setting fires). The notions of overt and covert behaviour can represent aggressors and stealers. Children higher in overt conduct problems are more irritable, negative, and resentful in their reactions to hostile situations, and they experience more family conflict (Kazdin, 1992).

Children higher in covert antisocial behaviour are less social, more anxious, view others more suspiciously, and come from homes lower in family cohesion. Children whose antisocial behaviours are diverse or mixed (i.e., overt and covert) may be at high risk for long-term dysfunction (Robins, 1978). A Canadian study of 1,037 males (Nagin & Tremblay, 1998) identified unique developmental pathways for those who engaged in overt antisocial behaviour (for example, physical violence) and those who engaged in covert antisocial behaviour (for example, theft) during adolescence.

Experimental and Persistent Antisocial Behaviour

Another distinction frequently made in the research literature relates to the stability or transient nature of antisocial behaviour. Childhood and adolescence are periods of high experimentation, during which many young people engage in behaviours that are not pro-social (for example, shoplifting, lying, bullying, annoying peers etc) (Kelley, Loeber, Keenan, & DeLamatre, 1997). Nevertheless, while many young people act in an antisocial manner, this behaviour is usually transitory (Dussuyer & Mammalito, 1998; Kelley et al., 1997; Moffitt & Harrington, 1996). Individuals who engage in antisocial behaviour for a relatively short period of time and then desist, are often referred to as 'experimenters'. On the other hand, for a small group of people, antisocial behaviour is much more stable (Kelley et al., 1997; Moffitt & Harrington, 1996), often beginning at a very early age and continuing well into adulthood. Those who maintain high levels of antisocial behaviour over long time periods are often labelled 'persisters'.

Life-course Persistent and Adolescence-limited Antisocial Behaviour

Consistent with the experimental-persistent distinction, Moffitt and colleagues (Moffitt & Harrington, 1996; Moffitt et al., 2001) propose two broad categories of antisocial behaviour: 'life-course persistent' antisocial behaviour (which emerges early in life and persists well into adulthood); and 'adolescent-limited' antisocial behaviour (which emerges alongside puberty and is transitory). According to these authors, adolescent-limited antisocial behaviour is quite common and may have few long-term deleterious consequences, whereas relatively few young people engage in life-course persistent antisocial behaviour.

Life-Course Persistent (LCP) group consists of individuals involved in antisocial behaviour long before they reach puberty. Difficult temperament, opposition to adults, impulsivity, and aggression toward peers characterize these children. As adolescents and adults, children with these characteristics are strongly involved in various forms of antisocial (drinking, driving, theft, staying away from home, etc.) and criminal behaviour, and they are disproportionally found in criminal registers. Approximately 5% of the population are considered LCP antisocial (less girls than boys).

Parallel with this group, a second much larger group co-exists. This group, which includes the majority of the adolescent population, shows no evidence of antisocial behaviour before the teen-age period. During the early years of puberty, however, these individuals become differentially involved in antisocial and criminal behaviour due to two phenomena: (1) Increasing motivation for performing antisocial acts, and (2) Increasing opportunity for performing antisocial behaviour through the affiliation with, and mimicry of, LCP adolescents. The motivational factor is governed by two subprocesses; pubertal status (biological maturity) and social status. Early mature individuals, fully cble of passing on their genes to the next generation, feel at odds with the social expectations directed towards them. Socially, they are, to a various degree, still considered immature and not cble of managing, or taking the full responsibility of, their lives. According to Moffitt's theory these individuals are caught in a time warp between biological and social status. Moffitt and her colleagues (2001) tested this taxonomy in a sample of 922 males and females from the Dunedin Multidisciplinary Health and Development Study. They found that 200 participants fulfilled the criteria for adolescent-limited antisocial behaviour, whereas 53 met the criteria for life-course persistent antisocial behaviour. Life-course persistent antisocial behaviour was considerably more common among males than females, with approximately 10 males to every female displaying this pattern of antisocial behaviour, whereas the gender difference in adolescent-limited antisocial behaviour was small (1.5:1 males to females).

THEORIES OF ANTISOCIAL BEHAVIOUR

Psychologists, sociologists and educationists have developed many theories to explain antisocial behaviour.

Biological Theories

The basis of these theories is that individuals vary in behaviour because their biological structures differ. Their belief in the biological inheritance of crime is viewed as a propensity, tendency or mental pre-disposition that is part of the physical environment.

Goring (1913), an English criminologist suggested that low intelligence is more responsible in developing criminal behaviour. He found that anatomical differences did not distinguish criminals from non-criminals. Schlapp (1924) held that excessive glandular secretions were the cause of antisocial behaviour. He confirmed from his studies that one third of the criminals suffered from emotional instability caused by malfunctioning of gland cells and central nervous system. All human beings were categorised into three body types (Sheldon et al., 1940). The endomorphic (round and fat), the mesomorphic (muscular) and the ectomorphic (lean). Geomorphic include most of the antisocial.

Physiological differences such as Frontal lobe dysfunction (Deckel et al., 1996) and increased testosterone (Olweus et al., 1980) are believed to influence behavioural inhibition, impulsivity, and aggression. Obstetric complications (Lewis et al., 1979; Raine, Brennan & Mednick, 1994) leading to brain damage are also considered as risk factors for antisocial personality disorder. Mineral toxicity and dietary risk factors include alcohol consumption during pregnancy (Rutter, 1989), exposure to lead (Needleman et al., 1996) and food intolerance (Taylor, 1991).

Psychological Theories

Psychological theories of antisocial behaviour attempt to link it with personality characteristics. Antisocial acts of adolescents, are considered are the result of defective family relationship and defects in learning.

Freud (1899) was the first psychologist who advocated that behaviour is not always consciously motivated but unconscious plays a major role in directing our behaviour. Psychoanalytically, the defects in early parent/child relationship results in failure to identify with parental figures. This finally results in faulty super-ego development resulting in lack of guilt and inability to restrain the antisocial activities of one's instincts.

Freud's contribution is largely based on his experiences. The major conclusions are as follows:

(i) Parents' reactions and early training of children is very important for the harmonicus development of personality. Feelings of insecurity, frustration and constant anxiety will create a disturbed personality.

(ii) The parent's attitudes and cultural environment play a vital role to determine the reaction of the child to them and the environment.

(iii) The unconscious mental process and motives are very important factors that shape the personality.

Green (1964) found that 60% of psychopathic sample had lost a parent during childhood. In other cases a child may be deprived of parental affection. High incidence of parental neglect, emotional disturbance in the family relationships, and parental inconsistency in discipline are the main causes of antisocial behaviour.

Behaviourists explain antisocial behaviour from learning point of view. According to them, all behaviour is learnt. Antisocial behaviour is also learnt from the environment. Eysenck (1964) combines the biological and learning theory approaches. He suggests that some people may suffer from an excess of anxiety because they have inherited an autonomically reactive nervous system that speeds up the acquisition of conditioned responses. Others have inherited a nervous system that leads to the under development of conditioned anxiety.

Eysenck (1994) further suggests that antisocial behaviour is egocentric and demands immediate gratification, he argues that because the introverts condition better, they are more likely to adapt to socially acceptable behaviour. The extravert who also scores high on neuroticism is more likely to engage in antisocial behaviour than normal controls (McGurk & Mc Dougal, 1981).

Numerous empirical studies have been conducted to link crime and antisocial behaviour to personality traits. Kulik, Stein, & Sarbin (1968) found that delinquents have a poor sense of future time perspective than non-delinquents. Eissler (1953) explained delinquent behaviour as a reaction to the value system of the individual. It involves a basic conflict with the value system of the society and is considered as aggressive behaviour that defies the established values in any given society.

Sociological Theories

Sociologists present a different explanation of antisocial behaviour. According to Durkheim (1951), 'serious economic or political stress can lead to breakdown of power in social system, whereby cultural norms no longer have inhibiting influence over group and individual behaviour'. Sociologists believe that many crimes are determined by factors operating outside individual choice, such as urban ecology, local culture, social change and structure. Gangs, lack of education, improper parenting, broken homes, association with thieves, and unemployment are considered to be the major causes of antisocial behaviour. Conger et al. (1995) identified poverty and socio-economic status as community risk factors for antisocial behaviour. Farrington et al. (1986) stated that unemployment raises the risk of criminal activities in individuals already at high risk.

As early as 1931, Shaw reported that 'contact with antisocial groups often marks the beginning of the student's career in antisocial acts and his initial behaviours are often identical with the traditions and established practices of the group'. It is probable that participation in the activities of such group is one of the very significant contributing factors in cases of antisocial behaviour.

Antisocial behaviour is more common in individuals with deviant peer groups (Sampson & Laub, 1993). Peer group influences are more likely in adolescent limited rather than life-course persistent antisocial behaviour. According to Coie, Dodge, & Kupersmidt (1990), peer rejection can act as risk factor for antisocial behaviour.

Culture is, however, an instrument of adaptation which is vastly more efficient than the biological processes which led to its inception and advancement. It is more efficient among other things because it is more rapid-changed genes are transmitted only to the direct descendants of the individuals in whom they first appear; to replace the old genes, the carriers of the new ones must gradually outbreed and supplant the former. Changed culture may be transmitted to anybody regardless of biological parentage, or borrowed ready-made from other peoples (Dobzhansky, 1962).

CAUSES OF ANTISOCIAL BEHAVIOUR

Shamsie (2000) has presented the following facts about violent youth that are suggestive of causes of antisocial behaviour:

Many antisocial youth have difficult temperaments from birth: Babies with difficult temperament are poor sleepers, difficult to feed and hard to toilet train. (Thomas, Chess, & Birch, 1969). These babies require extra patience and attention. Research has shown that children with difficult temperaments, who grow up in families where there have been serious difficulties, develop emotional and behavioural problems (Maziade et al., 1990). While some may perceive temperamental characteristics to be 'fixed', and as a consequence, not amenable to intervention, research indicates that such characteristics are moderately stable over childhood and thus not immutable (Sanson, Hemphill, & Smart, 2002). Furthermore, temperament's impact on a child's development depends largely on its 'fit'; with the environment. Hence, in striving to optimise a child's development, attempts should be made to maximise the 'fit' between the child and his/her environment, matching parenting and educational practices to the characteristics of the child, and helping the child to develop strategies to best manage his/her temperamental and behavioural tendencies.

Many antisocial youth suffer from a variety of disabilities: Learning disabilities, including reading disability, are common occurrences (Lewis et al., 1980). Lack of recognition of disabilities can cause serious problems to a child's progress and self-image. Many antisocial youth have serious psychiatric disorders. The most common is Attention-deficit hyperactivity disorder (ADHD), which makes it hard for these youth to do well academically (O'Brien et al., 1992). Impulsiveness is one of the symptoms of ADHD that often contributes to children getting into fights and trouble with the law. ADHD runs in families and has been linked to a genetic abnormality (Hauser et al., 1993). Besides the above, many antisocial youth have neurological disturbances such as psychomotor epilepsy, and symptoms of psychotic illnesses such as schizophrenia and manic-depressive psychosis (Lewis, 1993).

Many antisocial youth come from families that have experienced a great deal of difficulty and stress: Children growing up in these families may experience inconsistent discipline, neglect, and physical abuse (Reidy, 1977). There may be a history of mental illness in one or both parents. Very often the difficulties experienced by the families are further aggravated by poverty (Rae-Grant et al., 1989).

Many antisocial youth are unable to meet society's expectations: This may result from their disabilities, disorders and family backgrounds. They find it difficult to control their behaviour, unable to perform well in school and have difficulties in forming close and meaningful relationships. It is important to recognize that without help these youth are going to cause a great deal of harm to society through their antisocial and violent behaviour. Besides causing suffering to their families and society, they cost us millions of dollars through probation, jail, welfare and unemployment (Shamsie, 1990). The fact is that antisocial youth do not choose to be bad; with help they are cble of being good. It is in our interest to help them so that, instead of causing pain and expense to society, they can positively contribute.

NEED TO OVERCOME ANTISOCIAL BEHAVIOUR

Disruptive problems in childhood typically include hyperactivity, impulsivity, inattention, oppositional behaviours, defiance, aggression and disregarding the rights of others. When untreated, such children with antisocial behaviour are likely to experience peer rejection, school problems, and even grow into adults who experience low employment and socio-economic status, poor academic achievement, and high rates of automobile accidents, family problems, and mood problems.

Antisocial behaviour of youth at school may endanger their own or others' personal safety, or prevent themselves or other students from learning. Children's school experience should gradually replace external authoritarian controls with students' own internal controls and that students should be systematically taught the personal, interpersonal, communication and social skills that they need for maintenance of healthy family and community life (Ewashen et al., 1992; Tierney et al., 1993; Walker, 1993).

Antisocial behaviour problems in childhood are associated with serious negative consequences for both the child and those in the child's environment. So, gaining a greater understanding of antisocial behaviour of students is an important task for the mental health community (Frick, 1998; Hinshaw, 1994). Of even more concern is the clear failure of our society to effectively cope with these problems. Instead of offering prevention, early intervention and treatment, we have built more prisons and increasingly enacted laws that treat youth as adult criminals. These developments are more frustrating in light of the existence of well-proven methods of identifying young children who are at high risk for violent and destructive behaviours as teenagers or adults. We now know that certain specific antisocial behaviour patterns and high levels of aggression exhibited in preschool and kindergarten are not just correlated, but are highly predictive, of violent, delinquent and criminal behaviours in middle school, later adolescence and adulthood (Fagan, 1996; Walker et al., 1996).

As Letty Cottin Pogrebin (1983) stated, " Much is made of the accelerating brutality of young people's crimes, but rarely does our concern for dangerous children translate into concern for children in danger. We fail to make the connection between the use of force on children themselves, and violent antisocial behaviour, or the connection between watching father batter mother and the child deducing a link between violence and masculinity".

"Social development is an investment in people, in communities, and in society, and helps prevent crime; it is also cost effective." (Hepworth, 1996). We must, as a society, re-examine our beliefs and reprioritise our values, turning away from aggression, competition and dominance, toward empathy, mutuality, cooperation and interdependence. This will require a reinvestment of resources into social programmes that strengthen families, reduce substance abuse, eliminate poverty and increase a spirit of community belonging in order to decrease social alienation.

Currently, the lesson our children are being taught, whether it be through family, peers or media, is that antisocial behaviour is an acceptable way to solve problems or to get one's way. Antisocial behaviour exists in society as a whole as well as in the school, and so society as a whole must be involved in eliminating violence. Unless identified and tackled in the early years, antisocial behaviour will hamper the individual's integrity and social harmony thus paving the way for national disintegration. Our society needs to help young people recommit to the community rather than overvaluing individual needs. "Money invested in early prevention is money saved later on remedial services in school, social, physical and mental health services for families and correctional services for juveniles and adults" (Tremblay & Craig, 1995). The best efforts of schools, parents, peers, communities, business, the media and all the agencies that serve children and families are needed to overcome antisocial behaviour in students.

SUMMARY AND OVERVIEW OF REMAINING CHAPTERS

Antisocial behaviour causes harassment , alarm or distress to one or more persons. It involves violation of overall prescribed patterns of behaviour and thus represents a major social problem. Antisocial behaviour is the behaviour exhibited by troublesome children. Attention deficit hyperactivity disorcer, Oppositional defoiance disorder, and Conduct disorder are the characteristic behaviours exhibited by troublesome children and youth.

Antisocial behaviour of the adolescents accounts mostly for their unrest today. If Antisocial behaviours do not wax and wane over the course of normal development, they may become frequent, intense and chronic and pose a major threat to the entire society. Young people exhibit different patterns of antisocial behaviour differently classified as covert and overt, experimental and persistant, and life-course persistant and adolescence limited.

Antisocial behaviour may stem due to various causes such as difficult temperaments during birth, and a variety of disabilities or even due to social disadvantage. Family problems, negative peer pressure or media exposure to violence may also be the contributory factors. The solution in terms of understanding the unaccepted behaviours and identifying steps to ameliorate them have a long germination period. The schools, parents, peers, and communities have a greater role to play.

In the subsequent chapters, different types of antisocial behaviours will be elaborated. In Chapter 2, we will consider various Individual and Environmental factors related to Antisocial behaviour and examine how these factors may operate over the course of development. In Chapter 3, we will explain the different models proposed to describe the course of development of antisocial behaviour. The development of antisocial behaviour from ADHD to ODD to CD will also be discussed. In chapter 4, diagnosis and assessment of antisocial behaviour are examined. Different spources and measures of assessment are presented. In chapter 5, prevention and intervention strategies will be considered. The range of interventions that has been applied to antisocial youth or those who are at risk for antisocial behaviour is vast. Among the many innovative programmes, only a few related to individual, parental, peer group and school will be explicitly explained. In this, the final chapter, the need for using Comprehensive Intervention Strategy in ameliorating antisocial behaviour in children and adolescents will also be highlighted.

REFERENCES

Achenbach, T.M. (1991). *Manual for the Child Behaviour Checklist /4-18 and 1991 Profile*. Burlington: University of Vermont, Department of Psychiatry.

American Psychiatric Association. (1987). *Diagnostic and Statistical Manual* (3rd Edition-Revised). Washington DC.

Bachman, J.G., Johnston, L.D., & O'Malley, P.M. (1978). Delinquent Behaviour Linked to Educational Attainment and Post-high School Experiences. In L. Otten (Ed.), *Colloquium on the Correlates of Crime and the Determinants of Criminal Behaviour* (pp. 1-43). Arlington, VA: The MITRE Corp.

Bala, N. (1994). The Legal Response to Youth Violence. Paper Presented at the National Conference on Youth Violence in Canada. Ottawa, Ontario.

Biederman, J., Faraone, S.V., Keenan, K., Benjamin, J., Krifcher, B., Moore, C., Sprich-Buckminster, S., Ugaglia, K., Jellinek, M.S., Steingard, R., Spencer, T., Norman, D., Kolodny, R., Kraus, I., Perrin, J., Keller, M., & Tsuang, M.T. (1992). Further Evidence for Family-Genetic Risk Factors in Attention Deficit Hyperactivity Disorder. *Archives of General Psychiatry*, 49, 728-738.

Biederman, J., Newcorn, J., & Sprich, S. (1991). Comorbidity of Attention Deficit Hyperactivity Disorder with Conduct, Depressive, Anxiety, and Other Disorders. *American Journal of Psychiatry*, 148(5), 564-577.

Bland, N. and Read, T. (2000). *Policing Antisocial Behaviour*. Police Research Series Paper 123. London: Home Office.

Budd, T., & Sims, L. (2001). *Antisocial Behaviour and Disorder. Findings from the British Crime Survey*. Home Office Research Findings 145. London: Home Office.

Bullock, K., & Loxley, C. (1999). *Analysis of Antisocial Behaviour Within the 1998 Community Safety Strategies for the Most and the Least Deprived Areas in England and Wales*. (unpublished).

Cadoret, R.J. (1978). Psychopathology in Adopted-away Offspring of Biological Parents with Antisocial Behaviour. *Archives of General Psychiatry*, 35, 176-184.

Carlson, Caryn et.al. (1997). Gender Differences in Children with ADHD, ODD, and Co-occurring ADHD & ODD Identified in a School Population. (1997). *Journal of American Academy of Child Adolescent Psychiatry*, 36(12):1706-1714.

Carson, D.K., Chowdhary, A., Perry, C.K., & Pati, C. (1999). Family Characteristics and Adolescent Competence in India: Investigation of Youth in Southern Orissa. *Journal of Youth and Adolescence*, 28: 211-233.

Casaer, P., de Vries, L., & Marlow, N. (1991). Prenatal and Perinatal Risk Factors for Psychological Development. In M.Rutter & P. Casaer (Eds.), *Biological Risk Factors for Psycho-social Disorders* (pp. 139 -174). Cambridge, MA: Cambridge. University Press.

Chaudhari, A., & Choudhary, R. (1993). Exploring Research Strategies for Identifying Invulnerable Children: An Indian Contest. *Early Child Development and Car*, 93: 87-100.

Chauhan, S.S. (1983). Psychology of Adolescence (pp.179-180). Allied Publishers Pvt. Ltd.

Clark, C., Prior, M., & Kinsella, G.J. (2000). Do Executive Function Deficits Differentiate Between Adolescents with ADHD and Oppositional Defiant/Conduct Disorder? A Neuropsychological Study using the Six Elements Test and Hayling Sentence Completion Test. *Journal of Abnormal Child Psychology,* 28(5): 403-14.

Coie, J., Dodge, K., & Kupersmidt, J. (1990). Peer Group Behaviour and Social Status. In S. R. Asher & J. D. Coie (Eds.), *Peer Rejection in Childhood* (pp. 17-59). NY: Cambridge University Press.

Conger, R.D., Patterson, G.R., & Ge,X. (1995) It Takes Two to Replicate: A Mediational Model for the Impact of Parrents' Stress on Adolescent Adjustment. *Child Development*, 66: 80-97.

Connell H.M., Irvine L., & Rodney J. (1982). Psychiatric Disorder in Queensland Primary School Children. *Australian Paediatric Journal*, 18, 177-180.

Cook EH: The Early Development of Child Psychophamacogenetics. (1999). Journal of American Academy of Child and Adolescent Psychiatry, 38(12) 1478-1481.

Cornwall, A., & Bauden, H. (1992). Reading Disabilities and Aggression: A Critical Review. *Journal of Learning Disabilities*, 25(5), 281-288.

Costello, E.J., Angold, A., Burns, B., Strangl, D., Tweed, D., & Erkanli,A. (1996). The Great Smokey Mountain Study of Youth, I: Prevalence and Correlates of DSM-III-R Disorders. *Archives of General Fsychiatry*, 53, 1137-43.

Crime Reduction Toolkits (2000). *Antisocial Behaviour.* The Crime Reduction Website. *http://www.crimereduction.gov.uk/*

Dadds, M.R., & Powell, M.B. (1991). The Relationship of Interparental Conflict and Global Marital Adjustment to Aggression and Immaturity in Aggressive and Nonclinic Children. *Journal of Abnormal Child Psychology*, 19, 553-567.

Dash A.S., & Hariharan, M. (1988). Identification and Development of Talent in Disadvantaged Children. In M. K. Raina & S. Gulait (Eds.), *Identification and Development of Talent*, New Delhi: NCERT Publications.

Datta Banik, N.D., Nayyar, S., Krishna, L., & Lilaraj (1972). Behaviour Problems of School-going Children. *Indian Paediatrics*, 9, 757-761.

Deckel, A.W., Hesselbrock. V., & Bauer, L. (1996) Antisocial Personality Disorder, Childhood Delinquency, and Frontal Brain Functioning: EEG and Neuropsychological Findings. *Journal of Clinical Psychclogy*, 52, 639-650.

Disne, E,R., Elkins I.J. et al. (1999). Effects of ADHD, Conduct Disorder, and Gender on Substance Use and Abuse in Adolescence. *American Journal of Psychiatry*, 156:1515-1521.

Dobzhansky, T. (1962). *Mankind Evolving*. Yale University Press, New Haven.

Durkheim, Emile. (1951). Suicide: *A Study in Sociology.* Translated By George Simpson & John A. Spaulding. New York: The Free Press.

Dussuyer, I., & Mammolito, M. (1998). *Reoffending Patterns of Juveniles in Victoria*. Department of Justice, Victoria, Australia.

Dykman, R., Ackerman, P., & Raney, T. (1993). *Assessment and Characteristics of Children with Attention Deficit Disorder.* Washington, DC: U. S. Department of Education.

Easson , W. & Steinhilber, R.M. (1961). Murderous Aggression by Children and Adolescents. *Archives of General Psychiatry*, 4, 27-35.

Eaves, L., Silberg, J., Meyer, J., Maes, H., Simonoff, E., Pickles, A., Rutter, M., Neale, M.C., Reynolds, C.A., Erikson, M.T., Heath, A.C., & Loeber, R. (1997). Genetics and Developmental Psychopathology: 2. The Main Effects of Gene and Environment on Behavioural Problems in the Virginia Twin Study of Adolescent Development. *Journal of Child Psychology and Psychiatry*, 38, 965-80.

Eggar, J., Carter, C.M. et al. (1985). Controlled Trial of Oligoantigenic Diet Treatment in the Hyperkinetic Syndrome. *Lancet*, 540-545.

Eissler, K.R. (1953). The Effect of the Structure of the Ego on Psychoanalytic Technique. *Journal of the American Psychoanalytic Association*, 1, 1: 104-143.

Ewashen, G., Norrish, R. Weeks, G., Ormiston, S., & Taylor, S. (1992). Integrating Troubled Teens. *Education Canada*, Fall.

Eysenck, H. J. (1994). The Measurement of Creativity. In Boden M.A. (Ed.), *Dimensions of Creativity* (pp. 199-242). MIT Press.

Eysenck, H.J. (1964). *Crime And Personality* (1st Edition) London: Routledge & Kegan Paul. New York: Houghton Mifflin.

Fagan, J. (1996)..*Recent Perspectives on Youth Violence*. Keynote Address to Pacific Northwest Conference on Youth Violence, Seattle.

Farrington, D. P. (1989). Early Predictors of Adolescent Aggression and Adult Violence. *Violence and Victims*, 4, 79-100.

Farrington, D.P., & Loeber, R. (2000). Epidemiology of Juvenile Violence, *Juvenile Violence*, 9, 733-748.

Farrington, D.P. (1991). Childhood Aggression and Adult Violence: Early Precursors and Later Life Outcomes. In D.J. Pepler, K.H. Rubin (Eds.), *The Development and Treatment of Childhood Aggression* (pp. 189 -97). Hillsdale: N.J. Lawrence Erlbaum Associates.

Farrington, D.P. (1992). Explaining the Beginning, Progess and Ending of Antisocial Behaviour from Birth to Childhood. In J. McCord (Ed.), *Advances in Criminological Theory, Vol.3: Facts, Frameworks and Forecasts* (pp. 253-86). New Brunswick, NJ: Transaction Publishers.

Farrington, D.P. (1996): *Understanding and Preventing Youth Crime*. Social Policy Research & Joseph Rowntree Foundation. York: York Publishing Services.

Farrington, D.P. (1989). Early Predictors of Adolescent Aggression and Adult Violence. *Violence and Victims*, 4,79-100.

Farrington, D.P., Gallagher, B., Morley, R.J., & West, D.J. (1986) Unempoloyment, School Leaving and Crime. *British Journal of Criminology*, 26, 335-356.

Farrington, D.P., Loeber, R., & Van Kammen, W.B (1990b). Long-term Criminal Outcomes of Hyperactivity-impulsivity-attention Deficit and Conduct Problems in Childhood. In L. Robins & M. Rutter (Eds.), *Straight and Deviant Pathways from Childhood and Adulthood* (pp. 62-81). New York: Cambridge University Press.

Federal Bureau of Investigation. U.S. Department of Justice. (1989). *Uniform Crime Reports*. Washington, DC: Author.

Feingold, B.F. (1975). Interdependence as a Working Concept. In D. Mpoxon (Ed.), *Managing Criminal Justuce* (pp. 8-17). London: HMSO.

Feldman, R.A., Caplinger, T.E., & Wodarski, J.S. (1983). *The St. Louis Conundrum: The Effective Treatment of Antisocial Youths*. Engglwood Cliffs, N.J: Prentice Hall.

Fergusson, D.M., Horwood, L.J., & Lloyd, M. (1991). Confirmatory Factor Models of Attention Deficit and Conduct Disorder. *Journal of Child Psychology and Psychiatry*, 32, 257-274.

Fergusson, D.M., Lynskey, M.T., & Horwood, L.J. (1993). The Effect of Maternal Depression on Maternal Ratings of Child Behaviour. *Journal of Abnormal Child Psychology*, 21, 245-270.

Fischer, M., Barkley, R.A., Fletcher, K.E., & Smallish, L. (1993). The Adolescent Outcome of Overactive Children: Predictors of Psychiatric, Academic, Social, and Emotional Adjustment. *Journal of the American Academy of Child and Adolescent Psychiatry*, 32, 324-32.

Freud, S. (1899). Screen Memories. In J. Strachey (Ed.), (1962). *The Standard Edition of the Complete Psychological Works of Sigmund Freud*, Vol. 3. London: The Hogarth Press.

Frick, P.J. (1998). *Conduct Disorders and Severe Antisocial Behaviour*. New York: Plenum.

Gale Research (1998). Gale Encyclopaedia of Childhood and Adolescence: Antisocial Behaviour.

Garfinkel, B., & Wener, P.H. (1989). Attention Deficit Hyperactivity Disorder. In Kaplan HI, Sadock B. (Eds.), *Comprehensive Textbook of Psychiatry*, Fifth Edition (pp. 1828-1842). Baltimore: Williams and Wilkins.

Garnett, D. (1994). Dimensions of Youth Violence. In L. McCart (Ed.). *Kids and Violence* (pp. 15-24). Washington, DC: National Governor's Association.

Gold, D., Crombie, G., & Noble, S. (1987). Relations Between Teachers' Judgements of Girls' and Boys' Compliance and Intellectual Competence. *Sex Roles*, 16, 351-358.

Goodman, R., & Stevenson J. (1989). A Twin Study of Hyperactivity: I. An Examination of Hyperactivity Scores and Categories Derived from Rutter Teacher and Parent Questionnaires. II. The Aetiological Role of Genes, Family Relationships, and Perinatal Adversity. *Journal of Child Psychology and Psychiatry*: 30: 671-710. [Medline].

Goring, C. (1913). *The English Convict: A Statistical Study*. London: His Majesty's Stationary Office (Republished in 1972 by Patterson Smith, Monclair, N.J.).

Gottfredson, G. (1987). *American Education: American Delinquency. Today's Delinquent*. Pittsburgh, PA: National Center for Juvenile Justice.

Green (1964) Quoted in Chauhan, S.S. (1983). *Psychology of Adolescence* (pp.173-189). Allied Publishers Pvt. Ltd.

Halperin, J.M., Matier, K., Bedi, G., Sharma, V., & Newcorn, J. (1992). Specificity of Inattention, Impulsivity, and Hyperactivity to the Diagnosis of Attention Deficit Hyperactivity Disorder. *Journal of the American Academy of Child and Adolescent Psychiatry*, 31, 190-196.

Harvards Medical School (1989), Internet Mental Health, Long, P.W (1995-1997). Conduct Disorder. (Online) Available: *http://www.mentalhealth.com/mag1/p5h-cond.html*.

Hauser, P., Zametin A.J., Martinez, P., Vitiello, B., Metochik, J., Mixson, J.,& Weintraub, B.D. (1993). Attention Deficit Hyperactivity Disorder in People with Generalized Resistance to Thyroid Hormone. The New England Journal of Medicine, 328 (14): 997-1011.

Hawkins, J. (1995). Controlling Crime Before It Happens: Risk-focused Prevention. *National Institute of Justice Journal*, 229, 10-18.

Hechtman, L. (1996). Families of Children with Attention Deficit Hyperactivity Disorder. *Canadian Journal of Psychiatry*, 41: 350-360.

Henggler, S.W. (1989). Delinquency in Adolescence, 30, 208-217.

Hepworth, H.P. (1996). *The Economics of Crime Prevention Focus Magazine*, July.

Herrero, M.E., Hechtman, L., & Weiss, G. (1994). Antisocial Disorders in Hyperactive Subjects from Childhood to Adulthood: Predictive Factors and Characterization of Subgroups. American Journal of Orthopsychiatry, 64(4): 510-521.

Hinshaw, S.P. (1987). On the Distinction Between Attentional Deficits/ Hyperactivity and Conduct Problems/Aggression in Child Psychopathology. *Psychological Bulletin*, 101, 443-63.

Hinshaw, S.P. (1994). *Attention Deficits and Hyperactivity in Children* (Vol.29). Thousand Oaks, C.A: Sage.

Hinshaw, S.P., Lahey, B.B., & Hart, E.L. (1993). Issues of Taxonomy and Comorbidity in the Development of Conduct Disorder. Development and Psychopathology, 5, 31-49.

HMIC (1997). *Winning the Race: Policing Plural Communities*. London: HMSO.

HMIC (1999). *Winning the Race: Revisited*. HMSO: London.

Home Office (2002a). *A Guide to Antisocial Behaviour Orders and Acceptable Behaviour Contracts*. London: Home Office.

Home Office (2003). *Respect and Responsibility—Taking a Stand Against Antisocial Behaviour*. London: Home Office.

Homel, R., Cashmore, J., Gilmore, L., Goodnow, J., Hayes, A., Lawrence, J., Leech, M., O'Connor, I., Vinson, T., Najman, J., & Western, J. (1999). *Pathways to Prevention: Early Intervention and Development Approaches to Crime in Australia*. Attorney-General's Department, National Crime Prevention, Canberra.

Horner , B.R., Scheibe, K.E. (1997). Prevalence and Implications of Attention Deficit Hyperactivity Disorder Among Adolescents in Treatment for Substance Abuse. *Journal of the American Academy of Child and Adolescent Psychiatry*, 36, 30-36.

Huttenlocher, J., Haight, W., Bryk, A. Seltzer, M. and Lyons, T. (1991). Early Vocabulary Growth: Relation to Language Input and Gender. Developmental Psychology, 27, 236-248.

Jouriles, E., Murphy, C. and O'Leary, K. D. (1989). Interspousal Aggression, Marital Discord, and Child Problems. *Journal of Consulting and Clinical Psychology*, 57, 453-455.

Kazdin A.E. (1997) Parent Management Training: Evidence, Outcomes, and Issues. *Journal of American Academy of Child and Adolescent Psychiatry*, 36: 10-18

Kazdin, A.E. (1987). Treatment of Antisocial Behaviour in Children: Curremnt Status and Future Directions. *Psychological Bulletin*, 102(2), 187-203.

Kazdin, A.E. (1992). Overt and Covert Antisocial Behaviour: Child and Family Characteristics Among Psychiatric Inpatient Children. *Journal of Child and Family Studies*, 1, 3-20.

Kazdin, A.E., Siegel, T.C. and Bass, D. (1990). Drawing Upon Clinical Practice to Inform Research on Child and Adolescent Psychotherapy: A Survey of Practitioners. *Professional Psychology: Research and Practice*, 21, 189-198.

Keenan, K., Loeber, R. and Green S. (1999). Conduct Disorder in Girls: a Review of the Literature. *Clinical Child and Family Psychologocal Review*, 2(1):3-19, March.

Keilitz, I., & Dunivant, N. (1986). The Relationship Between Learning Disability and Juvenile Delinquency: Current State of Knowledge. *Remedial and Special Education*, 7(3), 18-26.

Kelley, B.T., Loeber, R., Keenan, K. & DeLamatre, M. (1997). Developmental Pathways in Boys' Disruptive and Delinquent Behaviour, *Juvenile Justice Bulletin*, December.

Klinteberg, B.A., Andersson, T., Magnusson, D., & Stattin, H. 1993. Hyperactive Behaviour in Childhood as Related to Subsequent Alcohol Problems and Violent Offending: A Longitudinal Study of Male Subjects. *Personality and Individual Differences*, 15:381-388.

Kuhne M, et. al (1997). Impact of Comorbid Oppositional or Conduct Problems on Attention-Deficit Hyperactivity Disorder. *Journal of American Academy of Child and Adolescent Psychiatry*, 36(12); 1715-1725.

Kuhne M, et. al. (1997). Impact of Comorbid Oppositional or Conduct Problems on Attention-Deficit Hyperactivity Disorder. *Journal of American Academy of Child and Adolescent Psychiatry*, 36(12); 1715-1725.

Kuhne M, et. al. (1997) . Impact of Comorbid Oppositional or Conduct Problems on Attention-Deficit Hyperactivity Disorder. .Journal of American *Academy of Child and Adolescent Psychiatry*, 36(12); 1715-1725.

Kulik, J.A., Stein, K.B., & Sarbin, T.R. (1968). Dimensions and Patterns of Adolescent Antisocial Behaviour. *Journal of Consulting and Clinical Psychology*, 32, 375-382.

Kuperman, S., Schlosser, S..S, et al. (1999). Relationship of Child Psychopathology to Parental Alcoholism and Antisocial Personality Disorder. *Journal of American Academy of Child and Adolescent Psychiatry*, 38(6):686-692.

Lavigne, J.V., Cicchettic, et al. (2001). Oppositional Defiant Disorder With Onset in Preschool Years: Longitudinal Stability and Pathways to Other Disorders. *Journal of American Academy of Child and Adolescent Psychiatry,* 40(12):1393-1400.

Leone, P.E., Mayer, M. J., Malmgren, K., & Misel, S.M. (2000). School Violence and Disruption: Rhetoric, Reality, and Reasonable Balance. *Focus on Exceptional Children*, 33, 1-20.

Letty Cottin Pogrebin (20th Century), U.S. Editor, Writer. *Famil; and Politics*, (1983). Ch. 5.

Levy, F., Hay, D.A., McStephen. M., Wood, C., & Waldman, I. (1997). Attention-deficit Hyperactivity Disorder: A Category of a Continuum? Genetic Analysis of a Large-scale Twin Study. *Journal of the American Academy of Child and Adolescent Psychiatry*, 36, 737-44.

Lewis, D.O. (1993). Conduct Disorder. In: R. Michels, A.M. Cooper, S.B. Guze, et al. (Eds.), *Psychiatry* (Vol. 2, Chap. 37, pp. 1-10). Philadelphia: J.B. Lippincott Co.

Lewis, D.O., Shanok, S.S., Balla, D.A. and Bard, B. (1980). Psychiatric Correlates of Severe Reading Disabilities in an Incarcerated Delinquent Population. *Journal of the American Academy of Child and Adolescent Psychiatry*, 19, 611-622.

Lewis, D.O., Shanok, S.S., Pincus, J.H. and Glaser, G.H. (1979) Violent Juvenile Delinquents: Psychiatric, Neurological, Psychological and Abyse Factors. *Journal of the American Academy of Child and Adolescent Psychiatry*, 18, 307-319.

Loeber, R. (1985). Patterns and Development of Antisocial Child Behaviour. In G.J. Whitehurst. (Ed.), *Annals of Child Development*, Vol. 2, NY: JAI Press, pp. 77-116.

Loeber, R. (1990). Development and Risk Factors of Juvenile Antisocial Behaviour and Delinquency. *Clinical Psychology Review*, 10, 1-41.

Loeber, R. (1996). Developmental Continuity, Change, and Pathways in Male Juvenile Problem Behaviours and Delinquency. In J. D. Hawkins (Ed.), *Delinquency and Crime*: Current Theories (pp. 1-27). New York: Cambridge University Press.

Loeber, R., & Hay, D.F. (1996). Key Issues in the Development of Aggression and Violence from Childhood to Early Adulthood. *Annual Review of Psychology*, 48: 371-410.

Loeber, R., Farrington, D. P., & Waschbusch, D. A. (1998). Serious and Violent Juvenile Offenders. In R. Loeber & D. P. Farrington (Eds.), *Serious and Violent Juvenile Offenders: Risk Factors and Successful Interventions* (pp. 13-29). Thousand Oaks, CA: Sage Publications.

Loeber, R., Farrington, D.P., Rumsey, E., Kerr, C.A. & Allen-Hagen, B. (1998). Serious and Violent Juvenile Offenders, *Juvenile Justice Bulletin*, May.

Loeber, R., Keenan, K., Lahey, B.B., & Thomas, C. (1991). Diagnostic Conundrum of Oppositional Defiance Disorder and Conduct Disorder. *Journal of Abnormal Psychology*, 100, 379-390.

Loeber, R., Wung, P., Keenan, K., Giroux, B., Stouthamer-Loeber, M., Van Kammen, W. B., & Maughan, B. (1993). Developmental Pathways in Disruptive Child Behaviour. *Development and Psychopathology*, 5, 101-133.

Lynam, D.R. (1996). Early Identification of Chronic Offenders: Who is the Fledgfling Psychopath? *Psychological Bulletin*, 120, 209-234.

MacDonald, V.M., & Achenbach, T.M. (1996). Attention Problems Versus Conduct Problems as Six-year Predictors of Problem Scores in a National Sample. *Journal of the American Academy of Child and Adolescent Psychiatry*, 35, 1237-1246.

Magnusson, D., Klinteberg., B., & Stattin, H. (1993). Autonomic Activity/ Reactivity, Behaviour, and Crime in a Longitudinal Prospective. In J. McCord (Ed.), *Facts, Frameworks and Forecasts*, pp. 287-318. New Brunswick, NJ: Transaction Publishers.

Mantzicopoulos, P.Y., & Morrison, D. (1994). A Comparison of Boys and Girls with Attention Problems: Kindergarten Through Second Grade. American Journal of Orthopsychiatry, 64, 522-533.

Matheny, K. B., Aycock, D. W., & McCarthy, C. J. (1993). Stress in School-Aged Children and Youth. *Educational Psychology Review*, 5, 109-134.

Matthys, W., Stephanie H. M. Goozen, Han de Vries Peggy T. Cohen-Kettenis, & Herman van Engeland. (1998). The Dominance of Behavioural Activation over Behavioural Inhibition in Conduct Disordered Boys With or Without Attention Deficit Hyperactivity Disorder. *Journal of Child Psychology and Psychiatry*, 39:643-651.

Maughan, B., Pickles, A., Rowe, R., Costello, E.J. & Angold, A. (2000). Developmental Trajectories of Aggressive and Non-aggressive Conduct Problems. *Journal of Quantitative Criminology*, vol. 16, pp. 199-221.

Mawson, A. R. and Jacobs, K. J. (1978). Corn Consumption, Tryptophan, and Cross-National Homicide Rates. *Journal of Orthomolecular Psychiatry*, 7: 227-30.

Maziade, M., Caron, C., Cote, R., Merette, C., Bernier, H., Laplante, B., Boutin, P., and Thivierge, J. (1990). Psychiatric Status of Adolescents Who Had Extreme Temperaments at Age 7. *American Journal of Psychiatry*, 147(11), 1531-1536.

McGee, R., Silva, P.A., & Williams, S. (1984). Perinatal, Neurological, Environmental and Developmental Characterisitics of Seven-year-Old Children with Stable Behaviour Problems. *Journal of Child Psychology and Psychiatry*, 25, 573-86.

McGurk, B.J., & Mc Dougall, C. (1981). A New Approach to Eysenck's Theory of Criminality. *Personality and Individual Differences*, 2, 338-340.

Microsoft Encarta Reference Library (2002) CD Version.

Milberger , S., Biederman, J., Faraone, S., Chen, L., & Jones, J. (1997). ADHD is Associated with Early Initiation of Smoking in Children and Adolescents. *Journal of American Academy of Child and Adolescent Psychiatry*, 36, 37-44.

Moffit, T.E. (1990b). Juvenile Delinquency and Attention Deficit Disorder: Boys; Developmental Trajectories from Age 3 to Age 15. *Child Development*, 61, 893-910.

Moffit, T.E. (1993a). Adolescent-limited and Life-course Persistent Antisocial Behaviour: A Developmental Taxonomy. *Psychological Review*, 100, 674-701.

Moffit, T.E. (1993b). The Neuropsychology of Conduct Disorder. *Development and Psychopathology*, 5, 135-151.

Moffitt, T.E., & Harrington, H.L (1996). Delinquency: The Natural History of Antisocial Behaviour . In P.A Silva., & W.R. Stanton (Eds.), *From Child to Adult: The Dunedin Multidisciplinary Health and Development Study*, Oxford University Press, Auckland, New Zealand.

Moffitt, T.E., Caspi, A., Harrington, H., & Milne, B.J. (2002). Males on the Life-course Persistent and Adolescence-limited Antisocial Pathways: Follow-up at Age 26 Years. *Development and Psychopathology*, 14, 179-207.

Moffitt, T.E., Caspi, A., Rutter, M., & Silva, P.A. (2001). *Sex Differences in Antisocial Behaviour: Conduct Disorder, Delinquency and Violence in the Dunedin Longitudinal Study*, Cambridge University Press, Cambridge.

Mooij & Funk (1977). *Revista de Educación: Monográfico sobre violencia en los centros educativos*, N°313, Madrid, MEC.

Moore, T., & Lawrence, E. (2000). The Concept of Antisocial Behaviour. *http://www.mdx.ac.uk/www/conel/dc2.htm.*

Moreno, J.M. (1998a). Le côte sombre de l'école: politique et recherche sur le Comportement Anti-social dans les écoles espagnoles. *Revue Francaise de Pédagogie*, n° 123, Avril-Juin, pp. 63-71.

Moreno, J.M. (1998b). Comportamiento Antisocial en los centros escolares: una visión desde Europa, *Revista Iberoamericana de Educación*, N° 18, Septiembre-Diciembre, pp. 189-204.

Moreno, J.M. y Torrego, J.C. (1999a). *Resolución de conflictos de convivencia en centros educativos*, Madrid, UNED.

Moreno, J.M. y Torrego, J.C. (1999b). Promoting Prosocial Behaviour in Spanish Schools: The 'Whole-school' Approach, *Emotional and Behavioural Difficulties*, 4, 2, 23-31.

Muralidharan, R. (1973). Age Trends in Behaviour Problem of Children in Shanmugam, T,E., (Ed)., *Researches in Personality and Social Problems*, Madras University, 107-128 (IPA, 4:372).

Murthy, S.R., Ghosh, A., & Verma, V.K. (1974). Behaviour Disorders of Childhood and Adolescence. *Indian Journal of Psychiatry*, 16: 229-Kazdin, Siege & Bass, 1990.

Nagin, D. & Tremblay, R.E. (1999). Trajectories of Boys' Physical Aggression, Opposition, and Hyperactivity on the Path to Physically Violent and Non-violent Juvenile Delinquency. *Child Development*, 70, 1181-1196.

Nanda. G.S., & Dash. A.S. (1996). *Disadvantage, Schooling, Competence and Invulnerability*. Bhubaneshwar, Orissa: Panchajanya Publications.

Needleman, H.L., Riess, J.A., Tobin, M.J., Biesecker, G.E., & Greenhouse, J.B. (1996) Bone Lead Levels and Delinquent Behaviour. *Journal of the American Medical Association*, 275, 363-369.

Neligan, G.A., Kolvin, I., Scott, D.M., & Garside, R.F. (1976). *Born Too Soon or Too Small: A Follow-up Study of Seven Years of Age*. London: Heinemann.

New Oxford English Dictionary (1989) Oxford: Clarendon.

Nichols, P.L., & Chen, T.C. (1981). *Minimal Brain Dysfunction: A Prospective Study*. Hillsdale, NJ: Erlbaum.

Nixon, J. Blandy, S. Hunter, C. Jones, A., & Reeve, K. (2003). *Developing Good Practice in Tackling Antisocial Behaviour in Mixed Tenure Areas*. Sheffield: Sheffield Hallam University.

O'Brien, J.D., Halperin, J.M., Newcom, J.H., Sharma, V., Wolf, L., & Morgänstein, A. (1992). ADDH, Conduct Disorder and Cognitive Functioning. *Developmental and Behavioural Pediatrics*, 130, 274-277.

Offord, D.R., & Bennett, K.J. (1994). Conduct Disorder: Long Term Outcomes and Intervention Effectiveness. *Journal of the American Academy of Child and Adclescent Psychiatry*, 33(8), 1069-1078.

Offord, D.R., Boyle, M.H., & Racine, Y.A. (1988). *The Epidemiology of Antisocial Behaviour in Childhood and Adolescence.* Unpublished Paper Presented at the Earlscourt Symposium on Childhood Aggression. Toronto, June 15-18.

Olweus, D. (1979) Quoted in James H. Derzon, Antisocial Behaviour and the Prediction of Violence: A Meta-analysis. *Psychology in the Schools*, 38(2), 93-106 Published Online: 28 Feb 2001.

Olweus, D., Mattson, A., Schaling, D., & Low, H. (1980). Testosterone Aggression, Physical, and Personality Dimensions in Normal Adolescent Males. *Psychosomatic Medicine*, 42, 253-269.

Oxford English Dictionary. (1885) Oxford: Clarendon.

Patterson, G., Reid, J., & Dishion T. (1992). *Antisocial Boys: A Social Interactional Approach*. Eugene, OR; Castalia Publishing.

Patterson, G.R. (1982). Coercive Family Process. Eugene, OR: Castalia.

Pine, D.S., Cohen, E., Cohen, P., & Brook, J.S. (2000). Social Phobia and the Persistence of Conduct Problems. *Journal of Child Psychology and Psychiatry* 41(5):657-65, July.

Piquero, A. (2000). Frequency, Specialisation and Violence in Offending Careers, *Journal of Research in Crime and Delinquency*, 37, 392-418.

Rae-Grant, N., Thomas, B.H., Offord, D.R., & Boyle, M.H. (1989). Risk, Protective Factors, and the Prevalence of Behavioural and Emotional Disorders in Children and Adolescents. *Journal of the American Academy of Child and Adolescent Psychiatry*, 28(2), 262-268.

Raine, A., Brennan, B., & Mednick, S. (1994). Birth Complications Combined with Early Maternal Rejection at age 1 Year Predispose to Violent Crime at age 18 years. *Archives of General Psychiatry*, 51, 984-988.

Raine, A., Brennan, B., & Mednick, S. (1994). Birth Complications Combined with Early Maternal Rejection at Age 1 Year Predispose to Violent Crime At Age 18 Years. *Archives of General Psychiatry*, 51, 984-988.

Raine, A., Brennan, P., Mednick, B., & Mednick, S.A. (1997). Interactions Between Birth Complications and Early Marternal Rejection in Predisposing Individuals to Adult Violence: Specificity to Serious, Early Onset Violence. *American Journal of Psychiatry*, 154, 1265-71.

Raine, A., Brennan, P., Mednick, B., & Mednick, S.A. (1996). High Rates of Violence, Crime, Academic Problems, and Behavioural Problems in Those with Early Neuromotor Deficits and Negative Family Environments. *Archives of General Psychiatry*, 46, 1003-7.

Reidy, T.J. (1977). The Aggressive Characteristics of Abused and Neglected Children. *Journal of Clinical Psychology*, 33(4), 1140-1145.

Rey, J.M. (1993). Oppositional Defiance Disorder. *American Journal of Psychiatry*, 150 (2): 1769-1778.

Robins, L., & Hill, S.Y. (1966). Assessing the Contributions of Family Structure, Class and Peer Groups to Juvenile Delinquency. *Journal of Criminal Law, Criminology and Police Science*, 57, 325-34.

Robins, L., West, P., & Herjanic, B. (1975). Arrests and Delinquency in Two Generations: A Study of Black Urban Families and their Children. *Journal of Child Psychology and Psychiatry*, 16, 125-140.

Robins, L.N. (1978). Sturdy Childhood Predictors of Adult Antisocial Behaviour: Replications from Longitudinal Studies. *Psychological Medicine* 8, 611-622.

Robins, L.N. (1981). Epidemiological Approaches to Natural History Research: Antisocial Disorders in Children. *Journal of the American Academy of Child Psychiatry*, 20, 566-680.

Rutter, M. (1979). Invulnerability, or Why Some Children are not Damaged by Stress. In: S.J. Shamsie (Ed.), *New Directions in Children's Mental Health* (pp. 53-76). New York: S.P. Medical and Scientific Books.

Rutter, M. (1989). Psychiatric Disorder in Parents as a Risk Factor for Children. In D. Shaffer, I. Philips, N.B. Enzer, M.M. Silverman, & V. Anthony (Eds.), *Prevention of Mental Disorders, Alcohol and Other Drug Use in Children and Adolescents* (OSAP Prevention Monograph No. 2), 157-189. Rockville, MD: Office for Substance Abuse Prevention, U.S. Department of Health and Social Services.

Rutter, M., Cox, A., Tupling, C., Berger, M. & Yule, W. (1975). Attainment and Adjustment in Two Geographical Areas: 1. The Prevalence of Psychiatric Disorder. British Journal of Psychiatry, 126, 493-509.

Rutter, M., Giller, H. & Hagell, A. (1998). *Antisocial Behaviour by Young People*. New York: Cambridge University Press.

Rutter, M., Tizzard, J., & Whitmore, K.(1970). Education, Health and Behaviour. London: Longman.

Sampson, Robert J., & John H. Laub. (1993). *Crime in the Making: Pathways and Turning Points Through Life*. Cambridge, MA: Harvard University Press.

Sanson, A., Hemphill, S. A., & Smart, D. (2002). Temperament and Social Development in P.K. Smith and C.H. Hart (Eds.), *Blackwell Handbook of Childhood Social Development*, Blackwell Publishing, Oxford, UK.

Sanson, A., Oberklaid, F., Pedlow, R., & Prior, M. (1991). Risk Indicators: Assessment of Infancy Predictors of Preschool Behavioural Adjustment. *Journal of Child Psychology and Psychiatry*, 32, 609-626.

Satterfield J.H., Hoppe, C., X., M., & Schell, A.M. (1982). A Prospective Study of Delinquency of 110 Adolescent Boys with Attention Deficit Disorder and 88 Normal Adolescent Boys. *American Journal of Psychiatry*: 139(6), 795-798.

Satterfield, J., & Schell, A. (1997). A Prospective Study of Hyperactive Boys with Conduct Problems and Normal Boys: Adolescent and Adult Criminality. *Journal of the American Academy of Child and Adolescent Psychiatry*, 36, 1726-1735.

Schachar , R., Tannock, R., Marriott, M., & Logan, G. (1995). Deficient Inhbibitor Control in Attention Deficit Hyperactivity Disorder. *Journal of Abnormal Psychology*, 23,411-437.

Schlapp (1924) as quoted in Chauhan, S.S. (1983). *Psychology of Adolescence* (173-189). Allied Publishers Pvt.Ltd.

Sendi, I.B., & Blomgren, P.G. (1975). A Comparative Study of Predictive Criteria in the Predisposition of Homicidal Adolescents. *American Journal of Psychiatry*, 132: 423-427.

Shamsie, J. (1999). Troublesome Children, Toronto, Ontario: IAY Publication.

Shamsie, J. (Ed.). (1990). *Youth with Conduct Disorder: What is to be done*? Toronto: Ministry of Community and Social Services.

Shamsie, J. (Ed.). (2000). *Why Do Some Youth Commit Antisocial and Violent Acts*? Toronto: Institute for the Study of Antisocial Behaviour in Youth.

Shanmugam, T.E. (1981). Factors Underlying Delinquency. Abnormal Psychology. Tata Mc Graw Hill Publishing Co. Ltd. Quoted in Tania Rehman. (2000). Perceived Parental Attitude of Delinquents and Non-Delinquents In Bangladesh. *Journal of Criminology*, 28(2), July.

Shaw, Clifford R. (1931). *The Natural History of a Delinquency Career.* Chicago: University of Chicago Press.

Shaw, D.S., Emery, R.E., & Tuer, M.D. (1993). Parental Functioning and Children's Adjustment in Families of Divorce: A Prospective Study. *Journal of Abnormal Child Psychology*, 21, 119-134.

Shaw, D.S., Vondra, J.I., Dowdell Hommerding, K., Keenan., & Dunn, M. (1994). Chronic Family Adversity and Early Child Behaviour Problems: A Longitudinal Study of Low Income Families. *Journal of Child Psychology and Psychiatry*, 35, 1109-1122.

Sheldon, W. H., Stevens. S. S., & Tucker, W. B. (1940). The Varieties of Human Physique; An Introduction to Constitutional Psychology. New York, London, Harper & Brothers.

Sherman, D.K., Iacono, W.G., & McGue, M.K. (1997). Attention-deficit Hyperactivity Dimensions: A Twin Study of in Attention and Impulsivity-hyperactivity. *Journal of the American Academy of Child and Adolescent Psychiatry*, 36, 745-53.

Shukla, M. (1994). India, pp. 191-206 in Hurrelmann (Ed.), *International Handbook of Adolescence.* Westport, CT: Greenwood Press.

Signals for Future Criminal Behaviour. Available Online: *http://www.minjust.nl/b_organ/dpjs/engels/pjs_reports.htm.* Retrieved 13th of October 2002.

Silberg, J.L., Meyer, J., Pickles, A., Simonoff, E., Eaves, L.J., Hewitt, J., et al. (1996a). Heterogeneity Among Juvenile Antisocial Behaviours: Findings from the Virginia Twin Study of Adolescent Behaviour Development. In Bock, G.R., Goode, J.A. (Eds.), *Genetics of Criminal and Antisocial Behaviour* (pp 76-86), 194. Ciba Foundation, Chichester: J Wiley.

Silberg, J.L., Rutter, M., Meyer, J., Maes, H., Somonoff, E., Pickles, A., Loeber, R., & Eaves, L. (1996b). Genetic and Environmental Influences on the Covariation Between Hyperactivity and Conduct Disturbance in Juvenile Twins. *Journal of Child Psychology and Psychiatry*, 37, 803-16.

Simcha-Fagen, O., Langner, T., Gersten, J., & Eisenberg, J. (1975). Violent and Antisocial Behaviour: *A Longitudinal Study of Urban Youth.* (OCD-CB-480). Unpublished Manuscript. Office of Child Development.

Simhadri, Y.C. 1989. *Youth in Contemporary World.* New Delhi: Mittal Publications.

Simonoff, E., Pickles, A., Meyer, J.L., Maes, H.H., Loeber, R., Rutter, M., Hewitt, J.K., & Eaves, L.J. (1997). The Virginia Twin Study of Adolescent Behavioural Development: Influences of Age, Gender and Impairment on Rates of Disorder. *Archives of General Psychiatry*, 54, 801-8.

Snyder, H. N., & Sickmund, M. (1995). *Juvenile Offenders and Victims: A Focus on Violence*. Statistics Summary. U.S. Office of Justice, Office of Juvenile Justice and Delinquency Prevention.

Speltz, M.L., McClelllan, J. et al. (1999). Preschool Boys with Oppositional Defiant Disorder: Clinical Presentation and Diagnostic Change. *Journal of American Child and Adolescent Psychiatry*, 38(7):838-845.

Steissguth A.P., Martin, D.C., Barr, H.M., & MacGregor Sandman, B. (1984). Intrauterine Alcohol and Nicotine Exposure: Attention and Reaction Time in 4 Year Old Children. *Developmental Psychology*, 20, 533-41.

Steissguth, A.P. (1993). Fetal Alcohol Syndrome in Older Patients. Alcohol, 2, 209-12.

Stuart Waiton, (2004). Who's Being Juvenile? http://www.tes.co.uk.

Taylor, E., Chadwick, O., Heptinstall E., & Danckaerts, M. (1996).Hyperactivity and Conduct Problems as Risk Factors for Adolescent Development. *Journal of American Child and Adolescent Psychiatry*, 35: 1213-26. [Medline].

Taylor, E. (1991). Toxins and Allergens. In M. Rutter & P. Casaer (Eds.), *Biological Risk Factors for Psychosocial Disorders*, pp.199-231. Cambridge: Cambridge University Press.

Taylor, E., Sanderberg, S., Thorley, G., & Giles, S. (1991). *The Epidemiology of Childhood Hyperactivity*. Oxford: Oxford University Press.

Thomas, A., Chess, S., & Birch, H.G. (1969). *Temperament and Behaviour Disorders in Children*. New York: New York University Press.

Thornberry, T. (1994). Risk Factors for Youth Violence. In L. McCart (Ed.), *Kids and Violence* (pp. 8-14). Washington, DC: National Governors Association.

Thornberry, T. P. (1998). Membership in Youth Gangs and Involvement in Serious Violent Offending. In R. Loeber & D. P. Farrington (Eds.), *Serious and Violent Juvenile Offenders: Risk Factors and Successful Interventions* (pp. 147-166). Thousand Oaks, CA: Sage Publications.

Tierney, J., Dowd, T., & O'Kane, S. (1993). Empowering Aggressive Youth to Change. *Journal of Emotional Behavioural Problems*, 2(1), 41-45.

Tremblay, R.E., & Craig, W.M. (1995). Developmental Crime Prevention, in Tremblay, R.E., Masse, L.C., Vitaro, F., & Dobkin, P.L. The Impact of Friends' Deviant Behaviour on Early Onset of Delinquency: Longitudinal Data from 6 to 13 Years of Age. *Development and*

Psychopathology, 7, 649-67.

Walker, H., Colvin, G., & Ramsey, E. (1995). *Antisocial Behaviour in School: Strategies and Best Practices.* Pacific Grove, CA: Brooks/ Cole Publishing Company.

Walker, H.M. (1993). Antisocial Behaviour in School. *Journal of Emotional and Behavioural Problems*, 2(1), 20-23.

Walker, H.M., Horner, R.H., Sugai, G., Bullis, M., Sprague, J.R., Bricker, D., & Kaufman, M.J. (1996). *Integrated Approaches to Preventing Antisocial Behaviour Patterns Among School-age Children and Youth*, 194-209, October.

Walker, Hill M., & Sprague, J. (1999). The Path to School Failure, Delinquency and Violence: Casual Factors and Some Potential Solutions. *Intervention in School and Clinic*, January.

Weiss, G., Hechtman, L., Milroy T., & Perlman, T. (1985). Psychiatric Status of Hyperactives as Adults: A Controlled Prospective 15-year Follow-up of 63 Hyperactive Children. *Journal of American Academy of Child Psychiatry*, 24:211-220.

Werner, E.E., & Smith, R.S. (1977). *Kauai's Children Come of Age.* Honolulu: University of Hawaii Press.

Williams, J. H., Ayers, C. D., & Arthur, M. W. (1997). Risk and Protective Factors in the Development of Delinquency and Conduct Disorder. In M. W. Fraser (Ed.), *Risk and Resilience in Childhood: An Ecological Perspective* (pp. 140-170). Washington, DC: NASW Press.

Williams, J.R., & Gold, M. (1972). From Delinquent Behaviour to Official Delinquency. *Social Problems*, 20, 209-229.

Wilson, G., & Kelling, J. (1982). Broken Windows: The Police and Neighbourhood Safety. *The Atlantic Monthly*, March, 29-37.

2

FACTORS ASSOCIATED WITH ANTISOCIAL BEHAVIOUR

OBJECTIVES

This chapter deals with the factors associated with Antisocial behaviour. After reading this chapter, the reader should be able to:

(i) Identify, explain and understand the role of individual factors related to antisocial behaviour in students;

(ii) Acquire knowledge and comprehend the environmental influences such as family, school, peer and neighbourhood on antisocial behaviour;

(iii) Cognisize the interaction of cultural and individual factors in antisocial behaviour of children and adolescents.

This is a time of high concern about antisocial behaviour by young people. As a nation, we are in a period of reflection as to what can done to stem this tide. In a world that prizes the consumer goods they cannot afford, young people may turn to illegal means to get material things. Several general factors put all children at risk for antisocial behaviour. The presence of multiple factors increases risk; conversely, their elimination reduces risk.

A risk factor is something negative in a young person or his environment that increases the likelihood of health or behaviour problems. For example, availability of drugs, poor parental supervision, or low achievement (Hawkins et al., 1999; Developmental Research and Programmes Inc, 2000; Farrington, 2000). Research indicates that the greater the number of risk factors to which an individual is exposed, the greater that individual's risk is of developing problems. Antisocial behaviour and drug abuse may be predicted by a common set of risk factors observable in childhood (Barton et al., 1997; Smith & Carlson, 1997).

'Young people have become a separate class. They have their own culture, their own dress sense, and have less contact with other age groups' (Rutter & Smith, 1995). Among a small percentage of young people, who would appear to have every risk indicator possible to predict future criminal behaviour, there is less of a chance that they go on to commit crimes in adult life (Asquith, 1998). There are huge individual differences in response to psychological factors, with some children being 'seriously affected' and others going on to show normal psychological development and social functioning.

There is a myriad of individual, social and psychosocial reasons for antisocial behaviour, and shows that with each round of research new additions to these possibilities are created (Rutter et al., 1998).

However, when we look at individuals, which indeed we must, we are not looking at the mere first hand experiences he or she is having, but rather that individual exists within an established political, economic and social framework. Hyperactive children may lash out and be labelled as antisocial. The conscious actions of adults who make moral choices about their actions, cannot be connected to this unconscious act of a child. That negative events and experiences may impact upon a young person's life is not in question here. Rather, the problem is the way in which events are, to a degree, seen as setting in stone a type of behaviour. With a relatively passive view of the subject that exists in Rutter's work the tendency towards a deterministic understanding of children, young people and adults is inevitable. Another problematic aspect of this deterministic approach and the attempt in practice to identify 'risk factors', is that, negative outcomes are immediately expected from young people who are labelled as having these risk factors. There are often more exceptions to the 'risk' rule than norms. Young people it appears are often far more robust than we imagine.

It is important to realize that, as suggested by Edwards (1996), 'the pathway to antisocial behaviour is multiple and diverse'. Most antisocial behaviour develops from a combination of risk factors associated with individuals, families, schools, and communities. The same factors apply across races, cultures, and classes, and their effects are cumulative exposure to multiple and interacting risk factors exponentially increases a child's overall risk. Also, antisocial behaviour evolves over the course of childhood, often beginning in the preschool and elementary years and peaking in late adolescence/early adulthood. Direct, early intervention can halt its progress; once firmly established, however, antisocial patterns become more difficult to change and can persist into adulthood (Gottfredson, 1987; Thornberry, 1994).

Antisocial behaviour, such as school misbehaviour, drug usage, and weapon carrying, is a disturbing issue confronting adolescents, parents, and teachers alike. Every five minutes a youth is arrested for some type of violent crime, and every two hours a child is killed by a gun (Edelman, 1995). Taken together, the increase in the number and severity of such acts and their overwhelming cost for society validates the notion that antisocial behaviour has become a prominent global issue. Continued efforts to decrease the number of antisocial acts have led many researchers to investigate the underlying factors that may lead youth to act out in delinquent ways. Indeed, many factors have been suggested to have correlational and/or causal links to antisocial behaviour. Webber (1997) has suggested that these can essentially be reduced to fundamental factors: Individual, and Environmental.

There are different views as regards the causal factors of antisocial behaviour. One view emphasises the importance of Individual factors and the other view, that of Environment in the development of antisocial behaviour. A third view emphasises that it is the combination of negative genetic and environmental factors which promotes the development of antisocial behaviour (Richters & Cichetti, 1993; Susman, 1993).

INDIVIDUAL/PERSONAL FACTORS

Some psychologists are of the view that antisocial behaviour is caused by temperamental factors that are the by-products of early learning and hereditary factors. Individual factors such as biological vulnerability, difficult temperament, early behavioural problems, school failure and being male might be contributory to risk for antisocial behaviour.

Prenatal

There is convincing evidence of correlations between complications of pregnancy and birth and behaviour disorder (Pasamanick et al.,1956). Behaviour disorders are caused by abnormalities of pregnancy and incidence of prematurity. Problems during pregnancy and the first few years of life are weakly, but significantly, correlated with the development of aggression, delinquency, and violence (Gibson & Tibbetts, 1998). Specifically, maternal problems during pregnancy that are associated with antisocial behaviour and other poor developmental outcomes include poor diet and nutrition, minimal weight gain, drug and alcohol use, smoking, and inadequate use of prenatal care. Child-related medical problems occurring during, or shortly after birth, that are suspected to be early risk indicators for delinquency include low heart rate, respiratory effort, poor muscle tone, reflex irritability, and anoxia-related colour (Gibson & Tibbetts, 1998). Pre-term delivery, low birth weight, and babies born affected by alcohol or other drugs are other developmental risks observed after the birth. It is believed that these risk factors impact the development of the child's central nervous system, which affects the child's ability to regulate stimuli and produces deficits in cognition and difficult temperament. Prenatal complications place children at greater risk for early onset delinquency and are thought to interact with impoverished environments (Tibbetts & Piquero, 1999).

Prenatal and early postnatal complications, a more specific set of medical conditions, have been found to have inconsistent effects across a number of studies (Hawkins et al., 1998c). These complications encompass a broad group of genetic conditions or physical injuries to the brain and nervous system that interfere with normal development, including low birth weight, oxygen deprivation, and exposure to toxins such as lead, alcohol, or drugs (Hawkins et al., 1998b). Low resting heart rate, a condition that has been studied primarily in boys, is associated with fearlessness or stimulation seeking, both characteristics that may predispose them to aggression and violence (Hawkins et al., 1998c; Raine et al., 1997), but there is not enough evidence to establish this condition as a risk factor for violence. Some studies have even questioned its effects on aggression (Kindlon et al., 1995; Van Hulle et al., 2000; Wadsworth, 1976). There is also no evidence that internalizing disorders—nervousness and withdrawal, anxiety, and worrying—are related to later violence (Hawkins et al., 1998c).

Sex and Age

Two moderate risk factors emerge in childhood, being male and aggression. Boys (and young men) are far more likely than girls to be violent, yet some researchers have suggested that sex is a risk marker rather than a risk factor (Earls, 1994; Hawkins et al., 1998a; Kraemer et al., 1997). A risk marker is a characteristic or condition that is associated with known risk factors but exerts no causal influence of its own (Earls, 1994; Patterson & Yoerger, 1997). For example, many more boys than girls are hyperactive, a risk factor with a small effect size, so some of the predictive power of being male may actually be the influence of hyperactivity. Moreover, boys have traditionally been exposed to more violence than girls, and socially approved male role models are more aggressive, suggesting that social learning plays a role in this risk factor. However, research indicates that being male confers risk even after accounting for other known risk factors. This suggests that being male is a risk factor rather than a risk marker, perhaps with some biological or biological-environmental interaction as the causal mechanism.

The tendency for aggression to be higher among males than females is a robust one (Daly & Wilson, 1988; Maccoby & Jacklin, 1980; Segall, Ember, & Ember, 1997). Many studies have found aggression—characterized as aggressive and disruptive behaviour, verbal aggression, and aggression toward objects—to be a moderate risk factor among boys, although there is some evidence that physical aggressiveness is actually responsible for most of the observed effect (Nagin & Tremblay, 1999).

Maccoby's (1998) review explores the findings that boys' activity level increases when they are interacting with playmates, that they become especially aroused when engaged in competition or meeting challenges, and that they may possess less ability than girls to regulate impulsive behaviour. Additional research is needed to sort out the unique influence of each of these types of aggression.

ADHD is seven times more common in boys than in girls (Garfinkel & Wener, 1989). Many ADHD children develop violent behaviour. Remarkably, studies reveal that ADHD is a risk factor for boys but not for girls. Girls with ADHD seldom develop violent and antisocial behaviour (Herrero et al., 1994). This is the same case with ODD (Shamsie, 1999) and CD (Shamsie & Hiluchy 1991). Boys report more physical forms of bullying; girls tend to bully in indirect ways, such as gossiping and excluding (Craig & Pepler, 1997).

In Indian society, irrespective of rural or urban background, boys are given more freedom and independency by their parents right from their childhood. It is the reverse with respect to girls. Perhaps, too much of freedom, in the adolescent stage, coupled with non-availability of proper counselling to channelise their energies might be the contributory factors for antisocial behaviour to be more prevalent among boys than in girls. Further, adolescence is the stage when students get easily motivated and attracted to their peers. It is also the stage when the students prefer to spend more time with their peer group than with their family. This gives them ample opportunities to get involved in acts such as stealing, bullying, smoking, drug addiction, and gambling for the sake of peer pressure and pleasure.

Until recently, research on adult outcomes of antisocial behaviour in youth has been primarily focused on males. This may stem in part from widespread beliefs that antisocial behaviour in females is rare and only a temporary stage that they will soon 'grow out of'. More recent research is providing evidence that antisocial behaviour in girls is neither rare nor temporary.

It is suggested that some antisocial adolescent girls begin their antisocial behaviour during early adolescence and continue to commit offences with increasing severity and frequency into adulthood. Others start with norm violation (such as coming home late and missing school) and continue into adulthood. Given the attitude of parents and guardians either to subdue the expressive feelings, opinions and emotions of girls right from the start, or to give uncontrolled freedom at all levels, the girls prefer to have better-time off their homes. School is the place where they group themselves with students of like-minds and similar stature and possibly violate social rules, perform poorly in academics and exhibit many unaccepted behaviours. They resort to antisocial behaviours ranging from stealing and blaming others to disobedience and aggression. Unlike boys, whose delinquent behaviour in adolescence is likely to result in criminal behaviour in adulthood, delinquent girls may manifest continued disturbed behaviour in different ways in adulthood.

In the male-dominated Indian society, boys exhibit their physical power more than girls, both in and out of their home environments. The greater vigour of boys is also depicted though theatre shows, video-films, CD games and popular teleserials. This is very much emulated by students. In order to exhibit their physical supremacy over the so-called weaker sex, boys develop more tendencies of bullying and aggression than girls. Girls, in general, are prohibited from learning and participating in activities involving physical stress such as karate, kabaddi and weight-lifting.

Type of brought-up (familial and societal rigidity) may well be the contributory factor for less tendency of bullying and aggression in girls than in boys. Due to various distractions that include television shows, wall posters, pamphlets, leaflets from exposure to obscene stuff through the internet, boys get tempted easily by peer group pressure to involve more in antisocial gang activities to show their muscle power. Imitation of their role models may also attribute to their involvement in bullying and aggression. As the concentration of boys get diverted to such activities, their concentration in studies also dwindles resulting in poor academic performance. They also do not seem to bother about wounding others either physically through their aggressive acts or verbally through utterance of unappreciated words to 'get' what they 'want'. It is of no wonder that boys thus exhibit more antisocial behaviours such as bullying and aggression and poor social and academic skills.

While girls may be less aggressive than boys, existing data indicates that girls engage in slightly more indirect aggression such as social manipulation, shutting a peer out of a group, becoming friends with another peer as a form of retaliation, and gossiping (Bell-Dolan et al., 1995; Mathews, 1999; Pepler & Sedighdeilami, 1998). Research also suggests that differences observed in friendship structures (i.e., boys socialise in large groups, while girls tend to prefer a small group often involving one best friend) may help in explaining some of the sex differences witnessed in antisocial activities by boys and girls (Osterman, 1999). Also, as girls mature and develop sooner than boys, age is also an important factor while assessing gender-specific variations in the manifestation of antisocial behaviour. Girls' involvement in antisocial behaviour begins earlier, but also ends sooner than boys (Appleby, 1998).

The number of young females charged with violent offences is growing more rapidly (Savoie, 1999) than their counterparts.

Research results for females are less consistent. McCord and Ensminger (1995) found similar results for males and females; however, Stattin and Magnusson (1989) did not find a relationship between early female aggression and later violent offenses.

In a sample of African American boys in the Woodlawn area of Chicago, IL, nearly half of the 6-year-old boys who had been rated aggressive by teachers were arrested for violent crimes by age 33, compared with one-third of their non-aggressive counterparts (McCord & Ensminger, 1995). This relationship also held for males in hyperactive samples (Loney, Kramer, & Milich, 1983).

The downward course of aggression with increasing age has been a steady finding in Western research (Coie & Dodge, 1998). Students in the age group of over 14 years were found to have greater intensity of antisocial behaviour than those below 14 years (Shyamala, 2004). These students might have acquired adolescent-limited antisocial behaviour. Evidence for the increased incidence of conduct disorder at about the age of 15 years with no corresponding increase in aggression has served as support for adolescent onset (McGee et al., 1992; Patterson, Reid & Dishion, 1992). Negative reinforcement of deviant behaviour, inattention to positive prosocial behaviour and coercive interactions between parent and child lead to escalation of antisocial behaviour in adolescents. This may lead to consequences such as poor peer relations, associations with deviant peers and school failure (Patterson, Cldi, & Bank, 1991).

Adolescence is the appropriate time for implementation of any designed strategy to overcome antisocial behaviour among students. As this is the most vulnerable stage to 'learn', anything that they learn at this stage will be ever-lasting in their lives. Recent gender-specific violence-related factors indicate that both boys and girls experience more emotional problems than their non-antisocial counterparts (Pepler & Sedighdeilami, 1998). They also experience high levels of conflicts and victimisations with their parents and peers. Thus, both boys and girls seem to experience similar problems within their living environment throughout their childhood and teen years. The causes for antisocial acts are equally problematic in both cases.

Early Initiation of Antisocial Behaviour

The earlier youths engage in crime, aggression/violence, drop out of school, or begin using drugs, the greater the likelihood that they will have chronic, and increasing problems in the future. McCord and Ensminger (1995) found, for example, that teacher ratings of aggression at age 6 predicted arrests for violent crimes up to age 33. Almost half of the aggressive boys in this study were arrested, compared with about a third of their non-aggressive counterparts. Another study reports that two-thirds of boys with official arrests for violence by age 26 had high teacher ratings of aggressive behaviour at ages 10 and 13 (Stattin & Magnusson, 1989). Both early and persistent school behaviour problems, characterized by physical and verbal aggression towards peers and adults, difficulties in peer situations, and stealing are both related to the development and maintenance of delinquency (McCord & Ensminger, 1995; Stattin & Magnusson, 1989).

Birth Order

Birth order is related to the onset of conduct disorder. Antisocial behaviour is greater among middle children in comparison to only children, first-born or youngest children (Glueck & Glueck, 1968; McCord et al., 1959) although there are some exceptions (Eron, Huesmann & Zelli, 1991). The effects are complex, and in the case of delinquency, may vary as a function of type of offence and duration of the only-child status (length of time before a sibling is born). However, in general, an extended period of time as the only or the youngest child before the sibling is born, reduces risk for antisocial behaviour. Children with older sibling are more likely to be antisocial; the older the siblings, (i.e., the greater the space in age between them), the greater the likelihood of antisocial behaviour (Wadsworth, 1979). Interestingly, the risk is said to be associated with number of brothers, rather than sisters in the family (Offord, 1982). If one of the brother is antisocial, the others are at increased risk for antisocial behaviour. Middle children and male children from large families have been found to be at an increased risk of delinquency and antisocial behaviours (Webster-Stratton & Dahi, 1995).

Food Additives and Refined Sugar

During the 1970's, strong claims were made that food additives were an important cause of hyperactivity (Feingold, 1975). At the population level, Mawson and Jacobs (1978) indicate that countries with significantly high homicide rates also have significantly high corn consumption. Such results, as perhaps with many correlations found between nutrition and criminality, may be spurious. Some children respond adversely to elements in their diet, sometimes showing hyperactivity (Carter et al., 1993; Eggar et al., 1985; Taylor, 1991). Feingold (1975) discovered that low molecular weight compounds, like artificial food dyes, produce neurophysiological disturbances and hyperactivity in susceptible children. Feingold was the first to reveal that 30-50% of children suffering from ADHD could be 'cured' using a dietary regimen, and follow up studies confirmed his findings.

In susceptible children, refined sugar consumption induces the production of cortisol, a chemical implicated in hyperactive behaviour. Sugar intake makes a marked contribution to hyperactive, aggressive, and destructive behaviour (Crook, 1999; Murray & Pizzorno, 1998; Prinz et al., 1980). A large study by Langseth and Dowd (1978) found 74 per cent of 261 hyperactive children manifested abnormal glucose tolerance in response to a sucrose meal.

Hormonal

Hormonal factors may also play a role. Body chemicals such as testosterone and serotonin can influence aggressive behaviour. Androgens (or "male" hormones, e.g. testosterone), like other hormones, may either have a direct influence on physiological mechanisms governing behaviour or organise the developing human brain to make particular behavioural responses more likely. Research suggests that men are more aggressive than women throughout all cultures because of their higher levels of testosterone (Lippa, 1990). Females exposed to excess androgenic activity show male characteristics such as increased aggression (Money & Erhardt, 1972), but such effects may be due to differential treatment during upbringing.

People's biological make-up influences their liability to antisocial behaviour—the evidence being strongest in the case of autonomic reactivity and diminished serotonic activity. The strongest biological effects are probabilistic. In addition, in some aggressive individuals there seems to be evidence of lower levels of serotonin, a neurotransmitter negatively associated with aggression and impulsivity (Lipsitt, 1990). But not all individuals with abnormal levels of serotonin are violent. The environment may also exacerbate aggressive behaviour, because even people without a chemical imbalance may behave violently (Myers, 1993). Thus, nature and nurture are both factors in aggression.

Psychological

The remaining individual risk factors have relatively small effect sizes. Various psychological conditions, such as hyperactivity, impulsiveness, daring, and short attention span, pose a small risk for violence. A consistent individual predictor is hyperactivity/low attention, the central components of attention-deficit/hyperactivity disorder (ADHD), a cognitive disorder that may be genetically influenced in some way (Hawkins et al., 1998a). ADHD is characterized by restlessness, excessive activity, and difficulty paying attention, traits that may also contribute to low academic performance, a risk factor in school. Hyperactivity is often found in combination with physical aggression, another risk factor. Some researchers question the independent effect of hyperactivity on later violence, suggesting that the effect is actually physical aggression (and perhaps low academic performance) that was not controlled for in earlier studies of hyperactivity (Nagin & Tremblay, 1999). There is little agreement about the mechanism linking hyperactivity to violence.

Antisocial beliefs and attitudes, including dishonesty, rule breaking, hostility to police, and a generally favourable attitude toward violence, usually constitute risk factors in adolescence, not childhood (Hawkins et al., 1998c). Only dishonesty in childhood is predictive of later violence or delinquency, and its effect is small.

Over the past few decades, researchers have identified deficient skills in empathy, impulse control, social problem solving, anger management and assertiveness to be consistently correlated with both adolescent and adult antisocial behaviour (Feshbach, 1984; Kendall & Braswell, 1985; Mehrabian, 1997; Spivack & Cianci, 1987). Several inborn traits and characteristics related to personality, temperament, and cognitive ability have been identified as risk factors for later antisocial behaviour. These do not doom children to misbehaviour or crime, but they do make them more susceptible to other risks in the environment such as impulsivity, the inability to adopt a future time perspective or to grasp future consequences of behaviour; the inability to delay gratification; the inability to self-regulate emotions, especially temper; the need for stimulation and excitement; low harm avoidance; low frustration tolerance; central nervous system dysfunction; low cortical arousal; a predisposition to aggressive behaviour; low general aptitude or intelligence; exposure to violence and abuse (as either a victim or a witness); alienation; rebelliousness; association with deviant peers; favourable attitudes toward deviant behaviour; peer rejection; alcohol and drug abuse; and early onset of aggressive or problem behaviour (Brier, 1994; Gibbs, 1995; Gotfredson, 1987; Hawkins, 1995; Keilitz & Dunivant, 1986; Martinez & Bournival, 1996; Thornberry, 1994; Wexler, 1996; Wright, 1995). Students with certain disabilities (e.g., emotional disturbance, attention deficit-hyperactivity disorders, specific learning disabilities) are more likely to display antisocial behaviour, suggesting that these conditions may be risk factors for later aggressive and violent actions (Leone et al., 2000). Individual factors exhibited early in childhood such as various forms of antisocial behaviours and difficult temperament have been found to predispose youth to problems later in life (Klein, 1995; Walker, Colvin, & Ramsey, 1995; Thomas, Chess, & Birch, 1969).

Cognitive

Dodge's (1986) research indicates that aggressive children tend to inaccurately detect and decipher the feelings and behaviours of other people. Because they lack skills in social perspective, aggressive youth are apt to misinterpret others' intentions (Selman & Kautz, 1989; Slaby & Guerra, 1988).

Constructivists hold that prior knowledge is used as a framework to learn new knowledge. A concept map, similar to an outline or a flowchart, is a way of representing or organizing knowledge. Joseph D. Novak of Cornell University first used concept maps in the 1960s (Lanzing, 1997). In particular, concept maps identify the way we think, the way we see relationships between knowledge. Concept maps can thus illustrate faulty views individuals may have.

Cognitive strategies are those procedures, such as self-questioning or inferring, that involve reflective mental activity. Met cognitive strategy involves monitoring of such cognitive efforts. Metacognition is an awareness and knowledge of one's own learning and thought processes, and the regulation of those processes. Therefore, there is a strong connection between critical thinking skills and those of metacognition.

Children who are at risk of becoming violent toward themselves or others need additional support. They often need to learn interpersonal, problem solving, and conflict resolution skills at home and in school. They also may need more intensive assistance in learning how to stop and think before they react, and to listen effectively (Gresham et al., 1998; Knoff & Batsche, 1995).

Thinking Errors

Human beings, to the best of our knowledge, are the only form of life with the city to stand off and examine their own thoughts while they engage in them. Although the human brain is able to generate reflective consciousness, however, not everyone seems to use it equally (Csikszentmihalyi,1990).

Thinking Errors are thoughts people exhibit and/or demonstrate during irresponsible behaviour. This thinking leads to and/or brings on antisocial behaviour. Antisocial thinking is the result of a number of mistaken cognitive beliefs. Errors in thinking are beliefs and thought patterns that permit the antisocial student to continue doing the things that seem so wrong to other people. Antisocial students, use cognitive distortions to justify socially unacceptable actions as acceptable. Antisocials lack interpersonal problem-solving skills. In addition, they have not acquired adequate critical reasoning and planning skills. They often seem unable to look at the world through another person's perspective and they don't seem to be able to distinguish their own emotional states and thoughts from those of others. They lack self-control, fail to self-regulate their behaviour and tend to be action-oriented, non-reflective, and impulsive. The end result is that they become caught in a cycle of 'thinking' errors—the most common error being blaming others for one's own fault.

As Shakespeare wrote in Hamlet, 'There is nothing either good or bad but thinking makes it so'. Many antisocials do not seem to have acquired a number of cognitive skills essential to social adaptation. (Ross & Fabiano, 1985; Zamble & Porporino, 1988). Indeed, there is evidence that young people who fail to learn how to think about their thinking, use logic and solve hypothetical problems are more likely to become involved in antisocial behaviour (Larson, 1998).

Antisocials find it acceptable to use cognitive distortions and, therefore use them frequently. These at risk youth tend to come from hostile and dysfunctional families in which very little emphasis is placed on structure and discipline. Their environments tend to be high in criticism, physical and emotional abuse, unnecessarily harsh punishments, and lack of positive parental influence. According to the social information processing theory, cognitive distortions may not be only due to environmental factors but due to the result of physiological processes. An individual's behaviour may be altered due to cognitive distortions interrupting the transfer of incoming information before the information activates a particular behaviour. The interruption may affect traditional schemas and/or the ability for the incoming information to continue to lead to an action (Liau, Barriga, & Gibbs, 1998).

The relationship between thinking errors and antisocial behaviour was suggested by few researchers (Barriga et al., 2000; Jerome R. Gardner, 1997; Raine et al., 2000). Children who are diagnosed with oppositional defiant disorder, attention deficit disorder, conduct disorder, and antisocial personality disorder exhibit more frequent use of cognitive distortions (Giancola, Mezzich, Clark, & Tarter, 1999). This is much in tune with the observations of Mussack (2000), Niolon (2000), Yochelson & Samenow (1995) and also the recent finding of Shyamala (2004) that, higher the thinking errors, more will be the antisocial behaviour.

It is necessary to identify the habits of thinking that directly relate to antisocial behaviour. Common themes of antisocial thinking include the belief and mind-set of those with antisocial behaviour themselves, that they are being victimised (Jerome R. Gardner, 1997). Thinking errors commonly associated with antisocial behaviours include excuse making, blaming, justifying, redefining, lying, making fools of, build-up, assuming I'm unique, vagueness, anger, power plays, victim playing, drama-excitement, closed channel, ownership, grandiosity (Mussack, 2000).

Adolescent antisocials commit thinking errors when faced with a problem. Four main categorisations of cognitive distortions (Barriga et al., 2000) are: self-centred, blaming others, minimizing/mislabelling, and assuming the worst. The first distortion is self-centred and is a primary distortion. An individual resorting to a self-centred cognitive distortion behaves according to his or her own views, expectations, needs, rights, immediate feelings, and desires to such an extent that the legitimate views of others (or even one's own long-term best interest) are scarcely considered or are disregarded altogether. The second distortion is blaming others. Blaming others is misattributing blame for one's harmful actions to outside sources, especially to another person, a group, or a momentary aberration (one was drunk, high, in a bad mood, etc.), or misattributing blame for one's victimization or other misfortune to innocent others. The third distortion is minimizing/ mislabelling in which an individual depicts antisocial behaviour as causing no real harm or as being acceptable or even admirable, or referring to others with belittling or dehumanising labels. The fourth distortion is assuming the worst. Assuming the worst is when an individual gratuitously attributes hostile intentions to others; considering a worst-case scenario for a social situation as if it were inevitable; or assuming that improvement is impossible in one's own or others' behaviour. The second, third, and fourth distortions are secondary distortions and are used to rationalize and diminish the bad feelings felt or enhanced due to the use of the primary or self-centred distortion (Barriga & Gibbs, 1996).

Cognitive Behavioural theorists say that Antisocials suffer from a number of mistaken cognitive beliefs. They probably learnt these and they were reinforced somewhere. It is worthwhile to look at the way they think (Niolon, 2000):

(i) Wanting something or wanting to avoid something is sufficient justification for acting in any way needed to obtain it or avoid it;

(ii) Thinking or feeling is a fact, and so if you think it is then it is true; the result is that you are always right;

(iii) Undesirable consequences will not happen to you or won't matter you're on your own in this world;

(iv) Why worry about tomorrow, focus on today.

Dodge (1980, 1986), and Dodge and Schwartz (1997) proposed that aggressive individuals have a distorted style of social information processing characterised, among other features, by a tendency wrongly to attribute hostile intent to neutral or ambiguous social approaches, a tendency to make negative misinterpretations (such as perceiving benign teasing as malicious), and a tendency to focus on aggressive social cues to the detriment of non-aggressive ones. The model has generated an immense body of research that is generally supportive of its basic proportions (Crick & Dodge, 1994; Rubin & Krasnor,1986).

Individuals perform antisocially because they lack the necessary skills for prosocial behaviour or because they have limited opportunities and have weak commitment to conformity (Cloward & Ohlin, 1960; Hirschi, 1969; Leiber & Mahwor, 1995). Social information processing patterns partially mediated the effects of early child abuse in predisposing to later conduct problems (but still in early childhood). To a significant albeit moderate extent, hostile attributional biases predict later aggressive behaviour (Dodge et al., 1995), the association being with angry or reactive aggression and violence rather than with crime generally.

Aggressive children have difficulties suppressing aggressive responses (Perry, Perry, & Rasmussen, 1986); they generally hold positive beliefs about aggression and believe that it is socially normative (Dodge & Schwartz, 1997). These positive evaluations tend to be associated with proactive aggression (such as bullying and grabbing other people's belongings) rather reactive anger (which is more associated with hostile attributional biases (Crick & Dodge, 1996). Also, Waldman (1996) has shown that the associations between aggression and both hostile perceptual biases and aggressive responses to non-hostile identified intentions remained even after controlling statistically for inattention and impulsivity.

Antisocials find it acceptable to use cognitive distortions and, therefore use them frequently. These at risk youth tend to come from hostile and dysfunctional families in which very little emphasis is placed on structure and discipline. Their environments tend to be high in criticism, physical and emotional abuse, unnecessarily harsh punishments, and lack of positive parental influence. Researchers have found children that have been raised in a negative type of environment are more aggressive, more often diagnosed with oppositional defiant disorder, attention deficit disorder, conduct disorder, and antisocial personality disorder, and exhibit more frequent use of cognitive distortions (Giancola, Mezzich, Clark, & Tarter, 1999). Children with less developed Interpersonal Cognitive Problem Solving skills, in particular deficient means-ends thinking, are more likely to display 'impulsive antisocial behaviours such as physical and verbal aggression, inability to delay gratification, over emotionality in the face of frustration, inability to make friends, and less tendency to show empathy or sympathy to others in distress'. Deficiencies in alternative solution thinking and consequential thinking are strongly associated with impulsiveness, withdrawn behaviour, and lack of prosocial skills (Shure, 1999).

The study by Raine et al. (2000) bolsters this link by taking people with lifelong antisocial tendencies. The 21 men studied were all diagnosed with Antisocial Personality Disorder (APD), which is characterized by irresponsibility, deceitfulness, impulsiveness, irritability, lack of emotional depth, lack of remorse, and life-long antisocial behaviour. All of them had psychopathic personalities.

Following are three reasons why prefrontal deficits may cause antisocial personality (Raine et al.,2000):

First, the region appears to be critical for self-restraint and deliberate foresight. 'One thing we know about antisocials is that they do not think ahead,' said Raine. *Second*, it is crucial for learning conditioned responses—essential, for example, to a child's linking the thought of a misdeed with anxiety over punishment. 'Unconscious mental-emotional associations such as these lie at the core of what we call conscience,' Raine said. *Third*, if prefrontal deficits underlie the APD group's low levels of autonomic arousal, these people may unconsciously be trying to compensate through stimulation-seeking. 'For some kids,' said Raine, 'one way of getting an arousal-jag is by robbing stores or beating people up'.

In a study by Brooklin (2001), The 'How I Think' questionnaire was used to measure the four different types of cognitive distortions Three questionnaires were administered. The 'How I Think' questionnaire was used to measure the four different types of cognitive distortions (Barriga & Gibbs, 1996). The Self-Reported Delinquency Scale was used to verify the types of crimes committed, if any, by the juvenile (Elliott & Ageton, 1980). The 'What I Am Like' scale was used to measure global self-esteem.

Three techniques were recommended by Vorrath and Brendtro (1985) to correct such faulty thinkings:

1. *Reversing* involves placing the responsibility for action back on those who must do the changing rather than allowing them to project it outside themselves;
2. *Relabelling* means assigning an accurate label to a behaviour. This counteracts the tendency of antisocial youths to engage in self-serving representations or interpretations, for instance, by placing a positive label on negative behaviour. For instance, if stealing is seen as slick, then it should be relabelled by adults, but more importantly by peers themselves, as 'sneaky and dumb';
3. *Confronting* entails addressing not only secondary but also primary (i.e., self-centered) cognitive distortions by making students aware of the effects of their actions on others. This confrontation highlights the harm to others resulting from their actions and thereby elicits and strengthens the empathic response. Such strengthening is crucial if empathic responses (and related emotions such as empathy-based guilt) are to counteract egocentric bias and to penetrate primary and secondary cognitive distortions.

Cognitive theorists believe that these types of strategies are necessary if cognitive distortions or thinking errors are to be corrected and more caring behaviours are to emerge. If biased cognitive processing plays a part in the persistence of antisocial behaviour, it may well be that interventions to prevent or alleviate antisocial behaviour should include steps designed to foster more positive and less biased ways of thinking and responding. By using restructured mind map, as a constructive perspective, it is possible to help children gain a deep understanding of themselves in relation to others in the world.

When an individual thinks about what he is doing, and the consequences of his actions in the form of cognising his acts, then he will be more rational thus causing less inconvenience to others. One cannot act differently than he thinks, therefore, change will occur only as he thinks differently. Cognitive change is based on the simple fact that how people think has a controlling effect on how they act. Understanding of self and others and considering others' feelings and beliefs is a part of the learning process.

It is possible to channelise the faulty thinking patterns of such students through well designed cognitive-behavioural strategies such as self-analysis and crisis intervention, for better inter-personal and pro-social behaviours. Family interventions that seek to promote the parent's ccity to monitor and discipline the adolescent's thinking patterns is also the need of the day. This will streamline thinking patterns and prevent antisocial thinking and antisocial behaviour (Reddy & Shyamala, 2003).

Genetic

Ted Grant and Alan Woods (1995) quote C. R. Jeffery as follows: "Science must tell us what individuals will or will not become criminals, what individuals will or will not become victims, and what law enforcement strategies will or will not work." Ted Grant and Alan Woods (1995) also quote Yudofsky with his assertion: "We are now on the verge of a revolution in genetic medicine. The future will be to understand the genetics of aggressive disorders and to identify those who have greater tendencies to become violent."

The role of chromosomal disorders has been implicated in criminality. The findings reported during the 1960s and 1970s suggested that certain chromosomal abnormalities (e.g., XYY and XXY anomalies) were mostly associated with a predisposition to violence (Casey et al., 1966; Forssman & Hambert, 1967; Hook, 1973; Nielson, 1968; Telfer, 1968; Witkin et al., 1976). The XYY chromosome abnormality (where males are born with an extra 'Y' or 'male' chromosome) has been associated with "super maleness" and thus increased aggressiveness and criminality. The criminality in women has been biologically considered, where delinquent girls are expected to show a higher rate of XXY genetic makeup. These girls are large for their age and have masculine traits,and show homosexuality. Later, these have been re-evaluated, and their conclusions questioned (Baker et al., 1970; Jacobs et al., 1971; Schiavo et al., 1984).

Jacobs et al. (1971) found that such a condition was over-represented in mental institutions, and that the afflicted had dangerous, violent or criminal propensities. Other studies have found no basis for such an assertion (Sarbin & Miller 1970), although Witkin et al. (1976) found that 41.7% of a very small sample of XYY subjects (n=12) had criminal convictions compared to only 9.3% of a matched XY sample (n=4111). However, XYY subjects were no more likely than their XY counterparts to have convictions for violent offences. Most probably, these abnormal constellations of chromosomes, like other abnormal conditions, predispose an individual to a variety of different kinds of adaptation problems that, depending on upbringing and stressors, may or may not be manifested by aggression. With the exception of Losch Nyhan Syndrome (Palmour, 1983), no genetic abnormality has yet been identified that predisposes an individual specifically to violent behaviour.

In an adoption study, the rate of criminality in adoptees who had non-criminal adoptive and biological parents was 2.9% (Cloninger et al., 1982). The rate increased to 6.7% when it was only the adoptive parents who were criminal, this can be seen as an environmental factor and the rate then increased to 12.1% when only the biological parents were criminal, suggesting a genetic link. Where both the adoptive and biological parents were criminals, the rate rose to 40%. Thus interaction between environment and genetics is more influential than either on its own, and suggests environmental factors are far more influential when interacting with genetics and heredity. It is likely that genetic factors do play a part in determining antisocial behaviour, but very little confirmatory research has been done in this arena.

In terms of ADHD, there is usually a history that some members of the family have suffered from this disorder. There is strong evidence that children with this disorder are born with a gene which makes them more likely to develop ADHD (Hauser et al., 1993). Inattention, hyperactivity and impulsivity are the characteristics expressed by students with ADHD. Owing to difficult temperament or ADHD, the child may get extra patience and energy and, due to inconsistent parenting, lack of parental care, and parental psychopathology, these children are prone to develop ODD or, these two disorders may co-occur (Biederman, Newcorn, & Sprich, 1991). These children often loose their temper, argue with adults, defy or refuse to comply with rules, deliberately annoy people, blame others, get easily annoyed, and are often angry and vindictive. The aggressive behaviour of oppositional defiant disordered children become more serious with age. Many of these children may go on to exhibit CD that includes hitting, stealing and destruction of property. Therefore, many children with ODD grow up to become conduct disordered youth also. When ADHD, ODD and CD persist and continue, the diagnosis would become Antisocial personality disorder (Shamsie, 1990).

Sex may also play a part in respect of genetic factors. It has been proposed that genetic loadings for antisocial behaviour may be greater in women than in men (Sigvardson et al., 1982; Widom & Ames, 1994). Raine and Dunkin (1990) suggest that the genetic predisposition for antisocial behaviour may find its base in Autonomous and Central Nervous Systems under arousal. This is because psycho-physiological measures of arousal have been shown to have a hereditary basis. Genetic influences play a larger role than environmental influences in physical aggression in male youth (Eley et al., 1999) arid hyperactivity (Silberg et al., 1996). Adoption studies suggest that genetically vulnerable children—that is, children whose birth parents were antisocial—may be especially susceptible to unfavourable family conditions, so that an interaction is clearly seen (Bohman, 1996). The genetic element seems to be stronger for adult criminality than childhood conduct disorder and delinquency (Rutter, 1996). Twin studies help psychologists to determine whether gene or environment has more impact on behaviour. The Monitor (1999) reports that identical twins are most likely to be similar in their degree of antisocial aggressive behaviour, such as bullying or hitting. Venter (2001) expresses the same idea by stating "We simply do not have enough genes for this idea of biological determinism to be right. The wonderful diversity of the human species is not hard-wired in our genetic code. Our environments are critical."

Individual factors (physical, mental and psychological) leading to antisocial behaviour reside in and around the 'self' or the individual, and are influenced by his 'environment'. Whether a person turns to be an antisocial or otherwise, is dependent on the kind of exposure he gets in his environment and how he reacts to it.

ENVIRONMENTAL FACTORS

As Goleman (1995) puts out, "genes alone do not determine behaviour; our environment, especially what we experience and learn as we grow, shapes how a temperamental predisposition expresses itself as life unfolds."

It appears that 'a greater genetic effect is required for the expression of aggression in more benign environments', whereas in more disadvantaged neighbourhoods disrupted family processes and context-dependent risks may promote aggressive behaviour even among individuals without a genetic predisposition (Rowe et al., 1999).

In recent years, the number of children and youth who have taken a path to school failure, delinquency and violence has grown significantly. Unfortunately, ineffective and punitive responses from their environments have taught many antisocial children 'that they do not like school or their parents and that following conventional rules does not yield rewards' (Gottfredson, 1987).

There are a number of factors contained within the home, community, and school that are related to antisocial behaviour (Mayer, 1995). A factor that cuts across all three of these areas is an aversive or punitive environment. Research has taught us that aversive environments predictably promote antisocial behaviours such as aggression, violence, vandalism, and escape (Azrin, Hake, Holz, & Hutchinson, 1965; Berkowitz, 1983).

Walker and Sprague (1999) have presented the path to long-term negative outcomes for at-risk children and youth as follows:

Exposure to Family, School and Societal Risk Factors

(Poverty, abuse, neglect, harsh and inconsistent parenting drug and alcohol use by caregivers, emotional and physical or sexual abuse, modelling of aggression, media violence, negative attitude toward schooling, family transitions (death or divorce), parent criminality)

↓

Leads to Development of Maladaptive Behavioural Manifestations

(Defiance of adults, lack of school readiness, coercive interactive styles, aggression toward peers, lack of problem solving skills)

↓

Produces Negative Short-term Outcomes

(Truancy, peer and teacher rejection, low academic achievement high number of school discipline referrals, large number of different schools attended early involvement with drugs and alcohol early age of first arrest—less than 12 years)

↓

To Negative, Destructive Long Term Outcomes

(School failure and dropout, delinquency drug and alcohol use; gang membership, violent acts, adult criminality, lifelong dependence on welfare system, higher death and injury rate).

Family characteristics, as well as community and societal factors, can increase risk for antisocial behaviour (Gottfredson, 1987; Hawkins, 1995; Thornberry, 1994). They are:

(i) Economic deprivation and unemployment that limit access to food, shelter, transportation, health care, etc.;

(ii) Parental history of deviant behaviour;

(iii) Favourable family/community attitudes toward deviant behaviour; harsh and/or inconsistent discipline;

(iv) Poor parental and/or community supervision and monitoring; low parental education (especially maternal education);

(v) Family conflict;

(vi) Disruption in care giving;

(vii) Out-of-home placement;

(viii) Poor attachment between child and family;

(ix) Low community attachment and community disorganization, as evidenced by low parent involvement in schools, low voter turnout, and high rates of vandalism and violence;

(x) Parental alcoholism;

(xi) Social alienation of the community;

(xii) Availability of drugs and guns;

(xiii) High community turnover; and

(xiv) Exposure to violence, including violence in the home, community, and media.

It has been shown that children exposed to these risk factors follow a well described and documented path beginning with behavioural manifestations and reactions such as defiance of adults, lack of school readiness and aggression toward peers (Walker & Sprague, 1999). This leads to negative short term outcomes including truancy, peer and teacher rejection, low academic achievement and early involvement in drugs and alcohol. These factors set a child up for school failure and eventual dropout, which leads finally to negative and destructive long term outcomes such as delinquency, adult criminality and violence. An increasing number of children are now exposed to these risk factors and then follow this unfortunate path. We know that a child can be diverted from this path, but success depends on early intervention. The farther the child goes down this destructive path, the more likely it is that he or she will reach the end, and adopt an antisocial behaviour pattern throughout life.

In the words of Reid (1993), "We have the ability to find these at—risk children and youth early, but we generally prefer to wait, to not do anything, and hope that they grow out of their problems. In far too many cases, in the absence of intervention and appropriate supports for their emerging behaviour problems, they grow into and adopt an antisocial behaviour pattern during their school careers".

Environmental variables can be classified into: i) Family-based, ii) School-based , iii) Peer-based, and iv) Neighbourhood or Community-based.

(i) Family-based

These include family history of high-risk behaviour, family management problems, family conflict, and negative parental attitudes and low involvement in children's lives. Factors that contribute to a particular child's antisocial behaviour vary, but usually they include some form of family problems.

Family Conflict and Disruption

Research has also indicated that the family environment is an important variable in the development of antisocial behaviour, although the exact nature of the relationship between family environment and antisocial behaviour remains debatable (Cashwell & Vacc, 1996; Clark & Shields, 1997; Featherstone, Cundick & Jensen, 1993; Flannery, Williams, Alexander, & Vazsonyi, 1999; Klein, Forehand, Armistead, & Long, 1997; Mathis & Yingling, 1990; McCord, 1991; Patterson, 1986; Rosenbaum, 1989; Shields & Clark, 1995; Simons, Whitbeck, Conger, & Conger, 1991). In particular, two specific aspects of the family environment seem to recur in the literature on antisocial behaviour. These may be best characterized as family status and family type.

Family status refers simply to the composition of the family. Mother alone families and those with stepfathers, has been linked to drug use and delinquency (Dornbusch et al., 1985; McCord, 1990). Those living with single parent have greater incidence of high antisocial behaviours (Shyamala, 2004). The reason may be lack of physical presence of other parent and the pre-occupation of the available parent in bread-winning activities. Over-autonomy and at times, stringent discipline practices by single parents might have also been the contributory factors. According to Bowlby (1969), prolonged absence of one parent has even more deleterious consequences: development of an 'affectionless character' which in turn, predisposed the children to delinquent behaviour. Among girls, this might lead them to turn to prostitution, among boys to thieving. Youth from intact two-parent families are less likely to report school problems than are children from single-parent families (Featherstone et al., 1993). Studies have consistently demonstrated that children from single-parent and reconstituted families may be more susceptible to problems than are children from traditional families (e.g., Featherstone et al., 1993; Thomas, Farrell, & Barnes, 1994).

Female headed single parent families are at the highest risk of poverty, since many single mothers are unable to work, and those who do work are more likely to be low paying positions. Accordingly, children raised in these family settings have a higher chance of encountering poverty and all its associated problems. For instance, research suggests that children living with single parents are more likely than other children to change schools frequently. These children, in turn, have lower academic achievements, more grade failures and more antisocial behaviours than children who stay in stable settings for many years (Ross, 1996). Students staying with guardians are more prone to antisocial behaviour than those staying with parents (Shyamala, 2004). Due to inability of the guardians to supplement the parental care and discipline effectively, and also due to mutual negligent attitude of the students and guardians alike.

Research indicates that children from families affected by divorce or separation are at increased risk for the development of delinquency and violence (Wadsworth, 1979; Farrington,

1992). However, it is not clear as to whether divorce is the primary risk factor for the development of delinquency, or whether divorce interacts with the potential consequences of divorce, such as poverty and a major life transition, to increase the risk of delinquency. When the effect of divorce is to disrupt the bond or attachment to one or both of the parents, the risk for delinquency increases (Williams & Van Dorn, 1999).

Effective parenting is disrupted when there are high rates of family conflict (e.g., domestic violence, arguing) which place children at risk for problem behaviours (McCord, 1979; 1996; Patterson, Reid, & Dishion, 1992). Family conflict per se appears to be more important than family structure (e.g., whether the child has both biological parents in the home or whether the home is single-parent headed) in the development of delinquency and other problem behaviours (Williams, Ayers, & Arthur, 1997; Williams, Stiffman, & O'Neal, 1998).

Family type refers to the way family members interact with each other, that is, levels of adaptability, cohesiveness, and communication demonstrated by the family unit. In assessing family type for research and clinical practice, the model most frequently cited and most widely accepted is Olson, Russell and Sprenkle's (1979) Circumplex Model (Green, Kolevzon, & Vosler, 1985; Maynard, & Olson, 1987; Olson, Russell, & Sprenkle, 1979; Rodick, Henggele, & Hanson, 1986). The Circumplex Model is measured by the Family Adaptability and Cohesion Evaluation Scales (Olson, Partner, & Lavee, 1985) and is based on the assumption that the difference between functional and dysfunctional families is determined by two interrelated dimensions: cohesion and adaptability.

Cohesion refers to the level of attachment and emotional bonding between family members. There are four graded levels to the cohesion dimension: disengaged, separated, connected, and enmeshed. Families that are disengaged lack closeness and/or loyalty, and are characterized by high independence. At the other end of the scale of cohesion are families identified as enmeshed. These families are characterized by high levels of closeness, loyalty, and/or dependency.

Adaptability is defined as the ability of the family to change in power structure, roles, and relationships in order to adjust to various situational stressors (Matherne & Thomas, 2001). It, too, has four graded levels: rigid, structured, flexible, and chaotic. Families with low levels of adaptability are considered rigid. Rigid family types are characterized by authoritarian leadership, infrequent role modification, strict negotiation, and lack of change. Families with high levels of adaptability are considered chaotic. Chaotic family types manifest a lack of leadership, dramatic role shifts, erratic negotiation, and are characterized by excessive change.

Previous studies have indicated that a number of family variables may effectively predict antisocial behaviour. For example, Thomas, Farrell and Barnes (1994) found that family structure generally influences the level of adolescent alcohol usage. Similarly, Kandel (1996) reported that family structure is a major variable in the development of drug use in adolescents. In addition, Cashwell and Vacc (1996) suggested that family relations may be even more important than peer relations in predicting antisocial behaviour.

Many family variables have been studied in an attempt to better understand the etiology of antisocial behaviour. For example, Rosenbaum (1989) found that adolescents who have a strong bond with their parents are less likely to be delinquent. Adolescents without parental supervision during after-school hours are more likely to engage in delinquent acts (Flannery et al., 1999).

Patterns of poor parent-child relationships can intensify the potential risk for peer rejection and antisocial behaviour during adolescence (Bagwell et al., 1998). In fact, the weaker a youth's links to his/her family, the greater the importance of association with other groups that play a central role in their daily lives. When young people cannot find what they want within their own family, they turn to other groups to have their needs met.

Researchers have found children that have been raised in a negative type of environment are more aggressive, more often diagnosed with oppositional defiant disorder, attention deficit disorder, conduct disorder, and antisocial personality disorder (Giancola, Mezzich, Clark, & Tarter 1999). Clark and Shields (1997) reported that the level of familial communication is related to adolescent delinquent behaviour. Cashwell and Vacc (1996) found that a cohesive family environment reduces the chances of delinquent behaviour. Similarly, Shields and Clark (1995) found that low levels of adaptability in the family result in higher levels of antisocial behaviour. Thus, there appears to be a relationship between family environment and the development of antisocial behaviour in adolescents.

Family background is related to behavioural changes. Child abuse, frequent changes in primary caregiver or in housing, learning or cognitive disabilities, or health problems are the probable causal factors related to antisocial behaviour. There is a link between childhood sexual abuse and later drug abuse, juvenile delinquency and criminal behaviour (Burgess, Hartman, & McCormack, 1987).

Family Income

Lipman, Offord and Boyle (1994) that there is significant relation between low income and psychosocial morbidity. Poverty (times of stress in the family) such as periods of unemployment and financial constraint can also contribute to family violence and child abuse (Krishnan, & Morrison, 1995). Poverty compromises access to material necessities, as well as the fulfilment of basic developmental needs such as safety and stability. Poor parents often have difficulty supplying their children with the best foods, with adequate clothing and housing, with appropriate child-care alternatives when parents are out working, with good education, with stimulating experiences such as books, toys, and outings, and with safe and pleasant residential neighbourhoods (Schor & Menaghan, 1995). Poverty also brings with it a high risk of exposure to harmful environmental conditions and stressful events (McLeod & Edwards, 1995). Children with a meagre monthly income among poor families often experience high residential mobility; frequent relocations of schools disturb children's academic routines, while the loss of familiar neighbourhoods may give rise to disturbances in peer relationships (McLoyd & Wilson, 1991).

Due to economic crunch in the family, it is probable that parents (single or both) or guardians are left with no choice but to go out to work all through the day. In the case of self-employed parents and privately employed parents, the time spent outside their homes as bread-winners is obviously more than the time spent by those in government jobs. In the present scenario of nuclear families, this may ultimately lead to their children being left to mend for themselves. At times, even these children have to work for their living. In such pathetic conditions, it is all the more natural for these students to disassociate themselves from academics, fall prey to money mindedness and associate themselves with antisocial peers. When parents confront financial constraints, they tend to be more stressed, less patient, and more likely to suffer from psychological instability. Alcoholism is more prevalent among people living in poverty. Given the high level of stress that exists within the environments, students with antisocial behaviour are most likely to develop low self-esteem and depression. So, there is higher incidence of domestic violence in lower income families. McLeod and Shanahan (1996) also provided evidence for the negative impact of poverty on students' development. They found that students who were persistently poor, showed higher rate of antisocial behaviour. Students who experienced persistent family economy hardship were found to be the least adjusted, showed low self-esteem, difficulties in peer relations, and showed externalising behaviour problems (Bolger et al., 1995). Socio-economic studies have suggested that the source of family income may affect child outcomes.

Parenting has been identified as an important link between poverty and children's developmental behaviours (Elder, Nguyen, & Capsi, 1985; Lempers, Clark-Lempers, & Simons, 1989). Halpern (1990) has suggested that poverty has an "organizing influence" on child-rearing by creating personal, situational and systemic obstacles that undermine attentive and nurturant parenting behaviours. Empirical studies have shown that impaired parenting can explain a large proportion of the total correlation between economic hardship and children's mental health (Conger et al., 1992; Dodge, Pettit, & Bates, 1994; McLoyd, 1995).

Parental Psychopathology

Parental psychopathology is another important causal pathway linking socio-economic disadvantage to children's mental health. Depressed and irritable mothers indirectly cause antisocial behaviour problems in children through inconsistent limit setting, emotional unavailability, and reinforcement of inappropriate behaviours through negative attention (Webster-Stratton & Dahi, 1995). Through a combination of financial strain, exposure to stressful life events, scarce social resources, and weak social supports, poverty jeopardizes the mental health of adults (Adler et al., 1994). In turn, parental psychopathology adversely affects the mental health of children (Downey & Coyne, 1990; Schor & Menaghan, 1995).

Parental Rearing Style

Five aspects of how parents bring up their children have been shown repeatedly to be strongly associated with long term antisocial behaviour problems: (a) poor supervision, (b) erratic, harsh discipline, (c) parental disharmony, (d) rejection of the child, and (e) low involvement in the child's activities (Farrington, 1994). Poor parental supervision has been found in a number of studies to be a risk factor for later violence (Patterson, Reid, & Dishion, 1992). There is a great deal of evidence to suggest that, in most cases, antisocial behaviour is learned (Natale, 1994; Shamsie & Hluchy 1991; Tierney et al., 1993; Walker, 1993). It has been further argued that antisocial behaviour in boys may follow directly from paternal incarceration (Sack, 1977). It is clear that boys are over-represented in mental health facilities and that boys are more likely than girls to demonstrate aggressive and antisocial behaviour (Gabel & Shindledecker, 1991).

The pioneering work of Patterson and his colleagues (1982) showed that parents had a causal role in maintaining antisocial behaviour by giving it attention and in extinguishing desirable behaviour by ignoring it. The risk of developing later antisocial problems is further increased if early onset conduct problems are combined with harsh and inconsistent parenting, low parental monitoring, and low parental involvement in school.

One study showed that among antisocial boys aged 10, differences in parenting styles predicted over 30% of the variance in aggression two years later (Patterson et al., 1992). Harsh, inconsistent parenting is strongly associated with antisocial behaviour in children (Farrington, 1995). A number of different factors have been identified which contribute to antisocial problems such as bullying. A number of child-rearing styles have been found to predict whether children will grow up to be aggressive bullies.

The family is considered to be the most violent institution (Myers, 1993) because problem situations within the family are often solved using aggressive behaviours. Discipline is one key element in the development of antisocial behaviours. When parents use physical means to discipline their children, children learn that battering or physical mishandling are normal, effective methods for expressing frustration. Exposure to these acts of force teaches children that aggression is an acceptable problem-solving technique.

Lack of attention and warmth towards the child, together with modelling of aggressive behaviour at home, and poor supervision of the child, provide the perfect opportunity for aggressive and bullying behaviour to occur (Loeber & Stouthamer-Loeber, 1986; Patterson, DeBaryshe, & Ramsey 1989; Olweus, 1993). Modelling of aggressive behaviour may include use of physical and verbal aggression toward the child by parents, or use of physical and verbal aggression by parents toward each other. The connection between witnessing wife assault by children, particularly male children, and bully behaviour by children toward peers, has not been well studied, but studies do indicate that aggressive behaviour of all kinds is elevated in children who witness violence by their father toward their mother (Jaffe, Wolfe, & Wilson, 1990).

Parent-child Interaction Pattern

Direct observation in the home shows that much aggressive behaviour in children is influenced by the way parents behave towards them. In many families with antisocial children the parents do little to encourage polite or considerate behaviour by the child—such behaviour is often ignored and rendered ineffective (Gardender, 1992). Yet frequently when the child yells or has a tantrum he or she gets attention; often the parent gives in, so the child wins and soon learns to adapt accordingly. The coexistent unresponsiveness to the child's communications and emotional needs contributes further to the child's disturbance. The relationship between parenting and child behaviour has been shown to be highly reciprocal, in that poor parenting seems to be related to the onset of conduct disorder, and children with behaviour problems appear to elicit poor parenting (Anderson, Lytton, & Romney, 1986; Caspi, Elder & Bem, et al., 1987).

Family management practices and parent-child interactions have been associated consistently with later antisocial behaviour (Capaldi & Patterson, 1996; Loeber & StouthamerLoeber, 1986). Theory and research suggest that risk for antisocial behaviour and violence is higher among youth whose parents ignore misbehaviour or fail to follow through with stated disciplinary actions because these youth do not learn associations between misbehaviour and negative consequences (Patterson, Reid, & Dishion, 1992; Wells & Rankin, 1988). Similarly, youth who are less closely supervised, have poor communication with their parents, and are less involved in family activities are at risk for associating with delinquent peers, also raising the risk for antisocial behaviour and violence (Elliott et al., 1985; Patterson et al., 1992). Lipsey and Derzon's meta-analysis identified antisocial peers as one of the strongest early adolescent predictors of later violent or serious antisocial behaviour (Lipsey & Derzon, 1998).

Parental Influence on Children's Emotions and Attitudes

Violence is mostly a learned behaviour, and it is often learned in the home or the community from parents, family members, or friends. Children are more aggressive and grow up more likely to become involved in violence—either as a victimizer or as a victim—if they witness violent acts. The home is the most fertile breeding place for this situation. A major example: A child who sees a parent or other family member abused is more likely to see violence as a way to solve problems and subsequently be more likely to abuse others.

Difficulties can often be traced back to infancy. A high proportion of toddlers who go on to develop conduct problems show disorganised attachment patterns, experiencing fear, anger, and distress on reunion with their parent after a brief separation. This behaviour is likely to be a response to frightening, unavailable, and inconsistent parenting (Lyons-Ruth, 1996). The security of infant attachment can be predicted with substantial certainty before the child is even born, from the emotionally distorted, confused style in which the mother talks about relationships with her own parents (Fonagy et al., 1991).

Traditional families have more resources than non-traditional families. With more resources, traditional families may provide a more balanced home environment and devote more time and energy to their children. For example, traditional families may allocate more time for family interaction, such as communication. As noted by Clark and Shields (1997), communication is an imperative factor in the family and may also be an important predictor of antisocial behaviour. Similarly, a key element in the development of antisocial behaviour is level of family communication (Klein et al., 1997). Good parenting skills may serve as a buffer for adolescent antisocial behaviour. Thus, it seems plausible that adolescents from traditional families may not need the same level of cohesion in the family because of various other compensating factors.

Non-traditional families may be operating under different circumstances. They may lack many of the above-mentioned compensatory mechanisms, and might benefit from communication and behaviour monitoring skill development. Parents, educators, and counsellors should be aware that adolescents from non-traditional families are more susceptible to antisocial behaviour. This is especially true for disengaged families. A collaborative effort by educators, counsellors, and parents may be the first step in preventing these at-risk youth from becoming antisocial.

Specific conditions within the family that may create antisocial behaviour in children are: Broken home, Lack of marital adjustment of the parents leading to children being left in the fray, Employed parents, Poverty, Disability of parents, Defective discipline, Lack of affection, Partiality, Tension in joint families, Lack of moral code, Lack of recreation, Crowded home, and Company of servants.

As confirmed by the studies of Manion and Wilson (1995), families that provide strong psychological support, a strong set of values and conventional role models, with parents who foster and establish strong relationships with their children, tend tc have lower rates of child antisocial activity. Good parental practices are believed to be as important as the family's socio-economic status (Mustard & Mcain, 1999).

The combined and unique ability of different aspects of family functioning was examined to predict involvement in antisocial behaviour in a large nonclinical (community) sample of adolescents (Dekovic et al., 2003). Distinction was made between global (e.g., family socio-economic status), distal (dispositional characteristics of parents), contextual (family characteristics), and proximal (parent-child interaction) factors that operate within families. Results showed that proximal factors were significant predictors of antisocial behaviour, independent of their shared variance with other factors.

(ii) School-based

Only in recent times, we have started to consider classroom and school variables as related to the appearance and the frequency of antisocial behaviour in schools; to the surprise of many, it is becoming increasingly clear that they can be as important as personal, family and social background variables (Vettenburg, 1999).

School is an important institution after home that is responsible for training children to shoulder the future responsibilities of life. School factors include low school involvement, academic and social failure, lack of clarity and follow-through in rules and policies, poor and/or inconsistent administrative support, and few allowances for individual differences. In addition, disciplinary practices in many schools are inconsistent and inequitable (Skiba & Peterson, 2000).

The following factors may lead children to antisocial behaviour: Location, Lack of discipline, Lack of proper emotional climate, Partiality of the school authorities, Lack of facilities, Lack of other extra-curricular activities, Religion and caste-system, Lack of guidance and counselling, Defective curriculum and examination system, and Lack of moral and sex education.

School and Classroom Size

Research indicates that larger classrooms and larger schools, including larger school districts, increase the risk for poor academic achievement, which is a risk factor for delinquency. The upper limits of the size of classrooms and schools vary by age group. While the research is controversial, it is believed that elementary schools with more than 400 students (Stockard & Mayberry, 1992) and/or more than 29 students per class when children are 6 years of age or younger (Robinson & Wittebols, 1986) are at increased risk for problem behaviours. When children are between the ages of 7 and 11, academic achievement is believed to suffer when classes have more than 36 students (Robinson & Wittebols, 1986). When youths reach secondary school, it is believed that schools with more than 900 students are at increased risk for poor academic achievement students (Stockard & Mayberry, 1992).

Disruptive School Environment

Schools with high incidences of discipline problems, fighting, and truancy appear to place children at increased risk for the development of antisocial behaviours. This occurs due to increased chances that children are in contact with antisocial others, which is a risk factor for the development of antisocial behaviour and other problem behaviours (Farrington, 1989,1993).

Academic Failure

Schools and classrooms have also been recognised as important contexts for the development of antisocial behaviour (Kellam et al., 1998). Success in school reduces the likelihood of antisocial behaviour (Rutter, 1978). Chronic school failure demoralizes children, can cause loss of status and rejection by peers, destroys self-esteem, and undermines feelings of competence. As a result, it can undermine a child's attachment to teachers, parents, school, and the values they promote. It also generates hopelessness and the children begin to feel that 'school is not a place of attachment and learning, but of alienation and failure' (Hawkins, 1995).

Academic failure beginning in elementary school; poor academic aptitude test scores especially in reading beginning in Grades 3 and 4; lack of commitment to school; lack of belief in the validity of rules; early aggressive behaviour (in Grades K-3); lack of attachment to teachers; low aspirations and goals; peer rejection and social alienation; association with deviant peers, including grouping antisocial children together for instruction and/or punishment; low student/teacher morale; school disorganization; ineffective monitoring and management of students; and poor adaptation to school, as evidenced by retention and attendance rates, assignment to special education, and student reports of not liking school, lack of effort, alienation, and punishment (Gottfredson,1986, 1987; Hawkins, 1995; Thornberry, 1994).

Chronic school failure demoralizes children, can cause loss of status and rejection by peers, destroys self-esteem, and undermines feelings of competence. As a result, it can undermine a child's attachment to teachers, parents, school, and the values they promote. It also generates hopelessness and helplessness. Children cease to believe that their efforts make a difference in outcomes (Brooks, 1992,1994). For delinquent youngsters, 'school is not a place of attachment and learning, but of alienation and failure' (Hawkins, 1995). In addition, an analysis of disruptive behaviour in 600 schools revealed that schools with discipline problems tend to be large and urban; lack teaching resources; lack fair, clearly stated, consistently enforced rules; have students who do not believe in the rules; lack leadership and cooperation among staff; and have punitive teachers.

Academic problems and dropping out of school appear to be correlated with current and later involvement in delinquent behaviour, drug use, violence, and teen pregnancy. Academic problems include grade repetition, low bonding to school, and lack of commitment to school (Cairns & Cairns, 1994; Hill et al., 1999; Loeber, Stuothamer-Loeber, Van Kammen, & Farrington, 1991; Maguin & Loeber, 1996). Low IQ, or low intelligence, includes learning problems and poor language ability. This risk factor has a small effect size and is often accompanied by other risk factors with small effect sizes, such as hyperactivity/low attention and poor performance in school.

Lack of Interpersonal Competencies for School Success

In order to succeed in school, children need to master certain minimal behavioural and interpersonal competencies, some related to teacher adjustment and others to peer adjustment. These have to do with the ability to affiliate, to adjust, to control anger, to comply and cooperate, to listen and communicate, to delay gratification, and to ask for help. Hostile, irritable, antisocial, aggressive and disrupting demanding behaviours are the major predictors of vulnerability among youth in India (Sarkar, 1988; Sethi & Manchanda, 1978; Sinha, 1988) and in all likelihood are closely associated with their academic performance (Nanda & Dash, 1996).

Almost all of the at-risk children do not possess even the minimal interpersonal and behavioural competencies essential to school success (Walker, 1997,1999) indicates that. Once rejected by their teachers and peers, these students often band together and tend to form deviant gangs which later run into trouble with the law (Dishion, Patterson, & Grisler, 1994; Dodge, Coie, & Brakke, 1982).

Punishment

Research indicates that schools too often emphasize punitive measures to manage student behaviour. One study found punishment and lack of praise by classroom teachers to be main factors related to delinquent behaviour (Farrington, 1987). This overemphasis occurs with all students, but disproportionately with males, minority students, and particularly students from low-income homes (McFadden, Marsh, Price, & Hwang, 1992; Shaw & Braden, 1990). Teachers in low income areas and/or low white-percentage schools more frequently endorse the use of punishment and the removal of students (Moore & Cooper, 1984). Similarly, adolescents from low income homes report a greater number and variety of penalties that tend to be disproportionate to the offenses and humiliating in nature (Brantlinger, 1991). Thus, not only are certain groups singled out for more punishment, but we also find that the total school environment often is too punitive for all students. For example, disapproval is used more frequently than approval as a consequence to student behaviour by many teachers (Heller & White, 1975; Thomas, Presland, Grant, & Glenn, 1978; White, 1975), though certainly not all teachers (Nafpaktitis, Mayer, & Butterworth, 1985; Wyatt & Hawkins, 1987). Similarly, results from a survey by the American Association of School Administrators (Brodinsky, 1980) indicated that school personnel spend more time and energy in implementing punitive than positive or preventive measures. In addition, Greenberg (1974) has pointed out that reliance on heavy security arrangements and punitive discipline strategies appears to aggravate, not reduce, vandalism as well as aggression towards others. Thus, it appears that schools, particularly urban schools, are indeed punitive for many students. What factors within our schools, then, contribute to punitive/aversive environments?

Mayer (1995) has identified and summarized a number of contextual factors within the school that appear to contribute to a punitive school environment that promotes antisocial behaviour. These include: (1) low student involvement in school activities; (2) unclear rules for student deportment; (3) weak or inconsistent administrative support for staff in carrying out student discipline (consistent follow-through), little staff support of one another, and a lack of staff agreement with policies;

(4) academic failure experiences; (5) students lacking critical social skills that form the basis of doing well academically and relating positively to others, such as persistence on task, complying with requests, paying attention, negotiating differences, handling criticism and teasing; (6) deficits in discriminating between prosocial and antisocial behaviour, as often seen in gang-on-gang conflicts (e.g., eye contact from a stranger, hand gestures, or a pat on the back might function as a challenge or threat rather than as a hello); and, (7) consequences unsuitable for individual students due to their distinctive learning histories.

These contextual factors have been found to relate significantly to both vandalism frequency and its resultant cost (Mayer et al., 1987). Also, research evidence (Mayer et al., 1979, 1981, 1983b, 1991, 1993) suggests that when these factors are considered and incorporated into a plan, a variety of antisocial behaviours (including vandalism costs) are reduced, attendance improves, more students spend increased time on assigned tasks, and cooperation and positive feelings among students and staff increase. In other words, changing contextual factors not only can help prevent antisocial behaviour, but also can help to create an environment more conducive to learning.

Because punitive school environments promote antisocial behaviour, the identified contextual factors need to be addressed to help reduce the emphasis that exists on punitive discipline measures. The importance of these contextual factors is further highlighted by the fact that they are similar to those identified in the home that promote antisocial behaviour (e.g., reliance on coercive or punitive discipline, inconsistent rule setting and delivery of consequences) (Loeber, Stouthammer-Loeber, & Green, 1987; Minuchin, 1974; Reid & Patterson, 1989).

Characteristics of Safe and Unsafe Schools

Research (Walker et al., 1996) has identified the major characteristics of safe and unsafe schools. Unsafe schools tend to lack cohesion. Their environments are chaotic, stressful, poorly structured and disorganized. There is a strong presence of gang activity, violence, and unclear academic and behavioural standards. On the other hand, in safe schools, students feel nurtured, cared for, accepted and protected. There is no violence and no sense of the possibility of physical or psychological harm. Other factors that contribute to higher school risk are overcrowding, lack of caring but firm disciplinary standards and procedures, insensitivity to multicultural diversity, high student alienation, neglect or overt rejection of high-risk students, and poor supervision. Interestingly, the design and use of the physical school space itself has been identified as an important factor in the level of risk for school alienation and violence.

Other factors that help prevent school violence are a positive atmosphere in the school, clear (and high) performance expectations for all students, strong student bonding to the school (school 'spirit'), high levels of student and parent involvement, opportunities for students to learn academic and social skills, school wide attention to conflict resolution, and a general sense of inclusion and non-discriminatory values. Large schools with high student-to-teacher ratios make it more difficult for teachers to form meaningful relationships with students or to identify individual student's needs. School overcrowding results in more problems with discipline and vandalism. Isolation of teachers from each other, from the administration, from parents and from the neighbourhoods in which they teach make them less effective. Obviously, schools can be made no safer than the communities in which they are located.

(iii) Peer-based

Peer influences have the greatest impact during adolescence (Thornberry & Krohn, 1997) when students prefer to spend more time with their friends than with their family. Hyperactivity and adverse family features make a major impact on the adolescents. In most cases, peers tend to replace the modelling environment provided by the family context during early childhood either for leisure activities or for sharing ideas and feelings. Peer influence then begins to contribute to shaping a young person's identification process and, to some extent, his/her values, sense of ethics and philosophy of life,social expectations, and school relationships and commitment (Walker,

1995). The relationships and identification with peers take an important meaning. The relationship is two-fold. On the one hand, students get the social acknowledgement they look for, and on the other, they are under a certain amount of pressure that drives them to abide by the peers' conventions for fear of rejection. Hence, peer influence is a vital component in a student's pro-and antisocial development.

Researchers suggest that contrary to popular opinion, 'adolescents are more likely to follow their peers and engage in 'neutral' or pro-social behaviours than in anti-social behaviours... evidence indicates that adolescents feel pressured to be involved with their peers and do not necessarily feel pressured towards misconduct' (Heaven, 1994). Antisocial peer influence and peer rejection and can exacerbate or create risk factors within a young person's environment, and so increases the likelihood of child and adolescent outcomes (Bagwell et al., 1998). Peer rejection and negative peer association are highly correlated to antisocial and criminal outcomes (Mayer, 1995).

Early Starters and Rejection by Peers and Teachers

Moffit (1993a) has identified a group of children referred to as the 'Early starters'. These children engage in such antisocial behaviours as defiance of adults, and also cruelty towards peers (taunting and provoking, bullying, hitting, yelling, mean-spirited teasing, throwing tantrums). They very often enter school with these behavioural patterns that got well rooted primarily because of their early exposure to many of the risk factors. These children's problems are exacerbated because their negative behaviour usually results in their rejection by both teachers and peers who are overwhelmed by their coercion, aggression and humiliation of others.

Patterson, Reid and Dishion (1992), and Reid (1993) have shown that this rejection by both teachers and peers is a key developmental stage on these children's path toward school failure and antisocial behaviourt. Rejection by teachers and peers, can lead to early school drop out which, in turn, increases a youth's risk for delinquent and criminal behaviour. Eighty per cent of day time crimes nationally and 90% of daytime burglaries in Los Angeles County are committed by truant or suspended juveniles (Bostic, 1994; Crowe, 1995). Rejection from pro-social peers in both school and the community places children at increased risk for delinquency and other social problems. Beginning in early elementary school, peer rejection and early aggressive behaviour are central risk factors for bullying, delinquency, and a variety of poor developmental outcomes (Crick & Dodge, 1994).

Delinquent acts are usually carried out in groups and co-offenders tend to live close to each other. Often a peer group provides the only source of approval and new attitudes and skills may be learned, albeit criminal ones. Chronically aggressive children as being more likely to be rejected by the peer group, more likely to disengage from school and academic pursuits, more likely to gravitate to antisocial peer groups, and more likely to engage in delinquent behaviour (Patterson, Reid, & Dishion, 1992).

Association with Peers Who Engage in Antisocial Behaviour

In most cases, positive peer influences strengthens early childhood- instilled prosocial values. For example, there exists a strong relationship between school adjustment and peer acceptance. Accordingly, strong and quality peer associations are related to good school performance and successful school transition (Bagwell et al., 1998). Just as prosocial peer association can benefit an individual, association with delinquent peers can prove to be extremely detrimental, both in terms of school performance and criminality.

Individuals who tend to have delinquent friends, have the opportunity to engage in antisocial activities. Young people who can not develop strong bonds with their siblings, are more likely to make negative peer association, which places them at great risk of school failure. Students who are at risk of dropping out usually establish stronger bonds with school dropouts and other at-risk students than most other students (Ellenbogen & Claire, 1997). It is believed that having a network of friends where school and prosocial behaviour are not valued, contributes to and accelerates the development of antisocial behaviour (Raine, 1993).

In the literature, negative peer association has also been linked with many mental health programmes and the development of antisocial behaviours (Bagwell et al., 1998). Association with delinquent peers and gang membership, along with other contextual factors, can lead to the development of aggressive behaviour, which further increases the risk of getting involved in violence, criminal activities, and drug use and abuse (Fraser, 1996; Jenkins, 1996).

Gang membership increases the risk of delinquency, specifically violence. Members of gangs are more likely to come from communities with high rates of poverty, crime, and violence. Gang members are more likely to experience school failure and show decreased levels of commitment to school and academics. Gang membership too is associated with a family history of gang membership, crime, and/or violence, poor family management practices, high levels of family conflict, and family poverty. Gang members themselves are more likely to have had early and persistent antisocial behaviour, favorable attitudes toward antisocial behaviour, and peers in gangs. Thus, gang membership represents the effect of a variety of developmental and community risk factors (Battin, Hill, Abbott, Catalano, & Hawkins, 1998; Hill et al., 1999; Williams & Van Dorn, 1999).

Gang members engaged in more antisocial behaviour when associated with a gang and less when they left it (Thornberry et al., 1993). There are two major models that try to explain why boys enter gangs. One model suggests that boys who already engage in antisocial behaviour enter gangs to join with people similar to themselves. The other model suggests that boys join gangs for such reasons as self-esteem, power, and protection. According to this model, it is through membership in the gang that these youths are encouraged to engage in antisocial behaviour. Both theories have some merit in explaining why youth join gangs and how further antisocial behaviour may be escalated through the gang membership. In early adolescence, friendships with delinquent peers may lead to gang membership, but in general, gang entry may reflect a tendency for antisocial boys to associate with one another. In early adolescence, boys with conduct problems who receive low parental supervision may be the first to join gangs, whereas boys who join gangs in later adolescence may have been deterred in earlier adolescence due to high parental supervision (Lahey et al., 1999).

Antisocial individuals tend to have antisocial friends and many antisocial activities are undertaken together with other people. According to Sheldon and Glueck (1950), associations with other delinquents amounted to no more than 'birds of a feather flock together'. Sutherland and Cressey (1978) opined that antisocial behaviour is largely learned through personal interactions in the peer group. Thus there are strong selection effects by which antisocial individuals tend to choose friends who are similarly antisocial. Delinquent activities may serve within an antisocial peer group, as a source of prestige or esteem (Emler & Reicher, 1995). There may be direct modelling of behaviour, but there may also be implicit pressures as a result of being with peers when the group is engaging in illicit or antisocial activities such as taking drugs, vandalizing property, stealing from shops, and the like. Youths who have peers who engage in antisocial behaviour or other problem behaviours are at an increased risk of engaging in antisocial behaviours themselves, including carrying weapons. Even when youths come from well-managed families and do not experience other risk factors, simply associating with peers who engage in problem behaviours increases risk and is associated with "late start" offending (Ageton, 1983; Bjerregaard & Smith, 1993; Elliott, 1994; Farrington, 1989).

Membership into a deviant peer group often plays an important role in antisocial involvement, and these friendships often serve to 'train' adolescents how to be delinquent (Dishion, Spracklen, Andrews & Patterson, 1996). Deviant friendships are often marked by higher conflict and lower supportive qualities (Dishion, Andrews, & Crosby, 1995), as well as higher levels of hostility within the friendship (Windle, 1994). Although alcohol and substance use is often considered as an antisocial behaviour, the relationship between substance use and antisocial behaviour may be declining (Adlaf, Smart, Walsh, & Ivis, 1994), and the two behaviours may be associated with different family and peer influences (Otero-Lopez et al., 1994).

(iv) Neighbourhood or Community-based

The behaviour of the young is a mirror that reflects back to the society the lessons they have learnt. The values, attitudes, and beliefs that guide their actions are acquired from the primary settings in which they grow up. Society-wide environmental influences might be more influential on adolescence-limited antisocial behaviour than life-course-persistent varieties.

An adolescent is more likely to become antisocial to the extent that risk factors within him, his family, and his neighbourhood are aggregated. However, it is also possible that effects of particular individual, family, and peer risk factors differ by type of neighbourhood. Research has suggested that societal factors such as accessibility of weapons (Edelman, 1995; Larson, 1994), media violence (Dorfman, Woodruff, Chavez, & Wallack, 1997; Webber, 1997), and inequitable educational opportunities (Mayer, 1995) may lead youth to become more antisocial (Webber, 1997).

Poverty and social disadvantage, Location of residence, Community drug and alcohol use, Community crime and violence, Presence of gangs, Availability of firearms and weapons, Exposure to violence in the mass media, Cultural discrimination and Lack of support services including transport, shopping, recreational facilities may contribute to antisocial behaviour among children and adolescents.

Poverty and Social Disadvantage

Social disadvantage refers to community characteristics that are associated with antisocial behaviour. These include poverty, poor housing, high rates of residential mobility, and parental or community unemployment. Children who grow up in neighbourhoods characterized by these problems are more likely to develop early behaviour and adjustment problems (Bursik & Webb, 1982; Farrington, 1998; Hill et al., 1999; Loeber & Dishon, 1983; Werner & Smith, 1992).

Social disorganization is also a risk factor for violence in rural areas. anti-social behaviour reflects an interaction between social-environmental conditions and individual or family influences. Most families who exhibit anti-social behaviour are poor and lack an employed person in the household. The concentration of disadvantaged families within the same area often fosters problems (Scott & Parkey, 1998). There may be a difference between factors affecting 'low level' nuisances and very serious anti-social behaviour, with life-style and perception differences being more important in the former and severe mental health or addiction issues figuring to a greater extent in the latter.

One study of rural communities found that poverty plays a less important role in predicting violence than residential instability, broken homes, and other indicators of social disorganization (Osgood & Chambers, 2000). In fact, very poor areas were not characterized by high residential instability or a large proportion of broken homes. In cities, however, the combination of poverty with instability and family disruption is predictive of violence (Bursik & Grasmick, 1993; Elliott et al., 1996).

Socially disorganized communities are characterized in part by economic and social flux, high turnover of residents, and a large proportion of disrupted or single-parent families, all of which lessen the likelihood that adults will be involved in informal networks of social control. As a result, there is generally little adult knowledge or supervision of the activities of teenagers and a high rate of crime. Moreover, in areas experiencing economic decline, there are likely to be few neighborhood businesses. In such an environment, it is hard for young people to avoid being drawn into violence. Not only are they on their own after school, they are exposed to violent adults and youth gangs, they have few part-time job opportunities, and their neighbourhood is not likely to offer many after-school activities such as sports or youth groups (Bursik & Grasmick, 1993; Sampson et al., 1997; Wilson, 1987).

Regional survey-based studies have shown that residing in a low-socio-economic status (SES) neighbourhood (defined using census-based indexes of socio-economic disadvantage) is associated with more frequent and severe delinquent and criminal behaviour among adolescents (Loeber & Wikstrom 1993; Peeples & Loeber, 1994; Sampson, Raudenbush, & Earls, 1997).

The classical view suggests that socio-demographic characteristics such as poverty and unemployment directly impact on antisocial behaviour by motivating an individual to offend. However, more recent research suggest that socio-demographic characteristics exert their effects on antisocial behaviour in a more indirect manner, for instance, by interfering with parents' ability to appropriately discipline and/or nuture their children (Barrera et al., 2002; Scaramella, Conger, Spoth & Simons 2002; Weatherburn & Lind, 1998). The findings from the current study lend support to the latter view. Significant group differences were observed on many aspects of the family environment often cited as important to the prediction of antisocial behaviour. For example, individuals in the experimental and persistent group reported lower attachment to parents, and poorer quality parenting (for example, less supervision of the adolescents' activities, less warmth in their relationships with their parents) than those in the low/non antisocial group.

Some communities lack features that help to prevent antisocial lifestyles, such as before- and after-school programmes, recreational opportunities, and adult mentors. In addition, the absence of emotional or financial support (e.g., friends, employment) may lead to efforts to gain such support through antisocial behaviour.

Antisocial behaviour in childhood precedes and predicts unemployment in adult life. These include easy accessibility to firearms and drugs, along with community laws and norms favourable toward their use, high transition and mobility, low neighbourhood attachment and cohesion coupled with community disorganization, and finally, severe economic and social deprivation. Antisocial behaviour is highly correlated to the social environment. The make-up of an area in terms of the people residing in it may turn out to be more important in the early development of antisocial behaviour than architectural or housing characteristics. Adolescents of various religions breed feelings of hatred against each other and results in communal clashes. Tension in time of war, flood, epidemics and other natural calamities and political conditions may also lead to antisocial behaviour. Some studies have shown that heredity for crime was stronger in twins from a higher social class and those that lived in a heavily rural area (Christiansen, 1977).

Social disadvantage and poverty are involved as risk factors to antisocial behaviour. The study by McLeod and Shanahan (1996) provided new evidence for the negative impact of poverty on children's development. The antisocial behaviour of children who were persistently poor during the entire five years period examined increased at a higher rate than that of other children. Children who experienced persistent family economic hardship were found to be the least adjusted, showed low self-esteem and difficulties in peer relations, showed externalising behaviour problems (Bolger et al., 1995).

The Rochester Youth Development Study was used to determine which aspect of social disadvantage was most related to which types of delinquency (Farnworth et al., 1994). Underclass status was the key risk factor, but its impact was mainly on street crime. Such antisocial behaviour is reported to be most acute among urban, lower-class minority youth. Yet, as the American Psychological Association's Commission on Violence and Youth (1993) points out, 'violence is most prevalent among the poor, regardless of race'.

Location of Residence

Students from semi-urban locality outnumber their urban counterparts in terms of high intensity of antisocial behaviour (Shyamala, 2004). The changing family support especially in urban areas (Lal & Sethi, 1977) has been considered as the contributory factor to antisocial behaviour in adolescents. Antisocial behaviour is highly correlated with the social environment. The make-up of an area, in terms of people residing in the nearby vicinity, may influence the behaviour pattern through various political and religious stigmas. Also, certain behaviour patterns, like smoking by male members of the family, are accepted as normal behaviours within the context of some localities. These are emulated by the adolescents in the family.

Community Drug and Alcohol Use

High rates of drug and alcohol use, including the availability of illicit drugs, present youths with opportunities to engage in the problem behaviour (Goldstein, 1989; Roncek & Maier, 1991; Sherman & Rogan, 1995). These problems also convey high acceptance of both drug and alcohol use and the selling of drugs. It appears that the availability of marijuana is a significant risk for not only adolescent delinquency but also gang involvement (Hill et al., 1999). Communities characterized by high rates of drug and alcohol use and availability of drugs are also at increased risk of experiencing problems with vandalism and crime (Bourgois, 1995; Fagan, 1993; Fagan & Chin, 1990; Fagan & Wilkinson, 1998; Goldstein, 1985).

Community Crime and Violence

Much like community drug use and availability, youths and adults living in communities with high rates of crime and violence tend to be exposed to attitudes and street codes (situational norms for behaviour) favourable to antisocial, aggressive behaviour and criminal involvement (Anderson, 1994, 1997). This occurs when one defends his reputation by confronting all transgressions, as a way of preserving the social capital believed to be crucial to his safety. Adolescents exposed to violence at home may experience some of the same emotions and difficulties as younger children—for example, fear, guilt, anxiety, depression, and trouble concentrating in school. In addition, adolescents may feel more vulnerable to violence from peers at school or gangs in their neighbourhood and hopeless about their lives and their odds of surviving to adulthood. These young people may not experience the growing feelings of competence that are important at their stage of development. Ultimately, their exposure to violence may lead them to become violent themselves. Studies have shown that adolescents exposed to violence are more likely to engage in violent acts, often as pre-emptive strikes in the face of a perceived threat (Fagan & Wilkinson, 1998; Loeber et al., 1998; Singer et al., 1994, 1995).

Presence of Gangs

The presence of gangs presents increased opportunities and social rewards for involvement in illegal activities. Some gang activity takes place in schools, but school gangs are generally younger and less violent than street gangs, which form in neighbourhoods (Laub & Lauritsen, 1998). First, communities with gangs tend to experience high rates of drug selling and drug use, specifically, marijuana. Also, communities with gangs tend to be characterized by extreme poverty, social disorganization (e.g., vandalism, poor surveillance in public places, little residential attachment to the neighbourhood, high rates of mobility), availability of firearms, and street codes favourable toward antisocial behaviuor (Curry & Spergel, 1992; Hill et al., 1999).

Availability of Firearms

Studies have shown an increase in the availability and use of illegal firearms among youths, specifically youth gangs (Block & Block, 1993; Cook & Laub, 1998; Howell, 1998; Maxson, Gordon, & Klein, 1985). Further evidence of an increase in the availability of firearms and its deleterious impact is shown by findings examining arrests for weapons offences, largely the result of illegally possessing or carrying firearms, armed robberies involving firearms, and male homicide-commission. Through the 1970s and early 1980s, adolescent arrest rates for weapon offences remained static (Cook & Laub, 1998). However, between 1985 and 1993 arrests for weapon offences doubled (Greenfeld & Zawitz, 1995; Cook & Laub, 1998).

According to the NCVS, robberies involving a firearm increased from 33 per cent in 1985 to 47 per cent in 1992. Of armed robberies that came to the attention of law enforcement, there was an increase from 60 to 67 per cent during that same period (Maguire & Pastore, 1996; Cook & Laub, 1998). Finally, male homicide-commission rates have increased dramatically when compared to non-gun rates. The non-gun homicide-commission rate for ages 13 to 17 is approximately 5:100,000. For gun related homicide-commission, the rate is approximately 21:100,000 (Cook & Laub, 1998).

Exposure to Violence in Mass Media

Watching dramatic violence on television and film affects aggressive thoughts and emotions, as well as aggressive behaviour. Many studies have also examined the immediate effect of media violence on aggressive thoughts or emotions (Rule & Ferguson, 1986), which have been shown to increase the risk of aggressive behaviour (Dodge & Frame, 1982; Huesmann & Guerra, 1997). All youths seem to be affected equally by media violence. Effects seem to be strongest on youths who are predisposed to be aggressive for some reason or who have been aroused or provoked (Berkowitz, 1993; Bushman, 1995; Geen & O'Neal, 1969).

There is now a very considerable body of research into the possible effects of watching TV or film violence on aggressive or antisocial behaviour. There can be no doubt that viewing violence can make it more likely that children and adolescents will behave aggressively (Huessman & Eron, 1986). Some researchers believe that viewing aggressive television shows can promote aggressive behaviour, and that the more violent the shows, the more aggressive the child (Myers, 1993). The effects will be more in a family situation in which children are left unsupervised to watch many hours of TV—rather than engaging in constructive activities of their own or participating in shared leisure activities with parents and siblings (Bronfenbrenner, 1976). Many Television programmes and movies immensely depict violence as the solution to stressful situations as a normal part of daily life. Children who see many programmes of this type may be unable to distinguish between real-life and fiction and may copy the role models they see on Television (British Columbia Teachers' Federation, 1993; Does TV Violence...,1992; How Safe are Our Schools? 1991). Heavy exposure to media violence does constitute a risk to children's health and safety. For example, the US Surgeon General's Report (Youth Violence, 2001) suggest that 'a small but statistically significant impact on aggression over many years' and that 'the science shows that media violence and this is primarily TV, can in fact in the short term increase aggressive behaviour'.

The American Academy of Paediatrics view media as constituting a learning environment in which children learn anti-social attitudes stating that children:

- Learn their attitudes about violence at a very young age and these attitudes tend to last;
- Although TV violence has been studied the most, researchers are finding that violence in other media such as computers and video games impacts children and teens in many of the same harmful ways;
- From media violence, children learn to behave aggressively toward others. They are taught to use violence instead of self-control to take care of problems or conflicts;
- Violence in the 'media world' may make children more accepting of real-world violence and less caring toward others. Children who see a lot of violence from movies, TV shows, or video games may become more fearful and look at the real world as a mean and scary place.

Psychological researchers present evidence that five major mechanisms help to explain the relationship between media violence and aggressive behaviour in the long term:

1. Imitation and Copycat (Bandura, 1977, 1986)

Developmental theories have noted that children will learn by means of imitation and reinforcement. The role models that children will imitate will be those individuals who are continually rewarded for their behaviours. Content analysis of TV shows by The National Television Violence Study (Mediascope, 1996) showed that 75% of violent acts go unpunished. Therefore heavy viewers of television will continually be exposed to unpunished and often rewarded act of violence. Studies of children's behaviour have indicated that their learned behaviours seem to rely on the direct reinforcement a child receives (Bandura, 1965). The imitation of a model is dependent on the attractive characteristics of that character. 40% of violent acts seen on TV were perpetrated by characters who possess attractive role model characteristics.

2. Scripts (Huesmann, 1988, 1998)

Observational learning theory suggests that children learn how to deal with everyday problems in a variety of ways. Overtime patterns become represented as scripts, which are applied and enacted in children's play and life. Therefore heavy viewers of violence may incorporate TV constructs into the development of their social scripts, which they enact and consolidate in their playful interactions.

3. Desensitization

Theorist have suggested that the more we view and experience violence the more we accept it as a way of life and a way of dealing with issues. Psychologists have suggested that children who are heavy viewers of violent media will not view violence in a negative respect and will become used to it and won't be as cautious about using aggression in dealing with issues (Dominick & Greenberg, 1972). Both theoretical and experimental studies have indicated the existence of children's desensitization to violence. Cline, Croft, & Courrier (1973) studied boys reception to new images of violence and found that prior viewing of violent images were the variable that determined how physically aroused the boys got while watching new images. It was suggested that the natural arousal reaction of viewers of violent images did not seem to exist with heavy viewers of violent images thus they had become desensitized to such images.

4. Identification/Justification (Huesmann, 1982)

It has been suggested that violent individuals may enjoy violent media because it justifies their own actions and behaviour as normal and acceptable. The notion that a child who behaves aggressively should be remorseful is in conjunction with the theory of desensitization. If a child becomes desensitized to acts of aggression their remorse for imitation and acting aggressively is also negated. Thus the child will view their acts as the norm and they way to deal with issues that arise (Fernie, 1981; Huesmann & Eron, 1986).

5. Mean world (Gerbner & Gross, 1976)

While children view television they may be cultivating a sense of risk associated with the real world experiences. Studies have shown that heavy TV viewers tend to be more anxious about becoming a victim of violence. These heavy viewers perceive the world to be a dangerous and scary place therefore developing a heightened sense of fear as well as a heightened need to protect themselves; therefore they may be more aggressive.

Other researchers (Lippa, 1990) argue that it is not a cause-effect relationship between viewing violence in the media and aggressive behaviour that predisposes individuals to view violent media programmes and display aggressive responses, but rather that additional factors, such as lower intelligence, are involved. Research suggests that not all youths are affected in the same way by viewing media violence. Factors that appear to influence the effects of media violence on aggressive or violent behaviour include characteristics of the viewer (such as age, intelligence, aggressiveness, and whether the child perceives the media as realistic and identifies with aggressive characters) and his or her social environment (for example, parental influences), as well as aspects of media content (including characteristics of perpetrators, degree of realism and justification for violence, and depiction of consequences of violence).

Overexposure to media violence can desensitise individuals to the tragedies they encounter in life (Huesmann et al., 1983). In addition, film and television portrayals may also contribute to feelings of deprivation as individuals compare their own lifestyles with the glamorous lifestyles, material goods, freedom, and social skills portrayed in the media. Thus, the perceived gap in lifestyles may create frustration leading to deviant acts (Lipsitt, 1990).

Evidence that these factors moderate the influence of media violence is limited, and it is more relevant to aggression than to violence. For example, studies of responses to violent television and films and violent video games have found that people who were initially more aggressive than other subjects were more affected in behaviour, thoughts, and emotions (Anderson & Dill, 2000; Bushman, 1995; Bushman & Geen, 1990; Friedrich & Stein, 1973; Josephson, 1987). Research in this area clearly suggests that the impact of violent television, film, and video games on aggression is moderated by viewers' aggressive characteristics.

Studies suggest that these factors may buffer or enhance effects, but few have tested for such influences. Although limited in scope and depth, such studies provide clues to potential avenues for prevention efforts. For example, preliminary data point to the potentially vital role of parents in supervising their children's exposure to violent media and in helping them interpret it (Nathanson, 1999). Playing computer games and, to a lesser extent, certain uses of the Internet may engage in a broad range of antisocial behaviour. Impulsive children with existing behavioural difficulties may get drawn to risk-taking and addictive behaviours.

Less Leisure

Some family and neighbourhood environments elevate a child's exposure to negative peer influence. For instance, a community that offers few after school hours activities is more prone to face gang activities, increasing the likelihood of a young person getting involved with delinquent peers (Bender & Losel, 1997).

Lack of Exercise and Free Play

A team at the National Institute of Mental Health discovered in 1985 that daily aerobic exercise reduced classroom disruptions and hyperactive behaviour among both normal children and those diagnosed with ADHD. Marilyn Wall, a psychologist at the University of Newcastle, later found that even as little as 4 minutes of vigorous in-class exercise raised arithmetic, spatial reasoning, and attention test scores in nearly all elementary school children. Follow up studies have confirmed all these findings. And yet the average amount of exercise given to American public school children has dropped every year of the last two decades. Today, less than 1/3 of American public school children get daily physical education. Even the amount of time children have to participate in free play shrank by 38% between 1981 and 1997.

Parents dictate priorities, and every parent wants his or her children to achieve success as defined by the culture. If a culture measures success by one's ability to indulge in pleasure, then success and money go hand in hand. For many parents, the higher the child's salary, the more successful he is. However embarrassing it is to admit, countless of our school principals have been told in no uncertain terms that the bottom line measure of a school's success is the percentage of its students who find their way into high paying careers. Because of the widespread belief that the path to cash runs straight though centum scores in school final examinations, elementary and high schools cram to accommodate heavy academic loads and produce State Ranks, and this often requires reducing or eliminating physical exercise from the schedule.

Cultural Discrimination

Although race/ethnicity can only be considered a gross proxy for cultural processes, examining differences in the development of conduct disorder across major U.S. racial/ethnic groups is a first step toward elucidating those cultural processes (Yung & Hammond, 1997). African American youth have higher rates of incarceration than youth from other racial/ethnic backgrounds (McCabe et al., 1999) and there is substantial evidence that racial bias plays a factor in this overrepresentation (Conley, 1994; Pope & Feyerherm, 1995; Wordes, Bynum, & Corley, 1994).

Dinges, Atlis and Vincent (1997) argue that the development of conduct disorder may be influenced by the discrimination and economic disadvantage that disproportionately affect ethnic minority youth. Barriers to achieving financial self-sufficiency through legitimate means may increase the acceptability of engaging in criminal behaviour within ethnic minority groups during adolescence, particularly when coupled with exposure to neighbourhoods with high rates of gang activity (National Center for Education Statistics, 1995; Yung & Hammond, 1997). In support of this position, they cite findings that African American detainees are less likely to have emotional/psychological dysfunction and troubled family backgrounds than their Caucasian counterpats, and more likely to associate with deviant peers (Dembo et al., 1994, cited in Dinges et al., 1997). In addition, there is some evidence to suggest that for some ethnic minority groups, involvement with traditional culture and lack of acculturation to mainstream American culture may protect the youth from delinquency involvement (Dinges et al., 1997). It is possible that the gap between biological maturity and the full rights and privileges that go along with social maturity may be lengthened for some ethnic minority groups that experience discrimination in combination with economic disadvantage and the protective influence of involvement with traditional cultures. Thus, according to Moffitt's theory, individuals from these ethnic minority groups would be disproportionately likely to have a later onset of conduct disorder as compared with Caucasians (Moffitt, 1993).

Consistent with this prediction, Stewart, Brown and Myers (1997) have found that non-Hispanic White adolescent substance abusers are more likely to have a history of childhood onset conduct disorder than Latino adolescent substance abusers. However, the relationship between race/ethnicity and age of onset of conduct disorder requires further investigation before firm conclusions can be reached.

INTERACTION OF CULTURAL AND INDIVIDUAL FACTORS

Cultural factors include such influences as changing social norms, decreased civility, increased divorce, social mobility, violence in the media and an increase in acceptance of violent behaviour.

A further theme appearing in much of the literature is the influence of the societal and cultural framework on coping skills and resilience at the individual level. Reporting on the youth suicide problem in New Zealand, Taylor (1990) offers this perspective: 'The reality is that many young people do have trouble in making the psychosocial adjustment of adolescence. Understandably, the very high rates of youth unemployment, the fear of joblessness, and the prevailing materialistic, worldly values that equate individual success with wealth, good looks and power make many young people feel quite worthless and cast out by society. Fatalistic attitudes are found more and more among young people—broken relationships, unhappy family backgrounds, confusion of cultural identity, or other influences can destabilise many young people, then their anxieties can become overwhelming'.

Several studies of self-harming among Aboriginal and Torres Strait Islander peoples (Hunter, 1993) come to essentially the same conclusion; i.e., that society is placing increasingly heavy demands on the resilience and coping skills of young people, and in such environments, underlying vulnerabilities can become powerful determinants of the outcomes in individual cases.

Behavioural aggression was observed among 192 three-to nine-year-old children in naturalistic settings in Belize, Kenya, Nepal, and American Samoa. (Robert et al,. 1999). Main results were that (a) boys exhibited aggression in approximately 10% of their social behaviours, girls in 6%, and in all four cultures the aggression of boys was more frequent than that of girls at a marginally significant level or better; (b) the aggression of boys, though not of girls, occurred in the presence of large numbers (and proportions) of same-sex peers; (c) aggression declined with age; (d) only 5% of children's aggressive interaction was directed toward adults (individuals aged 17 or older) whereas 30% of their other, non-aggressive interaction was directed toward adults; (e) the presence of either parent tended to be associated with less aggression, and; (f) aggression was displayed more frequently in the two patrilineal cultures (in Kenya and Nepal) and less frequently in the other two cultures.

Whiting and Edwards (1988), through their important 11-culture study reported that 'children who have been exposed to peers more than others have more opportunity to practice egoistic conflict behaviour and challenging styles' and that, toward mothers, the children display dependent and sociable behaviours due to the 'nurturing, training, and guiding dimensions of the maternal role'. Based on our findings, we would modify these generalizations to suggest the following: that aggression is most strongly affected by exposure to male peers (Butovskaya, 1997; Omark, Omark, & Edelman, 1975): that the dependent and non-aggressive style manifested toward mothers is also characteristic of behaviour toward fathers; and that in the presence of either parent, expression of physical aggression toward anyone is diminished.

The crime rate between countries can vary significantly, not just in total amount but also in the types of offences committed. There are some very significant problems with carrying out cross-cultural research into criminal behaviour, however one instance stands out as particularly relevant, that being the case of comparison between Japan and other Western nations, in particular the USA.

Research in the USA has suggested that young offenders from African-American populations are less likely to have emotional and psychological dysfunction and troubled backgrounds than their White counterparts, but more likely to associate with deviant peers (Dinges et al, 1997). Barriers to achieving financial self-sufficiency through legitimate means may increase the acceptability of engaging in criminal behaviour within ethnic minority groups during adolescence, particularly when coupled with exposure to neighbourhoods with high rates of gang activity (National Centre for Education Statistics, 1995; Yung & Hammond, 1997). In a study of children with conduct disorder, it was found that individual and familial factors were more strongly related to childhood-onset conduct disorder, whereas ethnic minority status and exposure to deviant peers were more strongly associated with onset in adolescence (McCabe et al., 2001). Longitudinal research is required into the criminal careers of Black men, and the possibility of higher rates of late-or adolescent-onset criminality, together with a third possibility that we could not measure in this study—that the threshold within the criminal justice system for their imprisonment may be lower.

In contrast, the prevalence of conduct disorder in South Asian children is lower than in White and Black children in Great Britain, and lower for girls than boys (Meltzer et al., 2000). This might partly explain the markedly lower rate of imprisonment of South Asian women. However, in circumstances where South Asian women do experience the same adverse childhood risk factors as White women prisoners, their risks of future criminality and psychiatric morbidity may be similar.

Japan is noted as being a country with low-recorded crime rates, especially in comparison with the USA. Wilson and Herrnstein (1985) suggest a number of cultural factors that could explain some of this difference:

(a) Higher clearance rates for serious crimes than in the USA (60% vs 20% in the early 1970's);

(b) Reporting rates are higher (more confessions, and less right to silence in Japan). This leads to more convictions in Japan;

(c) Japan is less culturally diverse than the USA and maintains closer familial links. These are known to prevent crime;

(d) Japanese people tend to be more concerned with obligation to the in-group over civil and individual rights. Again making crime less likely to occur, and when it does more likely to be reported;

(e) The average Japanese citizens IQ score is 110 compared to 100 in the USA. This may contribute to lower rates of criminal behaviour.

However the differences in economic factors and unemployment rates between the two countries also need to be taken into account. For instance, the USA has had relatively high unemployment in lower socio-economic groups for several decades whereas this is not true for Japan.

Parenting Style and Cultural Influences

The concept of parenting style is further complicated by cultural differences. In order to understand how parenting style influences child outcomes, one must disentangle what research refers to as three different aspects of parenting. These include (1) the goals of socialization, whereby parents help children conform to the demands of the family and society; (2) parenting practices, which are used to help children develop specific child behaviours such as table manners or school performance; and (3) parenting style, which are a "constellation of attitudes" that create an emotional climate through which parent's behaviours are expressed (Darling & Steinberg, 1993,). Separating parenting practice from style and recognizing parenting style as a context through which parents socialize their children for the culture in which they will most likely reside helps one understand the role of culture in the parent-child relationship.

Children may interpret the meaning of parents' behaviour differently depending on their cultural or ethnic background. For example, Chao (1994) notes that traditional Chinese parents have often been described as "authoritarian"—restrictive, controlling, or rejecting—but that many Chinese equate strictness, firm control, and parental obedience with parental care, concern, and involvement. Other studies have shown that greater parental control is associated with greater warmth and love by children in Korean families but is viewed far less positively by children in North American or European families (Deater-Deckard et al., 1996).

In another example of culturally specific parenting practices and outcomes, harsh physical discipline such as hitting and spanking is shown to be an early predictor of later hostility and aggressive behaviour in European American children but not in African American children. Harsh discipline in the form of physical abuse, however, has been shown to have negative effects for all socio-economic and ethnic groups (Deater-Deckard et al., 1996).

None of the above factors by themselves cause young persons to be antisocial. What makes the youth more than likely to be antisocial is the presence of more than two or three factors. In fact, most antisocial youth present 3 or 4 risk factors present (Rutter, 1979).

We have the ability to identify these at-risk children at very young ages and to successfully divert them from a destructive path, yet we too often ignore the problem in the hope that it will go way. But this problem will not disappear. In fact, without attention, it will severely worsen. In the absence of intervention and appropriate supports, many at-risk children adopt an antisocial behaviour pattern they will keep for the rest of their lives (Reid, 1993). For these reasons, we owe it to curselves, our children and our society as a whole to provide services of identification and treatment for all children everywhere.

SUMMARY

Several factors have been identified that place a child at risk for antisocial behaviour. Early signs of troublesome behaviour at home or school are salient predictors. In addition, a variety of parent and family chartacteristics have been identified as factors related to antisocial behaviour, such as Family conflict and disruption, Family Income, Parental psychopathology, Parental Rearing Style, Parent-child interaction pattern, & Parental influence on children's emotions and attitudes. Studies on peer factors relating to antisocial behaviour point out to negative peer relationships, peer rejection, and membership in gangs as salient factors. School and classroom size, disruptive school environment, academic failure, punishment, and lack of interpersonal competencies for school success lead to antisocial behaviour among the young. Poverty and social disadvantage, location of residence, community drug and alcohol use, community crime and violence, presence of gangs, availability of firearms and weapons, exposure to violence in the mass media, less leisure, and lack of exercise and free play are the neighbourhood or community factors related to antisocial behaviour. There is a classic interaction of individual and cultural factors in causing antisocial behaviour. Parenting Styles and Cultural Influences and the Interaction of Cultural and Individual Factors are dealt with in this chapter.

REFERENCES

Adlaf, E.M., Smart, R.G., Walsh, G.W., & Ivis, F.J. (1994). Is the Association Between Drug Use and Delinquency Weakening? *Addiction*, 89, 1675-1681.

Adler, N.E., Boyce, T., Chesney, M.A., Cohen, S.. Folkman et al. (1994). Socio-economic Status and Health: the Challenge of the Gradient. *American Psychology*, 49:15-24.

Ageton, S. S. (1983). *Sexual Assault Among Adolescents.* Lexington, MA: Lexington Books.

Anderson, C. A., & Dill, K. E. (2000). Video Games and Aggressive Thoughts, Feelings, and Behaviour in the Laboratory and in Life. *Journal of Personality and Social Psychology*, 78, 772-790.

Anderson, E. (1994). The Code of the Streets. *The Atlantic Monthly*, May, 81-94.

Anderson, E. (1997). Violence and the Inner-city Street Code. In J. McCord (Ed.), *Violence and Childhood in the Inner City* (pp. 1-30). New York, NY: Cambridge University Press.

Anderson, K. E., Lytton, H., & Romney, D. M. (1986). Mothers' Interactions with Normal and Conduct-disordered Boys: Who Affects Whom? *Developmental Psychology*, 22, 604-609.

American Psychological Association. (1993). *Violence and Youth: Psychology's Response*. Washington, DC: Author.

Appleby, Timothy. (1998). Youth Crime in Canada has Small Hard Core. *The Globe and Mail*, December 16.

Asquith, S et al. (1998). *Children, Young People and Offending in Scotland.* (The Scottish Office Central Research Unit).

Azrin, N. H., Hake, D. G., Holz, W. C., & Hutchinson, R. R. (1965). Motivational Aspects of Escape from Punishment. *Journal of the Experimental Analysis of Behaviour*, 8, 31-34

Bagwell, Catherine, et al. (1998). Preadolescent Friendship and Peer Rejection as Predictors of Adult Adjustment. *Child Development*, 69, No.1, February.

Baker, D., Telfer M.A., Richardson, C.E., & Clark, G.R. (1970). Chromosome Errors in Men with Antisocial Behaviour: Comparison of Selected Men with "Klinefelter's Syndrome" and XYY Chromosome Pattern. JAMA, 214:869-878.

Bandura, A. (1965). Behavioural Modification through Modeling Practices. In L. Krasner & I. Ullman (Eds.), *Research in Behaviour Modification* (pp. 310-340). New York: Holt, Rinehart & Winston.

Bandura, A. (1977). *Social Learning Theory*. Englewood Cliffs, NJ: Prentice-Hall.

Bandura, A. (1986). *Social Foundations of Thought and Action*. Englewood Cliffs, NJ: Prentice-Hall.

Barrera, M., Prelow, H.M., Dumka, L.E., Gonzales, N.A., Knight, G.P., Michaels, M.L., Roosa, M.W., & Tein, J. (2002). Pathways from Family Economic Conditions to Adolescents' Distress: Supportive Parenting, Stressors Outside the Family, and Deviant Peers. *Journal of Community Psychology*, Vol. 30, pp. 135-152.

Barriga, A. Q., & Gibbs, J. C. (1996). Measuring Cognitive Distortion in Antisocial Youth: Development and Preliminary Validation of the "How I Think" Questionnaire. *Aggressive Behaviour*, 22: 333-343.

Barriga, A.Q., Landau, J.R., Stinson, B.L., Liau, A.K., & Gibbs, J.C. (2000). Cognitive Distortion and Problem Behaviours in Adolescents. *Criminal Justice Behaviour*, 27, 36-56.

Barton, W.H., Watkins, M., & Jarjoura, R. (1997). *Social Work*, 42, 483-493.

Battin, S.R., Hill, K.G., Abbott, R.D., Catalano, R.F., & Hawkins, J.D. 1998. The Contribution of Gang Membership to Delinquency Beyond Delinquent Friends. *Criminology*, 36: 93-115.

Bell-Dolan, Debora, J. et al. (1995). Girls' Peer Relations and Internalizing Problems: Are Socially Neglected, Rejected, and Withdrawn Girls at Risk ? *Journal of Clinical Psychology*, 24: 4.

Bender, Doris, & Losel, Friedrich. (1997). Protective Risk Factors of Peer Relations and Social Support on Antisocial Behaviour in Adolescents from Multi-problem mileu. *Journal of Adolescence*, 20:6.

Berkowitz, L. (1983). Aversively Stimulated Aggression: Some Parallels and Difference in Research with Animals and Humans. *American Psychologist*, 38, 1135-1144.

Berkowitz, L. (1993). Pain and Aggression: Some Findings and Implications. Motivation and Emotion, 17, 277-293.

Biederman, J., Newcorn, J., & Sprich, S. (1991). Comorbidity of Attention Deficit Hyperactivity Disorder with Conduct, Depressive, Anxiety, and other Disorders. American Journal of Psychiatry, 148(5), 564-577.

Bjerregaard, B. & Lizotte, A. J. (1995). Gun Ownership and Gang Membership. *Journal of Criminal Law and Criminology*, 86, 37-58.

Block, C. R.; and Block, R. (1993). *Research in Brief: Street Gang Crime in Chicago*. Washington, DC: National Institute of Justice (CNJ 144782).

Bohman, M. (1996). Predisposition to Criminality Swedish Adoption Studies in Retrospect. In: Rutter M. ed. *Genetics of Criminal and Antisocial Behaviour*. Chichester: Wiley, (CIBA Foundation Symposium 194).

Bolger, K.E., Patterson, C.J., Thompson, W.W., & Kupersmidt, J.B. (1995). Psychosocial Adjustment Among Children Experiencing Persistent and Intermittent Family Economic Hardship. *Child Development*, 66:1107-29.

Bolger, K.E., Patterson, C.J. , Thompson, W.W., & Kupersmidt, J.B. (1995). Psychosocial Adjustment Among Children Experiencing Persistent and Intermittent Family Economic Hardship. *Child Development*, 66:1107-29.

Bostic, M. (1994). *Juvenile Crime Prevention Strategies: A Law Enforcement Perspective*. Paper Presented at the Council of State Governments Conference on School Violence, Westlake Village, CA.

Bourgois, Philippe. (1995). *In Search of Respect: Selling Crack in El Barrio*. Cambridge, United Kingdom: Cambridge University Press.

Bowlbv, J. (1969). *Attachment and Loss*. Vol. I. Attachment. London: Penguin, 1978.

Brantlinger, E. (1991). Social Class Distinctions in Adolescents' Reports of Problems and Punishment in School. *Behavioural Disorders*, 17, 36-46.

Brier, N. (1994). Targeted Treatment for Adjudicated Youth with Learning Disabilities: Effects on Recidivism. *Journal of Learning Disabilities*, 27(4), 215-222.

British Columbia Teachers' Federation. (1993). *Qualitative Research Study on Violence in B.C. Schools*. Vancouver, BC: Viewpoints Research.

Brodinsky, B. (1980). AASA *Critical Issues Report: Student Discipline, Problems, and Solutions* (Report No. 021 00334). Arlington, VA: American Association of School Administrators.

Bronfenbrermer , U. (1976). Ecology of the Family as a Context for Human Development Research Perspectives. *Developmental Psychology*, 22,723-742.

Brooklin K. Baker, (2001). Cognitive Distortions Among Juvenile Delinquents and Non-Delinquents. *http://clearinghouse.mwsc.edu/manuscripts/144.asp*.

Brooks, R. (1992). Fostering Self-esteem in Children with ADD: The Search for Islands of Competence. *Chadder*, pp. 14-15, Fall, Winter.

Brooks, R. (1994). Children at Risk: Fostering Resilience and Hope. *American Journal of Orthopsychiatry*, 64(4), 545-553.

Burgess, A. W., Hartman, C. R. and McCormack, A. (1987). Abused to Abuser: Antecedents of Socially Deviant Behaviours; *Annual Progress in Child Psychiatry and Child Development*, 20: 601-614.

Bursik and Webb. (1982). Community Change and Patterns of Delinquency. *American Journal of Sociology*, 88.

Bursik, R. J. Jr., & Grasmick, H. G. (1993). Neighbourhoods and Crime: *The Dimensions of Effective Community Control*. New York: Lexington Books.

Bushman, B. J. (1995). Moderating Role of Trait Aggressiveness in the Effects of Violent Media on Aggression. *Journal of Personality and Social Psychology*, 69, 950-960.

Bushman, B. J., & Geen, R. G. (1990). Role of Cognitive-emotional Mediators and Individual Differences in the Effects of Media Violence on Aggression. *Journal of Personality and Social Psychology*, 58, 156-163.

Butovskaya, M. Social Behaviour Among Kalmyk Primary School Children. *Noedus News*, 4(No. 2), 4-5.

Cairns, R.B. and B.D. Cairns. 1994. *Lifelines and Risks: Pathways of Youth in Our Time*. Cambridge: Cambridge University Press.

Capaldi, D. M., & Patterson, G. R. (1996). Can Violent Offenders be Distinguished from Frequent Offenders? Prediction from Childhood to Adolescence. *Journal of Research in Crime and Delinquency*, 33, 206-231.

Carter, C.M., et al. (1993). Effects of a Few Foods Diet in Attention Deficit Disorder, Archives of Disease in Childhood, 69 (5), 564-8.

Casey, L.J., Seagall, D.R., Street, K., & Blank, C.E. (1966). Sex Chromosomes Abnormalities in Two State Hospitals for Patients Requiring Special Security. Nature, 209:641-642.

Cashwell, C. S., & Vacc, N. A. (1996). Family Functioning and Risk Behaviours: Influences on Adolescent Delinquency. *School Counselor*, 44, 105-114.

Caspi, A., Elder, G. H., & Bem, D. J. (1987). Moving Against the World: Life-course Patterns of Explosive Children. *Developmental Psychology*, 23, 308-313.

Chao, Ruth. (1994). Beyond Parental Control and Authoritarian Parenting Style: Understanding Chinese Parenting Through the Cultural Notion of Training. *Child Development*, 65(4), 1111-1119. (ERIC Journal No. EJ491656).

Chris Gibson, & Stephen Tibbetts (1998). Interaction Between Maternal Cigarette Smoking and Apgar Scores in Predicting Offending Behaviour. *Psychological Reports*, 83: 579-586.

Christiansen, K.O., (1977). A Preliminary Study of Criminality Among Twins(pp45-48) in S. Mednick and K.O. Christiansen (Eds). *Biosocial Basis of Criminal Behaviour*. New York: Gardner.

Clark, R., & Shields, G. (1997). Family Communication and Delinquency. *Adolescence*, 32, 81-92.

Cline, V. B., Croft, R. G., & Courrier, S. (1973). Desensitization of Children to Television Violence. *Journal of Personality and Social Psychology*, 27, 360-365.

Cloninger, C. R., Sigvardsson, S., Bohman.M., & von Knorring, A. L. (1982). Predisposition to Petty Criminality in Swedish Adoptees. II. Cross-Fostering Analysis of Gene-environment Interaction. *Archives of General Psychiatry*, 39:1242-1247.

Cloward, R., and Ohlin, L. (1960). *Delinquency and Opportunity*. Glencoe, IL: Free Press.

Coie, J. D., & Dodge, K. A. (1998). Aggression and Antisocial Behaviour. In W. Damon & N. Eisenberg (Eds.), *Handbook of Child Psychology* (5th ed., Vol. 3) (pp. 779-862). New York: John Wiley.

Conger, R.D., Conger, K.J., Elder, G.H., Jr., Lorenz, F.O., Simons, R.L., & Whitbeck, L.B. (1992). A Family Process Model of Economic Hardship and Adjustment of Early Adolescent Boys. *Child Development*, 63, 526-41.

Conley, D. J. (1994). Adding Colour to a Black and White Picture: Using Qualitative Data to Explain Racial Disproportionality in the Juvenile Justice System. *Journal of Research in Crime and Delinquency*, 31, 135-148.

Crook, W.G. (1999). Sugar, yeast and ADHD: Fact or Fiction? In: Bellanti, J.A., Crook, W.G., & Layton, R.E. (Eds.), *Attention Deficit Hyperactivity Disorder: Causes and Possible Solutions (Proceedings of a Conference)*. Jackson, TN: International Health Foundation.

Cook, P.J., & J.H. Laub (1998). The Unprecedented Epidemic in Youth Violence. pp. 27-64 in Youth Violence, *Crime and Justice*, Vol. 24, M. Tonry and M.H. Moore,(Eds.), Chicago: University of Chicago Press.

Craig, W., & Pepler, D. (1997). *Naturalistic Observations of Bullying and Victimisation on the Playground*. Lamarsh Centre for Research on Violence and Conflict Resolution. York University, Unpublished Report.

Crick, N.R., & Dodge, K.A. (1994). A Review and Reformulation of Social Information-processing Mechanisms in Children's Social Adjustment. *Psychological Bulletin*, 115, 74-101.

Crick, N.R., & Dodge, K.A. (1996). Social Information-processing Mechanisms in Children's Social Adjustment,. *Child Development*, 67, 993-1002.

Crowe, T. (1995). *Youth Crime and Community Safety*. Keynote Address to the Eugene City Club, Eugene, OR.

Csikszentmihalyi, M. (1990). Flow: *The Psychology of Optimal Experience*. New York: Harper & Row Publisher.

Curry, G. D., & Spergel, I. A. (1992). Gang Involvement and Delinquency Among Hispanic and African-American Adolescent Males. *Journal of Research in Crime and Delinquency*, 29, 273-291.

Daly, M., & Wilson, M. (1988). *Homicide*. New York: Aldine de Gruyter.

Darling, Nancy, & Steinberg, Laurence. (1993). Parenting Style as Context: An Integrative Model. *Psychological Bulletin*, 113(3), 487-496.

Deater-Deckard, Kirby., Bates, John, E., Dodge, Kenneth A., & Pettit, Gregory S. (1996). Physical Discipline Among African American and European American Mothers: Links to Children's Externalizing Behaviours. *Developmental Psychology*, 32(6), 1065-1072. (ERIC Journal No. EJ543365)

Dekovic, Maja Janssens., Jan M.A.M.,. Van A.S., & Nicole M.C. (2003). Family Predictors of Antisocial Behaviour in Adolescence. *Family Process*: 6/22/2003

Dembo et al. (1994). Cited in Dinges, G., Atlis, M. M., & Vincent, G.M. (1997). Cross-cultural Perspectives on Antisocial Behaviour. In D. M. Stoff & J. Breiling (Eds.), *Handbook of Antisocial Behaviour* (pp. 474-495). New York: Wiley.

Developmental Research and Programmes Inc. (2000). Seattle, Washington.

Dinges, G6. G., Atlis, M. M., & Vincent, G.M. (1997). Cross-cultural Perspectives on Antisocial Behaviour. In D. M. Stoff & J. Breiling (Eds.), *Handbook of Antisocial Behaviour* (pp. 474-495). New York: Wiley.

Dinges, N., Atlis, M. M. & Vincent, G. M. (1997) Cross-cultural Perspectives on Antisocial Behaviour. In *Handbook of Antisocial Behaviour* (Eds.), D. M. Stoff & J. Breiling. New York: John Wiley & Sons.

Dishion, T., Andrews, D., & Crosby, L. (1995). Antisocial Boys and Their Friends in Early Adolescence: Relationship Characteristics, Quality, and Interactional Process. *Child Development*, 66, 139-151.

Dishion, T., Patterson, G.R., & Grisler, P. (1994). Peer Adaptation in the Development of Antisocial Behaviour. In L.Huesmann (Ed.), *Aggressive Behaviour: Current Perspectives* (pp.61-95). New York: Plenum.

Dishion, T.J., Spracklen, K., Andrews, D., & Patterson, G. (1996). Deviancy Training in Male Adolescent Friendships. *Behaviour Therapy*, 27, 373-390.

Dodge, K. A. (1986). A Social Information Processing Model of Social Competence in Children. In M. Perlmutter (Ed.), *Minnesota Symposium on Child Psychology*, 18, 77-125 Hillsdale, NJ: Erlbaum.

Dodge, K. A., & Frame, C. L. (1982). Social Cognitive Biases and Deficits in Aggressive Boys. *Child Development*, 53, 620-635.

Dodge, K., Coie, J., & Brakke, N. (1982). Behaviour Patterns of Socially Rejected and Neglected Adolescents: The Roles of Social Approach and Aggression. *Journal of Abnormal Child Psychology*. 10: 389-410.

Dodge, K.A. (1980). Social Cognition and Children's Aggressive Behaviour. *Child Development*, 51, 162-70.

Dodge, K.A., & Schwartz, D. (1997). Social Information-processing Mechanisms in Aggressive Behaviours. In D. Stoff, J. Breiling, & J.D. Maser (Eds.), *Handbook of Antisocial Behaviour*, pp.171-80. New York: Wiley.

Dodge, K.A., Petit, G.S., & Bates, J.E. (1994). Socialization Mediators of the Relation Between Socio-economic Status and Child Conduct Problems. *Child Development*, 65, 649-665.

Dodge, K.A., Pettitt, G.S., Bates, J.E. and Valente, E. (1995). Social Information-processing Patterns Partially Mediate the Effect of Early Physical Abuse on Later Conduct Problems. *Journal of Abnormal Psychology*, 104, 632-43.

Does TV Violence Lead to Violence at School? (1992). *Meeting the Challenge: Scarborough Board of Education's Community Newsletter, Spring*.

Dominick, J.R., & Greenberg, B.S. (1972). Attitudes Toward Violence: The Interaction of Television, Family Attitudes, and Social Class. In G.A. Comstock & E.A. Rubinstein (Eds.), *Television and Social Behaviour, Vol. 3: Television and Adolescent Aggressiveness* (pp. 314-335). Washington, D.C.: U.S. Government Printing Office.

Dorfman, L., Woodruff, K., Chavez, V., & Wallack, L. (1997). Youth and Violence on Local Television News in California. *American Journal of Public Health*, 87(8), 1311-1316.

Dornbusch, S.M, Carlsmith, J.M., Bushwall, S.J., Ritter, P.L., Leiderman,H., Hastorf, A.H., & Gross, R.T. (1985). Single Parents, Extended Households, and the Control of Adolescents. *Child Development*, 56, 326-341.

Downey, G., & Coyne, J.C. (1990). Children of Depressed Parents: An Integrative Review. *Psychological Bulletin*, 108, 50-76.

Earls, F. J. (1994). Violence and Today's Youth. *Critical Health Issues for Children and Youth*, 4, 4-23.

Edelman, M. W. (1995). United We Stand: A Common Vision. *Claiming Children*, 1, 6-12.

Edwards, J. E. (1996). A Measurement of Delinquency Differences Between a Delinquent and Non-delinquent Sample: What are the Implications? *Adolescence*, 31, 973-989.

Eggar, J., Carter, C.M. et al. (1985). Controlled Trial of Oligoantigenic Diet Treatment in the Hyperkinetic Syndrome. *Lancet*, 540-545.

Elder, G. H., Nguyen, T. V., & Caspi, A. (1985). Linking Family Hardship to Children's Lives. *Child Development*, 56, 361-375.

Eley, T. C., Lichtenstein, P., & Stevenson, J. (1999). Sex Differences in Etiology of Aggressive and Nonaggressive Antisocial Behaviour: Results from Two Twin Studies. *Child Development*, 70, 155-168.

Ellenbogen, Stephen, & Claire Chamberland. (1997). The Peer Relations of Dropouts: A Comparative Study of At-risk and Not At-risk Youth. *Journal of Adolescence*, 20.

Elliott, D. S. (1994). Serious Violent Offenders: Onset, Developmental Course, and Termination—The American Society of Criminology 1993 Presidential Address. *Criminology,* 32, 1-21.

Elliott, D. S., & Ageton, S. R. (1980). Reconciling Race and Class Differences in Self-reported and Official Estimates of Delinquency. *American Sociological Review*, 45: 95-110.

Elliott, D. S., & Menard, S. (1996). Delinquent Friends and Delinquent Behaviour: Temporal and Developmental Patterns. In J. D. Hawkins (Ed.), *Delinquency and Crime: Current Theories* (pp. 28-67). Cam bridge, United Kingdom: Cambridge University Press.

Elliott, D. S., Huizinga, D., & Ageton, S. S. (1985). *Explaining Delinquency and Drug Use*. Beverly Hills, CA: Sage.

Emler, N., & Reicher, S. (1995). *Adolescence and Delinquency: The Collective Management of Reputation*. Oxford: Balckwell.

Eron, L.D., Huesmann, L.R., & Zelli, A. (1991). The Role of Parental Variables in the Learning of Aggression. In D.P. Pepler and K.H. Rubin (Eds.), *The Development and Treatment of Childhood Aggression*, Hillsdale, NJ: Lawrence Erlbaum

Fagan, J., & Wilkinson, D. (1998). Social Contexts and Functions of Adolescent Violence. In D. S. Elliott, B. A. Hamburg, & K. R. Williams (Eds.), *Violence in American Schools: A New Perspective* (pp. 55-93). New York. Cambridge University Press.

Fagan, J.A. (1993). The Political Economy of Drug Dealing Among Urban Gangs. In *Drugs and Community*, R. Davis, A. Lurigio, & D. P. Rosenbaum (Eds.), (pp. 19-54). Springfield, IL: Charles Thomas.

Fagan, J.A. and K.L. Chin. (1990). *Violence as Regulation and Social Control in the Distribution of Crack*. National Institute on Drug Abuse Research Monograph Series 103: 8-43.

Farnworth, Margaret., Terence P. Thornberry., Marvin D. Krohn, & Alan J. Lizotte. (1994). *Journal of Research in Crime and Delinquency*, 31: 32-61.

Farrington D.P. (1995). The Development of Offending and Antisocial Behaviour from Childhood: Key Findings from the Cambridge Study in Delinquent Development. *Journal of Child Psychology and Psychiatry*, 36: 929-964 [Medline].

Farrington, D. (1987). Schools and Delinquency Prevention. *Today's Delinquent* (pp. 71-86). Pittsburgh, PA: National Center for Juvenile Justice.

Farrington, D. P. (1989). Early Predictors of Adolescent Aggression and Adult Violence. *Violence and Victims*, 4, 79-100.

Farrington, D. P. (2000) *Criminology*, 38, 1-24.

Farrington, D.P. (1992). Explaining the Beginning, Progess and Ending of Antisocial Behaviour from Birth to Childhood. In J. McCord (Ed.), *Advances in Criminological Theory*, Vol.3: Facts, Frameworks and Forecasts, pp. 253-86. New Brunswick, NJ: Transaction Publishers.

Farrington, D.P. (1993). Understanding and Preventing Bullying. In M. Tonry & N. Morris (Eds.), *Crime and Justice*, 17, 381-458. Chicago: University of Chicago Press.

Farrington, D.P. (1994). Early Developmental Prevention of Juvenile Delinquency. *Criminal Behaviour and Mental Health*, 4 (3), 209-27.

Farrington, D.P. 1998. Predictors, Causes and Correlates of Male Youth Violence. In Youth Violence, Crime and Justice, Vol. 24, (Ed.), Edited by M. Tonry and M.H. Moore. Chicago, IL: University of Chicago Press, pp. 421-475.

Featherstone, D. R., Cundick, B. P., & Jensen, L. C. (1993). Differences in School Behaviour and Achievement Between Children from Intact, Reconstituted, and Single-Parent Families. *Family Therapy*, 20, 37-48

Feingold, B. (1975). *Why Your Child is Hyperactive*. Random House: New York.

Fernie, D. E. (1981). Ordinary and Extraordinary People: Children's Understanding of Television and Real Life Models. In M. Kelly, & M. Gardner (Eds.), *Viewing Children Through Television*, (pp. 47-58). San Francisco: Jossey Bass.

Feshbach, N. D. (1984). Empathy, Empathy Training, and the Regulation of Aggression in Elementary School Children. In R. W. Kaplan, V. J. Konecni, & R. W. Novaco (Eds.), *Aggression in Youth and Children*. Boston: Martinus Nijhuff Publications.

Flannery, D. J., Williams, L. L., & Vazsony, A. T. (1999). Who are They with and What are They Doing? Delinquent Behaviour, Substance Use, and Early Adolescents' After School Time. *American Journal of Orthopsychiatry*, 69, 247-253.

Fonagy, P., Steele H., & Steele, M.(1991). Maternal Representations of Attachment During Pregnancy Predict the Organization of Infant-mother Attachment at One Year of Age. *Child Development*, 62: 891-905.

Forssman, H., & Hamber, G. (1967). Chromosomes and Antisocial Behaviour. *Exerpta Criminologica*, 7: 113-117.

Friedrich, L. K., & Stein, A. H. (1973). Aggressive and Prosocial Television Programs and the Natural Behaviour of Preschool Children. *Monographs of the Society for Research in Child Development*, 38, 1-64.

Gabel, S., & Shindledecker, R. (1991). Aggressive Behaviour in Youth: Characteristics, Outcome, and Psychiatric Diagnoses. *Journal of the American Academy of Child and Adolescent Psychiatry*, 30: 982-988.

Gardner, E. M. (1992). Parent-child Interaction and Conduct Disorder. *Educ Psychol Review*, 2:135-63.

Garfinkel, B. and Wener, P.H. (1989). Attention Deficit Hyperactivity Disorder. In: Kaplan HI, Sadock B. (Eds.), *Comprehensive Textbook of Psychiatry*, Fifth Edition, Baltimore: Williams & Wilkins, 1828-1842.

Geen, R. G., & O'Neal, E. C. (1969). Activation of Cue-elicited Aggression by General Arousal. *Journal of Personality and Social Psychology*, 11, 289-292.

Gerbner, G., & Gross, L. (1976). Living with Television: The Violence Profile. *Journal of Communication*, 26(2), pp. 173-199.

Giancola, P. R., Mezzich, A. C., Clark, D. B., & Tarter, R. E. (1999). Cognitive Distortions, Aggressive Behaviour, and Drug Use in Adolescent Boys With and Without a Family History of a Substance Use Disorder. *Psychology of Addictive Behaviours*, 13: 22-32.

Gibbs, W. (1995). Trends in Behavioural Science: Seeking the Criminal Element. *Scientific American*, 272(3), pp. 100-107.

Goldstein, P. (1985). The Drugs/violence Nexus: A Tripartite Conceptual Framework. *Journal of Drug Issues*, 15 (Fall), 493-506.

Goldstein, P. (1989). Drugs and Violent Crime. In N. Weiner & M. Wolfgang, (Eds.), *Pathways to Criminal Violence*. Newbury Park, CA: Sage.

Goleman, D. (1995). *Emotional Intelligence* (p. 224). New York: Bantam Books.

Gottfredson, D. (1986). *Promising Strategies for Improving Student Behaviour*. Paper Prepared for the Conference on Student Discipline Strategies of the Office of Educational Research and Improvement. Washington, DC: U. S. Department of Education.

Gottfredson, G. (1987). American Education: American Delinquency. *Today's Delinquent* (pp. 5-70). Pittsburgh, PA: National Center for Juvenile Justice.

Green, R. G., Kolevzon, M. S., & Vosler, N. R. (1985). The Beavers-Timberlawn Model of Family Competence and the Circumplex Model of Family Adaptability and Cohesion: Separate, but Equal? *Family Process*, 24, 385-398.

Greenberg, B. (1974). School Vandalism: Its Effects and Paradoxical Solutions. *Crime Prevention Review*, 1, 105.

Greenfeld, Lawrence A., & Zawitz, Marianne W. (1995). *Weapons Offences and Offenders. Selected Findings*. Bureau of Justice Statistics, U.S. Department of Justice. Washington, DC: U.S. Government Printing Office.

Gresham, F. M., Sugai, G., Horner, R. H., Quinn, M. M., & McInerney, M. (1998). *Classroom and School-wide Practices that Support Student's Social Competence: A Synthesis of Research*. Washington, DC: U.S. Department of Education.

Halpern, Robert. (1990). Parent Support and Education Programmes. *Children and Youth Services Review*, 12, 285-308.

Hauser, P., Zametin A.J., Martinez, P., Vitiello, B., Metochik, J., Mixson, J., & Weintraub, B.D. (1993). Attention Deficit Hyperactivity Disorder in People with Generalized Resistance to Thyroid Hormone. *The New England Journal of Medicine*, 328 (14): 997-1011.

Hawkins, J. (1995). Controlling Crime Before It Happens: Risk-focused Prevention. *National Institute of Justice Journal*, 229, 10- 18.

Hawkins, J. D., Catalano, R. F., Kosterman, R., Abbott, R. D., & Hill, K. G. (1999). *Archives of Paediatrics and Adolescent Medicine*, 226-243.

Hawkins, J. D., Farrington, D. P.. & Catalano, R. F. (1998b). Reducing Violence Through the Schools. In D. S. Elliott, B. A. Hamburg, & K. R. Williams (Eds.), *Violence in American Schools: A New Perspective* (pp. 188-216). New York: Cambridge University Press.

Hawkins, J. D., Herrenkohl, T. L., Farrington, D. P., Brewer, D., Catalano, R. F., & Harachi, T. W. (1998c). A Review of Predictors of Youth Violence. In R. Loeber & D. P. Farrington (Eds.), *Serious and Violent Juvenile Offenders: Risk Factors and Successful Interventions* (pp. 106-146). Thousand Oaks, CA: Sage Publications.

Hawkins, J. D., Laub, J. H., & Lauritsen, J. L. (1998a). Race, Ethnicity, and Serious Juvenile Offending. In R. Loeber & D. P. Farrington (Eds.), *Serious and Violent Juvenile Offenders: Risk Factors and Successful Interventions* (pp. 30-46). Thousand Oaks, CA: Sage Publications.

Heaven, Patrick C.L. (1994). *Contemporary Adolescence: A Social Psychological Approach.* Melbourne: Macmillan.

Heller, M. S., & White, M. A. (1975). Teacher Approval and Disapproval on Ability Grouping. *Journal of Educational Psychology*, 67, 796-800.

Herrero, M.E., Hechtman, L., & Weiss, G. (1994). Antisocial Disorders in Hyperactive Subjects from Childhood to Adulthood: Predictive Factors and Characterization of Subgroups. *American Journal of Orthopsychiatry* 64(4): 510-521.

Hill, K.G., Howell, J.C., Hawkins, J.D., and Battin-Pearson, S.R. (1999). Childhood Risk Factors for Adolescent Gang Membership: Results from the Seattle Social Development Project. *Journal of Research in Crime and Delinquency*, 36(3): 300-322.

Hirschi, T. (1969). *Causes of Delinquency*. Newbury Park, CA: Sage Publications.

Hook, E.B. (1973). Behavioural Implications of the Human XYY Genotype. *Science*, 179:139-150.

How Safe are Our Schools? (1991). *The Reporter*, December.

Howell, J. C. (1998). Youth Gangs: An Overview. Research Bulletin. Washington, DC: U.S. Department of Justice, Office of Juvenile Justice and Delinquency Prevention.

http://www.cognitiveBehaviour.com/practice/remedialoptions.html.

Huesmann, L. R. (1982). Video Games and Aggression. In D. Pearl, L. Bouthilet, & J. Lazar, (Eds.), *Television and Behaviour: Ten Years of Progress and Implications for the Eighties* (Vol. 2). Technical Reviews. Washington, DC: U.S. Government Printing Office.

Huesmann, L. R. (1998). The role of Social Information Processing and Cognitive Schema in the Acquisition and Maintenance of Habitual Aggressive Behaviour (pp. 73-109). In R. G. Geen & E. Donnerstein (Eds.), *Human Aggression: Theories, Research, and Implications for Policy*. New York: Academic Press.

Huesmann, L. R., & Guerra, N. G. (1997). Children's Normative Beliefs About Aggression and Aggressive Behaviour. *Journal of Personality and Social Psychology*, 72, 408-419.

Huesmann, L. R., Eron, L. D., Klein, 1~, Brice, P., & Fischer, P. (1983). Mitigating the Imitation of Aggressive Behaviours by Changing Children's Attitudes About Media Violence. *Journal of Personality and Social Psychology*, 44, 899-910.

Huesmann, L.R., & Eron, L.D. (Eds.). (1986). Television and the Aggressive Child: A Cross-national Comparison. Hillsdale, NJ: Erlbaum.

Hunter, Ernest, (1993). *Aboriginal Health and History: Power and Prejudice in Remote Australia*, Melbourne, Cambridge University Press.

Jacobs, P.A., Price, W.H., Richmond, S., & Ratcliff, B.A.W. (1971). Chromosomes Surveys in Penal Institutions and Approved Schools. *Journal of Medical Genetics*, 8:49-58.

Jaffe, P., Wolfe, D., & Wilson, S. (1990). *Children of Battered Women*. Newbury Park CA: Sage.

Jerome R. Gardner. (1997) Remedial Options—Cognitive Behaviour. Retrieved March 11, 2002 from Cognitive Behaviour Management Reference Web site: *http://www.cognitiveBehaviour.com/practice/remedialoptions.html*.

Josephson, W. L. (1987). Television Violence and Children's Aggression: Testing the Priming, Social Script, and Disinhibition Predictions. *Journal of Personality and Social Psychology*, 53, 882-890.

Kandel, D. B. (1996). The Parental and Peer Contexts of Adolescent Deviance: An Algebra of Interpersonal Influences. *Journal of Drug Issues*, 26(2), 289-315.

Keilitz, I., & Dunivant, N. (1986). The Relationship Between Learning Disability and Juvenile Delinquency: Current State of Knowledge. *Remedial and Special Education*, 7(3), 18-26.

Kellam, S. G., Mayer, L. S., Rebok, G. W., & Hawkins, W. E. (1998). Effects of Improving Achievement on Aggressive Behaviour and of Improving Aggressive Behaviour on Achievement Through Two Preventive Interventions: An Investigation of Causal Paths. In Dohrenwend, Bruce P. (Ed.), *Adversity, Stress, and Psychopathology* (pp. 486-505). New York, NY, USA: Oxford University Press. XV 567 pp.

Kendall, P. C., & Braswell, L. (1985). *Cognitive-Behavioural Therapy for Impulsive Children*. New York: Guilford.

Kindlon, D. J., Tremblay, R. E., Mezzacappa, E., Earls, F., Laurent, D., & Schaal, B. (1995). Longitudinal Patterns of Heart Rate and Fighting Behaviour in 9- Through 12-year-old Boys. *Journal of the American Academy of Child and Adolescent Psychiatry,* 34, 371-377.

Klein, K., Forehand, R., Armistead, L., & Long, P. (1997). Delinquency During the Transition to Early Adulthood: Family and Parenting Predictors from Early Adolescence. *Adolescence*, 32, 61-80.

Klein, M. W. (1995). *The American Street Gang: Its Nature, Prevalence, and Control*. New York: Oxford University Press.

Knoff, H. M. & Batsche, G. M. (1995). Project ACHIEVE: Analyzing a School Reform Process for At-risk and Underachieving Students. *School Psychology Review,* 24(4), 579-603.

Kraemer, H. C., Kazdin, A. E., Offord, D. R., Kessler, R. C., Jensen, P. S., & Kupfer, D. J. (1997). Coming to Terms with the Terms of Risk. *Archives of General Psychiatry*, 54, 337-343.

Krishnan, V., & Morrison, K.B. (1995). An Ecological Model of Child Maltreatment in a Canadian Province. *Child Abuse and Neglect*, 19:1.

Lahey, B.B., Gordon, R.A., Loeber, R. and Stouthamer-Loeber, M. and Farrington, D.P. (1999). Boys Who Join Gangs: A Prospective Study of Predictors of First Gang Entry. *Journal of Abnormal Child Psychology*, 27, 261-276.

Lal, N., & Sethi, B.B. (1977). Estimate of Mental Ill Health in Children of an Urban Community. *Indian Journal of Paediatrics*, 44: 55-64.

Langseth, L., & Dowd, J. (1978). *Glucose Tolerance and Hyperkinesis*. Fd Cosmet Toxicol, 16, 129-133.

Lanzing, J. W. A. (1997). The Concept Mapping. Retrieved March 13, 2002 from *http://users.edte.utwente.nl/lanzing/cm_home.htm*.

Larson, E. (1994). *Lethal Passage: How the Travels of a Single Handgun Expose the Roots of America's Gun Crisis*. New York: Crown.

Larson, K.A. (1998). Problem-Solving Training and Parole Adjustment in High-Risk Young Adult Offenders. *The Yearbook of Correctional Education*, 279-299.

Laub, J. H., & Lauritsen, J. L. (1998). The Interdependence of School Violence with Neighbourhood and Family Conditions. In D. S. Elliott, B. A. Hamburg, & K. R. Williams (Eds.), *Violence in American Schools: A New Perspective* (pp. 127-155). New York: Cambridge University Press.

Leiber, M.J., & Mahworr, T.L. 1995. Evaluating the Use of Social Skills Training and Employment with Delinquent Youth. *Journal of Criminal Justice*, 23:127-141.

Lempers, J. D., Clark-Lempers, D. C., & Simons, R. L. (1989). Economic Hardship, Parenting, and Distress in Adolescence. *Child Development*, 60, 25-39.

Leone, P.E., Mayer, M. J., Malmgren, K., & Misel, S.M. (2000). School Violence and Disruption: Rhetoric, Reality, and Reasonable Balance. *Focus on Exceptional Children*, 33, 1-20.

Liau, A. K., Barriga, A.Q., & Gibbs, J.C. (1998). Relations Between Self-Serving Cognitive Distortions and Overt Versus Covert Antisocial Behaviour in Adolescents. *Aggressive Behaviour*, 24: 335-346.

Lipman, E.L., Offord, D.R., & Boyle, M.H. (1994). Relation Between Economic Disadvantage Psychosocial Morbidity in Children. *Canadian Medical Association Journal*, 151, 431- 437.

Lippa, R. A. (1990). Introduction to Social Psychology. Belmont, CA: Wadsworth.

Lipsey, M. W., & Derzon, J. H. (1998). Predictors of Violence or Serious Delinquency in Adolescence and Early Adulthood. In R. Loeber & D. P. Farrington (Eds.), Serious and Violent Juvenile Offenders (pp. 86-105). Thousand Oaks, CA: Sage.

Lipsitt, L. P. (Ed.). (1990, January). Violence and Aggression in Adolescence. *The Brown University Child Behaviour and Development Letter*, 1-6.

Loeber, R. and Stouthamer-Loeber, M. (1986). Family Factors as Correlates and Predictors of Conduct Problems and Juvenile Delinquency. In M. Tonry and N. Morris (eds.), *Crime and Justice*, Vol. 7 Chicago: University of Chicago Press.

Loeber, R., & Dishon, T. (1983). Early Predictors of Male Delinquency: A Review. *Psychological Bulletin*, 94, 68-99.

Loeber, R., & Stouthamer-Loeber, M., Green, F. (1987). Prediction. In H. C. Quay (Ed.). *Handbook of Juvenile Delinquency* (pp. 325-382). New York: Wiley.

Loeber, R., & Wikstrom, P. O. (1993). Individual Pathways to Crime in Different Types of Neighbourhoods. In D. P. Farrington, R. J. Sampson, & P. O. Wikstrom (Eds.), *Integrating Individual and Ecological Aspects of Crime* (pp. 169-204). Stockholm: National Council for Crime Prevention.

Loeber, R., Farrington, D. P., & Waschbusch, D. A. (1998). Serious and Violent Juvenile Offenders. In R. Loeber & D. P. Farrington (Eds.), *Serious and Violent Juvenile Offenders: Risk Factors and Successful Interventions* (pp. 13-29). Thousand Oaks, CA: Sage Publications.

Loeber, R., M. Stouthamer-Loeber, W.B. Van Kammen, & D.P. Farrington. (1991). Initiation, Escalation and Desistance in Juvenile Offending and Their Correlates. *Journal of Criminal Law and Criminology*. 82: 36-82.

Loney, J., Kramer, J., & Milich, R. 1983. The Hyperkinetic Child Grows Up: Predictors of Symptoms, Delinquency, and Achievement at Follow-up: Birth and Childhood Cohorts. In (Eds.), S.A. Mednick, M. Harway, & K.M. Finello. *Handbook of Longitudinal Research*, Vol. 1., New York, NY: Praeger.

Lyons-Ruth, K. (1995). Attachment Relationships Among Children with Aggressive Behaviour Problems: The Role of Disorganized Attachment Patterns. *J Consult Clin Psychol*, 64(1),64-73.

Maccoby, E. E. (1998). *The Two Sexes*. Cambridge, MA: Harvard University Press.

Maccoby, E. E., & Jacklin, C. N. (1980). Sex Differences in Aggression: A Rejoinder and Reprise. *Child Development*, 51, 964-980.

Maguin, E, & R. Loeber. (1996). Academic Performance and Delinquency. In (Ed.), M. Tonry, Crime and Justice: A Review of Research. Chicago, IL: University of Chicago Press, 20: 45-264.

Maguire, K. & Pastore, A. L. (1996). *Sourcebook of Criminal Justice Statistics* 1995. Washington, DC: U.S. Department of Justice, Office of Justice Programmes, Bureau of Justice Statistics.

Manion, I.G., and S. Wilson (1995). *An Examination of the Association Between Histories of Maltreatment and Addescent Risk Behaviours*. Catalogue No. H72-21/ 139-1995E. Ottawa: National Clearinghouse on Family Violence, Health Canada.

Martinez, A., & Bournival, B. (1996). ADHD: The Tip of the Iceberg? *The ADHD Report*, 3(6), pp. 5-6.

Matherne, M. & Thomas, A. (2001). Family Environment as a Predictor of Adolescent Delinquency. *Adolescence*, Winter, 2001.

Mathews, Fred. (1999). Girls' Use of Violence and Aggression, *Orbit*, 29, 4.

Mathis, R. D., & Yingling, R. D. (1990). Divorcing Versus Intact Families on the Circumplex Model: An Exploration of the Dimensions of Cohesion and Adaptability. *Family Therapy*, 27(3), 261-272.

Mawson, A. R. and Jacobs, K. J. (1978). Corn Consumption, Tryptophan, and Cross-National Homicide Rates. *Journal of Orthomolecular Psychiatry*, 7, 227-30.

Maxson, C. L., M. A. Gordon, & M. W. Klein. (1985). Differences Between Gang and Nongang Homicides. Criminology, 23, 209-222.

Mayer, G. R. (1995). Preventing Antisocial Behaviour in the Schools. *Journal of Applied Behaviour Analysis*, 28, 467-478.

Mayer, G. R., & Butterworth, T. (1979). A Preventive Approach to School Violence and Vandalism: An Experimental Study. *Personnel and Guidance Journal*, 57, 436-441.

Mayer, G. R., & Butterworth, T. (1981). Evaluating a Preventive Approach to Reducing School Vandalism. *Phi Delta Kappan*, 62, 498-499.

Mayer, G. R., & Sulzer-Azaroff, B. (1991). Interventions for Vandalism. In G. Stoner, M. K. Shinn, & H. M. Walker (Eds.), *Interventions for Achievement and Behaviour Problems*. Washington, DC: National Association of School Psychologists Monograph.

Mayer, G. R., Butterworth, T., Nafpaktitis, M., & Sulzer-Azaroff, B. (1983b). Preventing School Vandalism and Improving Discipline: A Three-year Study. *Journal of Applied Behaviour Analysis*, 16, 355-369.

Mayer, G. R., Mitchell, L., Clementi, T., Clement-Robertson, E., Myatt, R., & Bullara, D. T. (1993). A Dropout Prevention Programme for At-risk High School Students: Emphasizing Consulting to Promote Positive Classroom Climates. *Education and Treatment of Children*, 16, 135-146.

Mayer, G. R., Nafpaktitis, M., Butterworth, T., & Hollingsworth, P. (1987). A Search for the Elusive Setting Events of School Vandalism: A Correlational Study. *Education and Treatment of Children*, 10, 259-270.

Maynard, P. E., & Olson, D. H. (1987). Circumplex Model of Family Systems: A Treatment Tool in Family Counseling. *Journal of Counselling and Development*, 65, 502-504.

McCabe, K. M., Hough, R., Wood, P. A., et al (2001) Childhood and Adolescent Onset Conduct Disorder: A Test of the Developmental Taxonomy. *Journal of Abnormal Child Psychology*, 29, 305-316. [Medline].

McCord, J. (1990). Problem behaviours. In S.S. Feldman, & G.R. Elliott (Eds.), *At the Threshold: The Developing Adolescent* (414-430; 602-614). Cambridge, MA: Harvard University Press.

McCord, J. (1991). Family Relationships, Juvenile Delinquency, and Adult Criminality. *Criminology*, 29, 397-417.

McCord, J. (1996). Family as Crucible for Violence: Comment on Gorman-Smith et al. (1996). *Journal of Family Psychology*, 10, 147-152.

McCord, J., & Ensminger, M. (1995, November). *Pathways from Aggressive Childhood to Criminality*. Paper Presented at the American Society of Criminology, Boston., MA.

McCord, W., McCord, J., & Zola, I.K. (1959). *Origins of Crime*. New York: Columbia University Press.

McFadden, A. C., Marsh, G. E., Price, B. J., & Hwang, Y. (1992). A Study of Race and Gender Bias in the Punishment of School Children. *Education and Treatment of Children*, 15, 140-146.

McGee, R., Silva, P.A., & Williams, S. (1984). Perinatal, Neurological, Environmental and Developmental Characterisitics of Seven-year-Old Children with Stable Behaviour Problems. *Journal of Child Psychology and Psychiatry*, 25, 573-86.

McLeod, J. D., & Shanahan, M. J. (1996). Trajectories of Poverty and Children's Mental Health. *Journal of Health and Social Behaviour*, 37, 207-220.

McLeod, J. D., & Edwards, K. (1995). Contextual Determinants of Children's Responses to Poverty. *Social Forces*, 73, 1487-1516.

McLoyd, V. C. (1995). Poverty, Parenting, and Policy: Meeting the Support Needs of Poor Parents. In H.E. Fitzgerald, B.M. Lester, and B. Zuckerman (Eds.), *Children of Poverty: Research, Health, and Policy Issues* (pp. 269-303). New York: Garland Publishing, Inc.

McLoyd, V., & Wilson, L. (1991). The Strain of Living Poor: Parenting, Social Support, and Child Mental Health. In A. Houston (Ed.), *Children in Poverty: Child Development and Public Policy* (pp. 105-135). Cambridge, U.K.: Cambridge University Press.

Mediascope, (1996). *National Television Violence Study*: Executive Summary. US: Mediascope.

Mehrabian, A. (1997). Relations Among Personality Scales of Aggression, Violence, and Empathy: Validational Evidence Bearing on the Risk of Eruptive Violence Scale. *Aggressive Behaviour*, 23, 433-445.

Meltzer, H., Gatward, R., Goodman, R. et al. (2000). *Mental Health of Children and Adolescents in Great Britain*. London: HMSO.

Minuchin, S. (1974). *Families and Family Therapy*. Cambridge, MA: Harvard University Press.

Moffit, T.E. (1993a). Adolescent-limited and Life-course Persistent Antisocial Behaviour: A Developmental Taxonomy. *Psychological Review*, 100, 674-701.

Money, J., Erhardt, A. A. (1972). *Man and Woman. Boy and Girl. Baltimore*: John Hopkins Press.

Moore, W. L., & Cooper, H. (1984). Correlations Between Teacher and Student Backgrounds and Teacher Perceptions of Discipline Problems and Disciplinary Techniques. *Discipline*, 5, 1-7.

Murray, M.T., & Pizzorno J,T. (1998). *Encyclopaedia of Natural Medicine*. Rocklin, CA: Prima Publishing.

Mussack, Steven, E. (2000). Thinking Errors. Retrieved March 16, 2002, from *http://www.choicesoforegon.com/thinking_errors.htm.*

Mustard, Fraser, & McCain, Margaret. (1999). ***Reversing the Real Brain Drain: Early Years Study,*** **Toronto, Ontario Children's Secretariat.**

Myers, J. (1993). ***Soc/a/psycho/ogy.*** **(3rd ed.). New York: McGraw-Hill.**

Nafpaktitis, M., Mayer, G. R., & Butterworth, T. (1985). Natural Rates of Teacher Approval and Disapproval and their Relation to Student Behaviour in Intermediate School Classrooms. *Journal of Educational Psychology*, 77, 362-367.

Nagin, D. & Tremblay, R.E. (1999). Trajectories of Boys' Physical Aggression, Opposition, and Hyperactivity on the Path to Physically Violent and Non-violent Juvenile Delinquency. *Child Development*, 70, 1181-1196.

Nanda. G.S., & Dash. A.S. (1996). *Disadvantage, Schooling, Competence and Invulnerability*. Bhubaneshwar, Orissa: Panchajanya Publications.

Natale, J. A. (1994). Roots of Violence. *American School Board Journal*, March, 33-40.

Nathanson, A. I. (1999). Identifying and Explaining the Relationship Between Parental Mediation and Children's Aggression. *Communication Research*, 26, 124-143.

National Center for Education Statistics. (1995). *The Pocket Condition of Education* 1995 (NCES 95-817). Washington, DC: U.S. Department of Education.

Nielson, J. (1968). The XXY Syndrome in a Mental Hospital. *British Journal of Criminology*, 8:186-203.

Niolon, Richard (2000), Antisocial Personality Style and Disorder, Resources Psychpage.com Retrieved from *http://www.psychpage.com/learning/library/person/asp.html.*

Offord, D.R. (1982). Family Backgrounds of Male and Female Delinquents. In J. Gunn & D.P. Farrington (Eds.), *Abnormal Offenders: Delinquency and the Criminal Justice System.* Chichester:, UK: Wiley.

Olson, D. H., Portner, J., & Lavee, Y. (1985). FACES III. St. Paul: *Department of Family Science*, University of Minnesota.

Olson, D., Russell, C., & Sprenkle, D. (1979). Circumplex Model of Marital and Family Systems II: Empirical Studies and Clinical Intervention. In J. Vincent (Ed.), *Advancement in Family Intervention, Assessment, and Theory* (pp. 128-176). Greenwich, CT: JAI.

Olweus, D. (1993). *Bullying at School: What We Know and What We Can Do*. Oxford UK: Blackwell Publishers.

Omark, D. R., Omark, M., & Edelman, M. (1975). Formation of Dominance Hierarchies in Young Children. In T. R. Williams (Ed.), *Psychological Anthropology* (pp. 289-315). The Hague: Mouton.

Osgood, D. W., & Chambers, J. M. (2000). Social Disorganization Outside the Metropolis: An Analysis of Rural Youth Violence. *Criminology*, 38, 81-111.

Osterman, Karin. (1999). *Developmental Trends and Sex Differences in Conflict Behaviour*, Abo Akademi University, Department of Developmental Psychology.

Otero-Lopez, J., Luengo-Martin, A., Miron-Redondo, L., Carrillo-De-La-Pena, M., & Romero-Trinanes, E. (1994). An Empirical Study of the Relations Between Drug Abuse and Delinquency Among Adolescents. British Journal of Criminology, 34, 459-478.

Palmour, R.M. (1983). Genetic Models for the Study cf Aggressive Behaviour. Prog. Neuropsychopharmacol. Biol. Psychiatry. 7: 513-517.

Pasamanick, B., Rogers, M. E., & Lilienfeld, A. M. (1956) Pregnancy Experience and the Development of Behaviour Disorder in Children. *American Journal of Psychiatry*, 112, 613-618.

Patterson, G. (1986). Performance Models for Antisocial Boys. *American Psychologist*, 41, 432-444.

Patterson, G. R., & Yoerger, K. (1997). A Developmental Model for Late-onset Delinquency. *Nebraska Symposium on Motivation*, 44, 119-177.

Patterson, G., Reid, J. and Dishion T. (1992). *Antisocial Boys: A Social Interactional Approach*. Eugene, OR; Castalia Publishing.

Patterson, G.R., Capaldi, D.M., & Bank, L. (1991). An Early Starter Model for Predicting Delinquency. In D.J. Pepler and K.H. Rubin (Eds.), *The Development and Treatment of Childhood Aggression*, Hillsdale, NJ: Erlbaum, pp. 139-168.

Patterson, G.R., Chamberlain, P. & Reid, J.B. (1982). A Comparative Evaluation of a Parent Training Programme. *Behaviour Therapy*, 13, 638-650.

Patterson, G.R., DeBaryshe, B.D. and Ramsey, E. (1989). A Developmental Perspective on Antisocial Behaviour. *American Psychologist*, 44, 329-35.

Peeples, F., & Loeber, R. (1994). Do Individual Factors and Neighborhood Context Explain Ethnic Differences in Juvenile Delinquency? *Journal of Quantitative Criminology*, 10, 141-157.

Pepler, Debra & Sedighdeilami, Farrokh. (1998). Aggressive Girls in Canada, Hull, Human Resources Development Canada. *Applied Research Branch Paper* No. W-98-30-E.

Perry, D.G., Perry, L.C., & Rasmussen, P. (1986). Cognitive Social Learning Mediators of Aggression. *Child Development*, 57, 700-11.

Pope, C. H., & Feyerherm, W. F. (1995). *Minorities and the Juvenile Justice System* (OJJDP Publication No. NCJ 145849). Washington, DC: U.S. Department of Justice.

Prinz, R.J., Roberts, W.A., Hantman, E., et al. (1980). Dietary Correlates of Hyperactive Behaviour in Children. Journal of Consulting and Clinical Psychology, 48, 760-769.

Raine, A. , Lencz, T., Bihrle, S., LaCasse, L., & Colletti, P. (2000). Reduced Prefrontal Gray Matter Volume and Reduced Autonomic Activity in Antisocial Personality Disorder. Archives of General Psychiatry, 57:119-27.

Raine, A., & Dunkin, J.J. (1990). The Genetic and Psychophysiological Basis of Antisocial Behaviour: Implications for Counselling and Therapy. *Journal of Counselling and Development*, 68: 637-644.

Raine, Adrian, (1993). The Psychology of Crime, Delinquency, and Special Education Placement. *Adolescence*, 32: 126, Summer.

Raine, et al. (1997). *Biosocial Bases of Violence*. NY: Plenum.

Reddy, G.L. and Shyamala, V. (2003). Thinking and Constructivism: Approaches in the Classroom. *University News*,. 41, 17, May.

Reid, J. (1993). Prevention of Conduct Disorder Before and After School Entry: Relating Interventions to Developmental Findings. *Development and Psychopathology*, 5 (1/2), 243-262.

Reid, J. B., & Patterson, G. R. (1989). The Development of Antisocial Behaviour Patterns in Childhood and Adolescence. *European Journal of Personality*, 3, 107-119.

Reid, J.B., & Patterson, G.R. (1996). Early Prevention and Intervention with Conduct Problems: A Social Interactional Model for the Integration of Research and Practice. In Stoner, G., Shinn, M.R., & Walker, H.M. (Eds.), *Interventions for Achievement and Behaviour problems* (pp. 715-739). Bethesda, MD: The National Association of School Psychologists.

Richters, J., & Cicchetti, D. (1993). Mark Twain Meets DSM-III-R: Conduct Disorder, Development, and the Concept of Harmful Dysfunction. *Development and Psychopathology*, 5, 5-29.

Robert L. Munroe., Robert Hulefeld., James M. Rodgers., Damon L. Tomeo., & Steven K. Yamazaki. (1999). *Aggression Among Children in Four Cultures*. Paper Presented at the Annual Meeting of the Society for Cross-Cultural Research in Santa Fe, NM, February.

Robinson, Glen & J. H. Wittebols (1986). *Class Size Research: A Related Cluster Analysis for Decision Making*. Educational Research Service (Arlington VA).

Roddick, J. D., Henggeler, S. W., & Hanson, C. L. (1986). An Evaluation of the Family Adaptability and Cohesion Evaluation Scales and the Circumplex Model. Journal of *Abnormal Child Psychology*, 14, 77-87.

Roncek, D. & Maier, P. A. (1991). Bars, Blocks and Crime Revisited: Linking the Theory of Routine Activities to the Empiricism of Hot Spots. *Criminology*, 29, 725-753.

Rosenbaum, J. (1989). Family Dysfunction and Delinquency. Crime and Delinquency, 35, 31-44.

Ross, David (1996). Rethinking Child Poverty, Insight, CCSD.

Ross, R.R. and Fabiano, E. (1985). Time to Think: *A Cognitive Model of Delinquency Prevention and Offender Rehabilitation*. Johnson City, Tennessee: Institute of Social Sciences and Arts, Inc.

Rowe, D.C., Almeida, D. M., & Jacobsen, K. C. (1999). School Context and Genetic Influences on Aggression in Adolescence. *Psychological Science*, 10, 277-280.

Rubin, K.H and Krasnor, L.R. (1986). Social Cognitive and Social Behavioural Perspectives on Problem-solving. In M. Perlmutter (Ed.), *The Minnesota Symposium on Child Psychology*, 18, 1-68. Hillsdale, NJ: Erlbaum.

Rule, B. G., & Ferguson, T. J. (1986). The Effects of Media Violence on Attitudes, Emotions, and Cognitions. *Journal of Social Issues*, 42, 29-50.

Rutter, M., & Smith, D. (1995). *Psychosocial Disorders in Young People*. John Wiley & Sons.

Rutter, M. (1996). *Genetics of Criminal and Antisocial Behaviour*. Chichester: Wiley and Sons.

Rutter, M. (1978). Family, Area, and School Influences in the Genesis of Conduct Disorder. In pp. 95-113 L.A. Hersov and M.Berger (Eds.), *Aggression and Antisocial Behaviour in Childhood and Adolescence*. Oxford: Pergamon Press.

Rutter, M. (1979). Invulnerability, or Why Some Children are Not Damaged by Stress. In: S.J. Shamsie (Ed.), New Directions in *Children's Mental Health* (pp. 53-76). New York: S.P. Medical and Scientific Books.

Rutter, M. (1979). Protective Factors in Children's Responses to Stress and Disadvantage. In M.W. Kwnt and J.E. Rolf (Eds.), *Primary Prevention of Psychopathology*, Vol. 3: Social Competence in Children, pp. 49-74. Hanover, NH: University Press of New England.

Rutter, M., Giller, H., & Hagell, A. (1998). *Antisocial Behaviour by Young People*. New York: Cambridge University Press.

Sack , W. H. (1977). Children of Imprisoned Fathers, *Psychiatry*, 40: 163-174.

Sampson, R. J., Raudenbush, S. W., & Earls, F. (1997). Neighbourhoods and Violent Crime: A Multilevel Study of Collective Efficacy. *Science*, 277, 918-924.

Sarbin, T. R. and Miller, J. E. (1970). Demonism Revisited: The XYY Chromosome Anomaly. Issues in Criminology, 5, pp. 199-208.

Sarkar, C. (1988). Juvennile Delinquency in India. Delhi: Daya Publishing House.

Savoie, Jose, (1999). Youth Violent Crime, Juristat, Ottawa, Statistics Canada, 19: 13.

Scaramella, L.V., Conger, R.D., Spoth, R., & Simons, R.L. (2002). Evaluation of a Social Contextual Model of Delinquency: A Cross-Study Replication. *Child Development*, 73, 175-195.

Schiavo, R., Theilgaard, A., Owen, D. et al. (1984). Sex, Chromosome Anomalies, Hormones and Aggressivity. *Archives of General Psychiatry*, 4:93-99.

Schor, E. L., & E. G. Menaghan. (1995). Family Pathways to Child Health. In B. C. Amick, S. Levine, A. R. Tarlov, and D. C. Walsh (Eds.), *Society and Health*. New York: Oxford University Press, pp. 18-45.

Schor, E. L., & E. G. Menaghan. (1995). Family Pathways to Child Health. In B. C. Amick, S. Levine, A. R. Tarlov, and D. C. Walsh (Eds.) *Society and Health*. New York: Oxford University Press, pp. 18-45.

Scott, S., & H. Parkey. (1998). Myth and Reality: Anti-social Behaviour in Scotland. *Housing Studies*, 13(3): 324-345.

Segall, M. H., Ember, C. R., & Ember, M. (1997). Aggression, Crime, and Warfare. In J. W. Berry, M. H. Segall, & C. Kagitcibasi (Eds.), *Handbook of Cross-cultural Psychology* (2nd ed, Vol. 3) (pp. 213-254). Boston: Allyn and Bacon.

Selman, B., & H. Kautz. (1989). The Complexity of Model-Preference Default Theories. In M. Reinfrank, M., J. de Kleer, & M. Ginsberg (Eds.), *Nonmonotonic Reasoning*. (Berlin: Springer) pp. 115-130.

Sethi, B.B., & Manchanda, R. (1978). Family Structure and Psychiatric Disorders. *Indian Journal of Psychiatry*, 20 (3), 283-288.

Shamsie , J. (1999). *Troublesome Children*. Toronto, Ontario: IAY Publication.

Shamsie, J. (Ed.). (1990). *Youth with Conduct Disorder: What is to be Done?* Toronto: Ministry of Community and Social Services.

Shamsie, J., & Hluchy, C. (1991). Youth with Conduct Disorder: A Challenge to be Met. (Review). Canadian Journal of Psychiatry, 36 (6):405-414, (Summary). (Online) Available: *http:// www.mentalhealth.com/dis/p20-ch02.html*.

Shaw, S. R., & Braden, J. P. (1990). Race and Gender Bias in the Administration of Corporal Punishment. *School Psychology Review*, 19, 378-383.

Sheldon Glueck, & Eleanor Glueck, (1950). Unraveling Juvenile Delinquency. New York: The Commonwealth Fund, 133.

Sherman, L. W., & Rogan, D. P. (1995). The Kansas City Gun Experiment. Research in Brief. Washington, DC: National Institute of Justice.

Shields, G., & Clark, R. D. (1995). Family Correlates of Delinquency: Cohesion and Adaptability. Journal of Sociology and Social Welfare, 22(2), 93-106.

Shure, M. (1999). Preventing Violence the Problem-Solving Way. Washington, DC: Office of Juvenile Justice and Delinquency Prevention. Available online: *http://www.ncjrs.org/pdffiles1/172847.pdf.*

Shyamala, V. (2004). *Effectivenss of Certain Strategies in Overcoming Antisocial Behaviour Among High School Students.* Ph.D. Thesis. Alagappa University.

Sigvardsson, S., Cloninger,C.R., Bohmam, M., & Von Knorring, A. (1982). Predisposition to Petty Criminality in Sewdish Adoptees: III. Sex Differences and Validation of Male Typology. *Archives of General Psychiatry*, 39, 1248-1253.

Silberg, J.L., Rutter, M., Meyer, J., Maes, H., Somonoff, E., Pickles, A., Loeber, R., & Eaves, L. (1996b). Genetic and Environmental Influences on the Covariation Between Hyperactivity and Conduct Disturbance in Juvenile Twins. *Journal of Child Psychology and Psychiatry*, 37 :803-16.

Simons, R., Whitbeck, L., Conger, R., & Conger, K. (1991). Parenting Factors, Social Skills, and Value Commitments as Precursors to School Failure, Involvement with Deviant Peers, and Delinquent Behaviour. *Journal of Youth and Adolescence*, 20, 645-664.

Singer, M., Anglin, T. M., Song, L., & Lunghofer, L. (1994). *The Mental Health Consequences of Adolescents' Exposure to Violence*. Cleveland, OH: Case Western Reserve University Press.

Singer, M., Anglin, T. M., Song, L., & Lunghofer, L. (1995). Adolescents' Exposure to Violence and Associated Symptoms of Psychological Trauma. *Journal of the American Medical Association*, 273, 477-482.

Sinha, D. (1988). The Family Scenario in a Developing Country and Implications for Mental Health: The Case of India.in Jasen D.W Berry and N. Sartorious (Eds.), *Health and Cross-cultural Psychology: Toward Implications*. Newbury Park, CA; Sage Publications.

Skiba, R.J., & Peterson, R.L. (2000). School Discipline at a Crossroads: From Zero Tolerance to Early Response. *Exceptional Children*, 66, 335-347.

Slaby, R. G. and Guerra, N. G. (1988). Cognitive Mediators of Aggression in Adolescent Offenders: I. *Assessment. Developmental Psychology*, 24, 580-588.

Smith, C. and Carlson, B. E. (1997) Social Servic s Review, 71, 231-255.

Spivack, G. and Cianci, N. (1987). High Risk Early Behaviour Pattern and Later Delinquency. In J.D. Burchard & S. Burchard (Eds). *Prevention of Delinquency and Antisocial Behaviour*, Washington, DC: US Government Printing Office.

Stattin, H., and Magnusson, D. (1989). The Role of Early Aggressive Behaviour in the Frequency, Seriousness, and Types of Later Crime. *Journal of Consulting and Clinical Psychology*, 57: 710-718.

Stewart, D. G., Brown, S. A., & Myers, M. G. (1997). Antisocial Behaviour and Psychoactive Substance Involvement among Hispanic and Non-Hispanic Caucasian Adolescents in Substance Abuse Treatment. *Journal of Child and Adolescent Substance Abuse*, 6, 1-22.

Stockard, J., & Mayberry, M. (1992). *Effective Educational Environments*. Newbury Park, CA: Corwin Press, Inc.

Studer, Jeannine (1996). Understanding and Preventing Aggressive Responses in Youth. Excerpted From Elementary School Guidance & Counselling/February 1996/Vol. 30, PRIVATE PRACTICE 194-203. Available on the Worldwide web: *http://ericcass.uncg.edu/virtuallib/violence/9006.html*.

Susman E. J. (1993). Psychological, Contextual, and Psychobiological Interactions: A Developmental Perspective on Conduct Disorder. *Development and Psychopathology*, 5(1/2): 181-190.

Sutherland, Edwin H., & Donald R. Cressey. (1978). *Criminology*. Philadelphia: J.B. Lippincott Company.

Taylor, B. (1990). In A Time of Crisis, Office of Youth Affairs, Wellington.

Taylor, E. (1991). Toxins and Allergens. In M. Rutter & P. Casaer (Eds.), *Biological Risk Factors for Psychosocial Disorders*, pp.199-231. Cambridge: Cambridge University Press.

Ted Grant and Alan Woods. (1995). Reason in Revolt: Marxism and Modern Science, Wellred Books. *http://www.marxist.com/science/preface_spanish_2nd_ed.html*.

Telfer, M.A. (1968). Are Some Criminals Born That Way? Think, 34: 24-28.

The APA Monitor Quoted in Vitality, 1999, 4(3). Retrieved from http://www.wilsonbanwell.com/assets/vitality/ vit99_4_3.pdf.

Thomas, A. C., Chess, S., & Birch, H. (1969). Temperament and Behaviour Disorders in Children. New York: New York University Press.

Thomas, G., Farrell, M. P., & Barnes, G. M. (1994). The Effects of Single-Mother Families and Non-resident Fathers on Delinquency and Substance Abuse in Black and White Adolescents. *Journal of Marriage and the Family*, 58(4), 884-894.

Thomas, J. D., Presland, I. E., Grant, M. D., & Glynn, T. (1978). Natural Rates of Teacher Approval in Grade-7 Classrooms. *Journal of Applied Behaviour Analysis*, 8, 367-372.

Thornberry, T. (1994). Risk Factors for Youth Violence. In L. McCart (Ed.), *Kids and Violence* (pp. 8-14). Washington, DC: National Governors Association.

Thornberry, T. P. and Krohn, M. D. (1997). Peers, Drug Use, and Delinquency. In D. M. Stoff, J. Breiling, & J. D. Maser (Eds.), Handbook of Antisocial Behaviour (pp. 218-233). New York: Wiley.

Thornberry, T.P., Krohn, M.D., Lizotte, A.J., & Chard-Wierschem, D. (1993). The Role of Juvenile Gangs in Facilitating Delinquent Behaviour. *Journal of Research in Crime and Delinquency*, 30(1): 55-87.

Tibbetts, S. G., & Piquero, A. (1999). The Influence of Gender, Low Birth Weight, and Disadvantaged Environment in Predicting Early onset of Offending: A Test of Moffitt's Interactional Hypothesis. *Criminology*, 37, 843-877.

Tierney, J., Dowd, T., and O'Kane, S. (1993). Empowering Aggressive Youth to Change. *Journal of Emotional Behavioural Problems*, 2(1), 41-45.

Van Hulle, C. A., Corley, R., Zahn-Waxler, C., Kagan, J., & Hewitt, J. K. (2000). Early Childhood Heart Rate does not Predict Externalizing Behaviour Problems at Age 7 Years. *Journal of the American Academy of Child and Adolescent Psychiatry*, 39, 1238-1244.

Venter, Craig in *Observer*, 11/ 2/ 2001.

Vettenburg, N. (1999). *School Influence on Juvenile Delinquency*. Paper Presented to the European Conference on Educational Research, Liubjana, Slovenia, 17-20 September.

Vorrath, H., & Brendtro, L. (1985). *Positive Peer Culture*. New York: Aldine (Second Edition).

Wadsworth, M. (1979). *Roots of Delinquency: Infancy, Adolescence and Crime*. New York: Barnes and Noble.

Wadsworth, M. (1976). Delinquency, Pulse Rates and Early Emotional Deprivation. *British Journal of Criminology*, 16, 245-255.

Waldman, I.D. (1996). Aggressive Boys' Hostile Perception and Response Bias: The Role of Attention in Impulsivity. *Child Development*, 67, 1015-34.

Walker, H. M., Colvin, G., & Ramsey, E. (1995). *Antisocial Behaviour in School: Strategies and Best Practices*. Pacific Grove, CA: Brooks/ Cole Publishers.

Walker, H.M. (1993). Antisocial Behaviour in School. *Journal of Emotional and Behavioural Problems*, 2(1), 20-23.

Walker, H.M. (1999). Psychology of Domestic Violence Around the World. *American Psychologist*, 54, 21-29.

Walker, Hill M., & Sprague, J. (1999). The Path to School Failure, Delinquency and Violence: Casual Factors and Some Potential Solutions. *Intervention in School and Clinic* January.

Walker, Hill M., Homer, Robert., Sugai, George, Bullis, Michael, Sprague, Jeffrey R., Bricker, Diane, & Kaufman, Martin J. (1996). Integrated Approaches to Preventing Antisocial Behaviour Patterns Among School-Age Children and Youth. *Journal of Emotional and Behavioural Disorders* 4.4 ,194-204, October.

Walker, Robert N. (1995). *Psychology of the Youthful Offender*. Springfiled, Charles C Thomas Publisher.

Walker, S. (1997). Preschool Children's Social Judgments: The Effect of Reputation. Paper Presented at the ARECE Conference, Canberra, January.

Weatherburn, D., & Lind, B. (1998). Poverty, Parenting, Peers and Crime-Prone Neighbourhoods. *Trends and Issues in Crime and Criminal Justice*, April.

Webber, J. (1997). Comprehending Youth Violence. Remedial and Special Education, 18, 94-109.

Webster-Stratton, C., & Dahi, R.W. (1995). Conduct Disorder. In M. Hersen & R.T. Ammerman (Eds.), *Advanced Anbormal Child Psychology* (pp.333-352). Hilsdale, New Jersy: Lawrence Erlbaum Associates.

Webster-Stratton, C., & Dahi, R.W. (1995). Conduct Disorder. In M. Hersen & R.T. Ammerman (Eds.), *Advanced Anbormal Child Psychology* (pp.333-352). Hilsdale, New Jersy: Lawrence Erlbaum Associates.

Wells, L. E., & Rankin, J. H.(1988). Direct Parental Controls and Delinquency. *Criminology*, 26, 263-285.

Werner, E. E., & Smith, R. S. (1982). Overcoming the Odds: *High Risk Children from Birth to Adulthood*. Ithaca, NY: Cornell University Press.

Wexler, H. (1996). AD/HD Substance Abuse and Crime. *Attention*, 2(3), pp. 27-32.

White, M. A. (1975). Natural Rates of Teacher Approval and Disapproval in the Classroom. *Journal of Applied Behaviour Analysis*, 8, 367-372.

Whiting, B. B., & Edwards, C.P. (1988). Children of Different Worlds. Cambridge.

Widom, C. S. (1991). Does Violence Beget Violence? A Critical Examination of the Literature. *Psychology Bulletin*, 109: 130.

Williams, J. H., & Van Dorn, R. A. (1999). Delinquency, Gangs, and Youth Violence. In J. Jenson & M. O. Howard (Eds.), *Youth Violence: Current Research and Recent Practice Innovations* (pp. 199-228). Washington, DC. NASW Press.

Williams, J. H., Ayers, C. D., & Arthur, M. W. (1997). Risk and Protective Factors in the Development of Delinquency and Conduct Disorder. In M. W. Fraser (Ed.), *Risk and Resiliency in Childhood: An Ecological Perspective* (pp. 140-170). Washington, DC: NASW Press.

Williams, J. H., Stiffman, A. R., & O'Neal, J. L., (1998). Violence Among Urban African-American Youths: An Analysis of Environmental and Behavioural Factors. In P. L. Ewalt, E. M. Freeman, S. A. Kirk, & D. L. Poole (1999) (Eds.), *Multicultural Issues in Social Work: Practice and Research* (pp. 195-212). Washington, DC: NASW Press.

Williams, J.H., & Van Dorn, R. A. (1999). *Predictors of Male Violence: An Analysis of Psychological, Social, Community, and Family Correlates Across Racial Groups*. Society for Social Work and Research, Austin, TX, January.

Wilson, & Herrnstein. (1985). Crime & Human Nature. New York: Simon and Schuster.

Wilson, W. J. (1987). *The Truly Disadvantaged: The Inner City, the Underclass and Public Policy*. Chicago: University of Chicago Press.

Windle, M. (1994). A Study of Friendship Characteristics and Problem Behaviours Among Middle Adolescents. *Child Development*, 65, 1764-1777.

Witkin, H. A., Mednick, S. A., Schulsinger, F., Bakkestrom, E., Christiansen, K. O., Goodenough, D. R., Hirschhorn, K., Lundsteen, S. Owen, D. R., Phillip, J., Rubin, D. B. & Stocking, M. (1976). Criminality in XYY and XXY men. *Science*, 196, 547-555.

Wordes, M., Bynum, T. S., & Corley, C. J. (1994). Locking up Youth: The Impact of Race on Detention Decisions. *Journal of Research in Crime and Delinquency*, 31, 149-165.

Wright Mills, C. (1956). *The Power Elite*. Oxford University Press, New York.

Wright, L. (1995). A reporter at Large: Double Mystery. *The New Yorker*, pp. 45-62, August 7.

Wyatt, W. J., & Hawkins, R. P. (1987). Rates of Teacher Verbal Approval and Disapproval: Relationship to Grade Level, Classroom Activity, Student Behaviour, and Teacher Characteristics. *Behaviour Modification*, 11, 27-51.

Yochelson, S., & Samenow, S. (1995). *The Criminal Personality: A Profile for Change. Jason Aronson.*

Youth Violence: A Report of the Surgeon General January 2001 *http://www.surgeongeneral.gov/library/youthviolence/youvioreport.htm.*

Yung, B. R. & Hammond, W. R. (1997) Antisocial Behaviour in Minority Groups: Epidemiological and Cultural Perspectives. In (Eds.), D. M. Stoff & J. Breiling, *Handbook of Antisocial Behaviour*, New York: John Wiley & Sons.

Zamble, E., & Porporino, F.J. (1988). Coping, Behaviour and Adaptation in Prison Inmates. Secaucus, N.J.: Springer-Verlag.

3

DEVELOPMENT OF ANTISOCIAL BEHAVIOUR

OBJECTIVES

This chapter deals with the Development of Antisocial behaviour. After reading this chapter the reader should be able to:

(i) Understand the different models proposed to explain the development of Antisocial behaviour;

(ii) Identify the different stages of development of Antisocial behaviour;

(iii) Perceive the course of development of Antisocial behaviour;

No single factor can predict who is likely to engage in antisocial behaviour, but longitudinal studies have established developmental pathways that lead to antisocial and delinquent behaviour, which includes patterns of aggression and violence.

MODELS

Many models have been proposed to explain the development of antisocial behaviour.

1. Pathways

Some models propose different pathways leading to the development of antisocial behaviour. For example, Loeber and his colleagues (1993) suggest that three different pathways can explain the development of antisocial behaviour in males. The first of these, the overt pathway, involves an escalation in aggressive acts (for example, minor aggression, physical fighting, physical violence) over time; the second, the covert pathway, involves an escalation in less overt antisocial acts (for example, minor covert behaviours, property damage, moderate to severe delinquency); while the third pathway, the authority conflict pathway, involves a sequence of stubborn behaviour, leading to defiance, and ultimately authority avoidance (for example, running away from home, truancy). Less serious behaviours precede more serious behaviours in these pathways and boys may proceed along more than one pathway at a time.

2. Social Learning

The Social Development model of Catalano and Hawkins (1996) emphasises the role of social learning in the development of antisocial behaviour. According to this model, children learn patterns of behaviour, whether they are prosocial or antisocial, from their family, their school, religious and other community institutions, and their peers. Hence, an individual's behaviour is determined by the predominant behaviours, norms and values held by those to whom the individual is attached. Consequently, youth attachment to prosocial individuals, developed particularly through involvement in rewarding experiences, is posited to be protective against the development of antisocial behaviours, conduct problems and substance use.

3. Economic Stress

Weatherburn and Lind (2001) propose a role for economic stress in the development of criminal behaviour. According to their model, parents who experience higher levels of economic stress are more likely to neglect or abuse their children or engage in harsh, erratic and inconsistent disciplinary practices than other parents. This kind of parenting behaviour may lead a child to affiliate more strongly with their peers than their parents, making the child susceptible to the negative influence of antisocial peers. The effects of economic stress are reduced when parents have a strong social support network, but increase if such a support network is absent, or other sources of stress are present (for example, crowded household, large family, difficult child, family conflict, parental disorder).

4. Parental Role

Patterson and his colleagues (Patterson, 1986; Patterson, Reid, & Dishion, 1992) have shown that the development of antisocial behaviour patterns follows a predictable sequence that begins when the child is an infant and escalates as he or she grows older. They believe that many of the aversive behaviours manifested by antisocial children are merely attempts to alter their social environment. Moreover, they suggest that the development of antisocial behaviour patterns begins with a breakdown in parent effectiveness and discipline, for example, when difficult infants realize that their own aversive behaviours such as whining, crying, or temper tantrums can be used to stop the demands of their parents. The performance of aversive behaviours is reinforced when the parent gives in, thus these behaviours tend to increase in frequency, intensity, and duration over time until the parent finds it difficult to monitor the coercive child's whereabouts. Unsupervised time in turn increases the opportunity for such children to get into more trouble. Finally, they begin to notice that they are not as well liked as other members of their family and they become at-risk for rejection by their parents (Patterson, 1986).

Patterson, Reid and Dishion (1992) also suggest a critical role for parenting in the development of antisocial behaviour among males. They suggest that individuals who experience poor 'basic training' as children are more susceptible to poor academic performance and peer rejection later on. These problems may lead to association with antisocial peers and engagement in antisocial acts in adolescence, and eventually, to poor adjustment in adulthood. It should be noted that many of these 'pathways' models have been developed to explain antisocial behaviour among males, with relatively little attention to antisocial behaviour among females.

By the time children with antisocial behaviours enter school, they have learned many coercive behaviours but are not equipped with the necessary prosocial skills to develop healthy peer and adult relationships (Patterson, 1986; Patterson et al., 1992). Goldstein, Sprafkin, Gershaw, and Klein (1980) report that antisocial children display dysfunctional and antisocial behaviours and show a lack of prosocial or developmentally appropriate behaviours. On measures of social skills, Walker, Shinn, O'Neill, and Ramsey (1987) found that the mean scores of elementary and middle school students who displayed antisocial behaviours were approximately one standard deviation below the mean for their 'normal' peers. These children deal with the teacher and other students in the only way they know how—through the use of coercive behaviours. Such behaviours make it extremely difficult for the student to learn the basic academic skills necessary to function in the school setting. Children with antisocial behaviour patterns begin to sense that their teachers and peers do not like them, and that they are outsiders within their own classroom community. This, coupled with their academic failure, lowers their self-esteem. By the time the child reaches the age of 10 or 11, rejection by parents and peers contributes to pervasive sadness that is so acute that it can be recognized by those adults who interact with the child (Patterson et al., 1992).

The child who does not feel a sense of community within their classroom will begin to seek out the company of others who are unskilled in prosocial behaviours and likewise feel rejected by their family, peers, or teachers. These children often form deviant peer groups that are characterized by negative attitudes toward adult authority and school. By the time the child reaches the ages of 12 or 13, they often become recognized members of deviant peer groups. Membership in these groups increases the risks for substance abuse, truancy, and delinquency later in adolescence (Robins & Ratcliff, 1978-9).

If this behaviour pattern is allowed to persist, the child is in danger of becoming a 'career antisocial adult'. Such individuals lack the social skills necessary to move beyond a marginal existence and have little hope for a quality life.

Longitudinal studies show that antisocial children and adolescents have unhappy adulthoods plagued with marital problems (Caspi, Elder, & Bem, 1987), erratic employment (Robins, & Ratcliff, 1978-9), and heightened risk for multiple arrests, drug and alcohol abuse, and institutionalization for crimes or mental disorders (Caspi, Bem, & Elder, 1989; Robins, West, & Herjanic, 1975). Finally, antisocial adults are people who tend to be both lonely and loved by few (Patterson et al., 1992).

5. Risk Factors

Another approach to understanding the development of antisocial behaviour is the Risk Factors approach. A large body of research has been dedicated to the identification of risk and protective factors associated with the development of antisocial behaviour. Risk factors can be defined as those factors that 'increase(s) the likelihood that a subsequent negative outcome will occur' (Loeber, 1990), whereas protective factors operate in the context of risk and 'offset risk factors and promote social development, well-being and resilience' (Bond et al., 2000). Risk and protective factors associated with the development of antisocial and criminal behaviour can occur across a number of domains. These include the characteristics of the child, the family and its experience of stressful life events, the school context, and community and cultural factors (Homel et al., 1999).

Research suggests that no single risk factor can explain the development of antisocial behaviour. Rather, the more risk factors an individual is exposed to, the greater the likelihood that he or she will exhibit antisocial or criminal behaviour (Bond et al., 2000; Loeber & Farrington, 2000). Similarly, the greater the number of protective factors possessed by a young person, the more likely he or she is to display resilience despite the presence of risk (Howard & Johnson, 2000). Hence, the risk of a child becoming antisocial appears to be dependent upon the balance of risk and protective factors in their lives (Loeber & Farrington, 2000).

STAGES OF DEVELOPMENT

Over the past few decades, researchers have identified early indicators of antisocial behaviour. Persistent delinquent acts in adolescence emerge as the outcome of a predictable developmental trajectory of behaviour problems beginning in childhood (Farrington, 1994; Robins, 1966). Adults, who are diagnosable as having anti-social personality, had almost all been anti-social children; that is, anti-social personality rarely or never arose de novo in adulthood. The child's own behaviour is a better predictor of his adult behaviour than are his family characteristics or social status. Family variables matter more for moderately than for severely anti-social children. Severely anti-social children are found to be at high risk, no matter how good or bad their environment, but moderately anti-social children with anti-social fathers are more likely to be highly anti-social adults than are others. Severe antisocial behaviour may emerge in adulthood without a childhood history of such behaviour (Tweed et al., 1994).

Research has shown that early onset of violence and antisocial behaviour is associated with more serious and chronic violence (Farrington, 1991; Piper, 1985; Thornberry, Huizinga, & Loeber, 1995; Tolan & Thomas, 1995). Antisocial behaviour has considerable stability across time, making early conduct problems a strong predictor of later antisocial behaviour (Elliott, Huizinga, & Ageton, 1985; Loeber & Dishion, 1983). Hyperactivity, impulsivity, and inattention problems in childhood, related to antisocial behaviour through impaired cognitive processes (e.g., difficulty evaluating consequences of actions), have been shown to predict later convictions, independent of conduct disorder (Farrington, Loeber, & van Kammen, 1990). Risk factors reflecting less constraint by conventional norms and institutions (Hirschi, 1969), such as lower commitment to school (Cernkovich & Giordano, 1992) and positive attitudes toward deviance (Elliott, 1994; Zhang, Loeber, & Stouthamer-Loeber, 1997), have also been related to increased antisocial behaviour. In a meta-analysis of prospective longitudinal studies, Lipsey and Derzon (1998) found that early adolescent aggression, psychological condition (e.g., hyperactivity), and school attitude/performance were among the most predictive risk categories for later serious antisocial behaviour and violence. The result of the long-term course and outcome of juvenile obsessive-compulsive disorder (OCD) revealed that earlier age-at-onset was associated with better course and outcome (Janardhan Reddy et al., 2003).

From Infancy to Preschool to Adolescence

We now know that certain specific antisocial behaviour pasterns' and high levels of aggression exhibited in preschool and kindergarten are not just correlated, but are highly predictive, of violent, delinquent and criminal behaviours in middle school, later adolescence and adulthood (Fagan, 1996; Walker et al., 1996).

Aggressive behaviour at 5 years was the strongest predictor of later antisocial behaviour (at age 14) in a sample of 3, 792 Australian children (Bor et al., 2001). Aggressive behaviour measured from ages 6 to 13 consistently predicts later violence among males. Many researchers have noted the continuity in antisocial behaviour from early aggression to violent crime (Loeber, 1990; 1996; Loeber & Hay, 1996; Olweus, 1979). A study in Orebro, Sweden, found that two-thirds of boys with high teacher-rated aggression scores at ages 10 and 13 had criminal records for violent offences by age 26. They were more than six times more likely than boys who were not rated aggressive to be violent offenders (Stattin & Magnusson, 1989).

A study by Griffin (1987) reported that children who exhibited a greater number of antisocial behaviours as well as developmental and academic problems before age 9 displayed more aggressive tendencies as adults than did those individuals who did not exhibit such early behaviour and problems. Farrington (1995) found that one-half of boys adjudicated delinquent for a violent offense between age 10 and age 16 were convicted of a violent crime by age 24, compared with only 8 per cent of juveniles between age 10 and age 16 not adjudicated delinquent for a violent crime as juveniles.

In a longitudinal study in Sweden, 15 per cent of boys with both restlessness and concentration difficulties at age 13 were arrested for violence by age 26. Boys with restlessness and concentration difficulties were five times more likely to be arrested for violence than boys without these characteristics (Klinteberg et al., 1993). In another study, Farrington (1989) found that teacher ratings of male children's concentration problems and restlessness—including difficulty sitting still, the tendency to fidget, and frequent talkativeness—predicted later violence. Concentration problems also predicted academic difficulties, which predict later violence. Multivariate models are needed to understand the pathways leading to violent behaviour.

Social class of rearing is a remarkably unimportant variable. It adds nothing significant once the levels, of child's and his parents' antisocial behaviour are taken into account in predicting severe adult antisocial behaviour. Children reared in a poor but conforming family who do not develop anti-social behaviour in childhood are not likely to show antisocial behaviour as adults. A child may exhibit antisocial behaviour in response to a specific stressor (such as the death of a parent or a divorce) for a limited period of time, but this is not considered a psychiatric condition. Children and adolescents with antisocial disorders have an increased risk of accidents, school failure, and early alcohol and substance use, suicide and criminal behaviour. The elements of moderate to severely antisocial personality are established as early as kindergarten. Antisocial children score high on traits of impulsiveness, but low on anxiety and reward-dependence—that is, the degree to which they value, and are motivated by, approval from others. Yet, underneath their tough exterior, antisocial children show low self-esteem. The early indicators-deficient skills in empathy, impulse control, social problem solving, anger management, and assertiveness—have been consistently correlated with adolescent and adult antisocial behaviour. The teen years pose some of the most difficult challenges for families.

Teenagers, as adolescents, mostly in their high schools, may feel that no one can understand their feelings. As a result, they may feel angry, alone and confused while facing complicated issues about identity, peers, sexual behaviour, drinking and drugs. They consistently do not listen to authority, pay no attention to the feelings or rights of others, seem to rely on physical violence to solve problems, do poorly in academics, cut classes, miss school very frequently for no identifiable reasons, get suspended or dropped out, join gangs, get involved in lying, truancy, bullying, fighting, stealing or destroying property, drink alcohol or may take to drugs.

Life-course Persistent Antisocial Behaviour Theory

Longitudinal research has identified types of youth who progress to adolescent antisocial behaviour, multiple pathways through which it develops and persists, and the multiple factors that shape this risk. Loeber (1988) has identified that individuals pass through stages of increasingly serious antisocial acts. There are two possible pathways: childhood versus adolescent onset. Life-course persistent antisocial behaviour theory developed by Moffit (1993a) suggests that antisocial behaviour consists of two possible outcomes: Life Course Persistent antisocial behaviour (LCP) where antisocial behaviour begins in childhood and persists throughout life, or Adolescence-Limited (AL) behaviour where antisocial behaviour commences in adolescence but stops in adulthood.

The theory suggests that LCP behaviour is a personality defect in the brain that occurs during development whereas AL is a result of environmental factors. Thus, Life course persistent antisocial behaviour is viewed as a form of psychopathology, and adolescence limited antisocial behaviour is identified only in select social situations. The distinction between these two types of individuals is very useful, both as a way of thinking about developmental knowledge and as a tool for targeting the right interventions for antisocial youth. The LCP type shows persistent, severe and frequent antisocial behaviour across time and situation. Early age of onset is related to more serious and persistent antisocial behaviour (Earls, 1994; Tolan & Thomas, 1995)..

It has been suggested that these youth are born with neuropsychological deficiencies which adversely effect such functioning as; reading, writing, listening, problem solving, speech, memory, attention and impulsivity. Thus, higher comorbidity of AD/HD, learning disability and other academic difficulties are identified in these children. These deficits make it harder to raise these very difficult children, and when these youth are raised without understanding and support their difficulties are magnified often resulting in antisocial and aggressive behaviour. In contrast to LCP, the AL youth whose antisocial behaviour is limited to adolescence, do not have any neuropsychological deficiencies and displays of antisocial behaviour is an attempt to show their autonomy and independence.

Adolescent onset is more common developmental pathway characterised by isolated antisocial acts, less severe behaviours, is less aggressive and is less likely to persist in later years. Life course persistent individuals begin antisocial behaviour early in childhood and continue into adulthood, after their adolescence limited counterparts stop. Life course persistent behaviour has been correlated with neurological deficits and pathological behaviours (e.g. impulsivity) that are exacerbated when they are combined with stressful home situations. Estimates of prevalence of life-course persistent antisocial behaviour in the general population are in the region of six per cent (Kratzer & Hodgins 1996; Moffit et al., 1996).

Aguilar et al. (2000) reported that the factor that distinguishes the two groups (LCP and AL) is psychological history in early years and not temperament and neuropsychological functioning. It was suggested that normal development of neuropsychological systems require a supportive and growth promoting environment. Therefore, a child will show deficits in neuropsychological functioning, as a result of growing up in an adverse environment.

THE TIMING AND SEVERITY OF ANTISOCIAL BEHAVIOUR

Early onset youth are significantly more likely to engage in aggressive offences than youth with late onset conduct disorder (Lahey et al., 1999). Evidence from longitudinal studies indicates that conduct problems in early childhood are significant predictors of adult antisocial behaviour and psychopathology (Loeber, 1990; Quinton, Rutter, & Gulliver, 1990). Studies of young offenders have found that 50-70% of youth who are arrested for crimes committed during childhood or adolescence go on to be rearrested as adults (Loeber, 1982; McCord, 1979). The stability of conduct disorder is significantly related to the age of onset of the disorder, with earlier onset predicting greater persistence of the disorder over time (Loeber, 1990; Tolan, 1987). Although most young children with conduct problems do not go on to become antisocial adults, childhood onset conduct disorder has been associated with severe and aggressive antisocial behaviour that persists over the life course (Lahey et al., 1998; Loeber, 1982; Loeber & Stouthamer-Loeber, 1987) and with chronic substance abuse that is resistant to treatment (Brown et al., 1996; Myers, Brown, & Mott, 1995).

The relationship between age of onset and chronic offending has led some to theorize that conduct disorder that begins in early childhood may be qualitatively distinct from conduct disorder that emerges during adolescence (Brown et al., 1996; Hinshaw, Lahey, & Hart, 1993; Loeber, 1988; Moffitt, 1993; Patterson, 1986; Tolan, 1987). The DSM-IV currently recognizes this distinction by including two subtypes of conduct disorder based on age of onset. 'Childhood Onset Type,' is diagnosed when 'at least one criterion characteristic of conduct disorder begins prior to age 10 years,' and 'Adolescent Onset Type,' when there is an 'absence of any criteria characteristic of conduct disorder prior to age 10 years' (American Psychiatric Association [APA], 1994). The identification of subtypes of conduct disorder has been recognized as an important goal that may shed light on etiological processes and assist interventionists in tailoring their treatments to specific populations (Hinshaw et al., 1993; Lahey et al., 1998). Although evidence suggests that there is an important distinction between early and late onset conduct disorder, Lahey et al. (1999) caution that further research is still needed before final conclusions about the relationship between age of onset and conduct problems can be drawn. For example, further research is needed to determine whether childhood and adolescent onset conduct disorder show differential relationships with risk and protective factors, indicating distinct etiologic pathways as well as developmental course.

Moffitt (1993) proposes a theoretical framework that makes specific predictions about which risk and protective factors should be related to early onset conduct disorder. She argues that 'life-course persistent antisocial behaviour' (i.e., early onset conduct disorder) has its earliest roots in both neurological deficits and exposure to environmental risk, such as poor parenting and parental antisocial behaviour. Neurological deficits give rise to difficult temperament that leaves the affected child vulnerable to poor parenting, as well as more likely to elicit poor parenting from caretakers. These early risk factors start the child on a trajectory of increasing antisocial behaviour that escalates throughout adolescence and persists into adulthood.

By contrast, Moffitt (1993) theorizes that individuals with 'adolescent-limited antisocial behaviour' begin their antisocial behaviour during the adolescent period and desist after reaching young adulthood. She argues that the spike in rates of antisocial behaviour observed in adolescence is in part caused by the long gap between biological maturity (occurring in early adolescence), and social maturity (i.e., adult status) that exists in industrialized societies with a long period of formal education and dependency. In such societies, adolescents without developmental histories of conduct problems may engage in antisocial behaviour in order to gain access to adult privileges and will imitate deviant peers who appear to have achieved autonomy from parents through antisocial behaviour. These individuals will tend to desist from antisocial behaviour when they reach young adulthood and autonomy is no longer a motivating reinforcer. Therefore, cultures or subcultures that have a longer gap between biological and social maturity will produce larger numbers of adolescent-limited offenders, and those with a shorter gap will produce fewer.

Moffitt (1993) hypothesizes that measures of individual and family characteristics (e.g., gender, hyperactivity, parental deviance and child rearing practices) should be associated with early onset conduct disorder. Late onset conduct disorder, by contrast, should be better predicted by societal and environmental factors such as exposure to delinquent peers, access to adult roles, and the cultural context that determines the length of time between biological and social maturity. Second, the theory predicts that adolescent limited offenders will engage primarily in crimes that symbolize adult privilege or which demonstrate autonomy from parental control. Moffitt (1993) indicates that these offences would include vandalism, public order offences, running away, truancy, and theft. Individuals with childhood onset antisocial behaviour, on the other hand, will commit both: offences that demonstrate autonomy and offences that are violent and victim-oriented. Therefore, youth with early onset conduct disorder should be expected to commit more aggressive and violent crimes than those with adolescent onset conduct disorder.

Several studies have examined the correlates of early and late onset conduct disorder and have generated partial support for this theory. Loeber and his colleagues (1995) examined a longitudinal sample of boys in treatment at outpatient clinics, and found that, consistent with Moffitt's theory (Moffitt, 1993), having a diagnosis of Attention Deficit Hyperactivity Disorder (ADHD) was a significant predictor of conduct disorder onset before age 12. Using data from the Methods for the Epidemiology of Child and Adolescent Mental Disorders Study (MECA) and DSM-IV field trials, Lahey et al. (1998) reported that youth with onset of conduct disorder before age 10 displayed more aggressive behaviours. In addition, meeting criteria for oppositional defiant disorder, being male, and having parents with antisocial behaviour were associated with early onset in the DSM-IV field trial sample. Finally, Tolan (1987) examined the ability of demographic, individual, and family characteristics to predict age of Onset in a cross-sectional sample of normal adolescent boys. He found that boys who were born later in the birth order, who scored lower on achievement tests, and whose families were low on cohesion and high on conflict were more likely to have an earlier age of onset of delinquent behaviour. Taken together, these studies begin to suggest a profile of individual and family characteristics associated with early onset conduct disorder that are consistent with Moffitt's theory (Moffitt, 1993). However, conclusions are limited by small sample sizes, the exclusion of girls and racial/ethnic groups other than Caucasians and African Americans, the examination of only a small subset of the known risk factors for conduct disorder, and the exclusion of variables reflecting exposure to deviant peers.

COURSE OF DEVELOPMENT FROM ADHD TO ODD TO CD

The restless, overactive and fidgety child who stands out from his peers has been around, presumably, as long as children have been around. The first known reference to a hyperactive child or one with attention deficit hyperactivity disorder (ADHD) occurs in the poems of the German physician Heinrich Hoffman, who in 1865 described 'fidgety Philip' as one who 'won't sit still, wriggles, giggles, swings backwards and forwards, tilts up his chair... growing rude and wild'. These children, described by Tredgold as early as 1908, are today diagnosed as suffering from ADHD with associated oppositional defiant disorder or conduct disorder.

Children who exhibit antisocial behaviour tend to fall under three subclasses of disruptive behaviour disorders: Attention deficit hyperactivity disorder, Oppositional defiant disorder, and Conduct disorder. The fact that these three subclasses are grouped together under antisocial behaviour suggests that they have a common characteristic, disruptiveness, which is more distressing to others than to the individual with the disorder. ADHD, ODD and CD may transform from one to the other. This usually happens in a particular order.

Given the progression from ADHD to ODD to CD, Robins (1991) queries whether one should consider each of these as separate disorders or whether conduct disorder might be better seen as 'the middle phase of a very chronic psychiatric disorder which typically begins early in life and continues into adulthood but which can also abort at any point along the way'.

There is a great deal of comorbidity. Some children develop one disorder after another, thus experiencing all the three disorders as they grow from early childhood to adolescence. The literature abounds with studies indicating the co-mordid relationships between Attention Deficit Hyperactivity Disorder, Conduct Disorder, Oppositional Defiant Disorder, Learning Difficulties, Mood Disorders, Depressive symptoms, Anxiety Disorders, Communication Disorders, and Tourette's Disorder (American Psychiatric Association,1994; Biederman, Newcorn, & Sprich 1991). A high level of comorbidity (almost 95%) was found among 236 ADHD children (aged 6-16 yrs) with conduct disorder, ODD and other related categories (Bird, Gould, & Staghezza Jaramillo 1994). In an 8 year follow-up study, Barklay and his colleagues (1990) found that 80% of the children with ADHD were still hyperactive as adolescents and that 60% of them had developed Oppositional Defiant or Conduct Disorder.

Research shows that many children with ADHD develop a very bothersome behaviour pattern during childhood and adolescence that is known as Oppositional Defiant Disorder or ODD. About 65% of boys with Attention Deficit Disorder and 25% of girls have ODD. About 25% of boys and 8% of girls with ADHD also go on to develop, in addition to the oppositional defiant behaviour, a more serious condition called Conduct Disorder (Biederman et al. 1996). This individual has not only the symptoms of ADHD but also the symptoms of Oppositional Defiant Disorder and the symptoms of Conduct Disorder. This is what is known as the high-risk group. These individuals are set up for some very poor outcomes in the absence of intervention.

Either Conduct Disorder or Oppositional Defiant Disorder may co-occur among youth with attention deficit disorders as well as with depression and anxiety disorders. Similarities between youth who are diagnosed with Oppositional Defiant Disorder, Conduct Disorder and those with attention deficit disorders have been studied.

Hinshaw (1987) found that between 30% to 90% of youth can be classified with both ADHD and Conduct Disorder, depending upon the sample tested. It is generally accepted that ADHD is more likely associated with cognitive impairment and neuro-developmental abnormalities, while Conduct Disorder and Oppositional Defiant Disorder are thought to be more related to psychosocial disadvantages (Wicks-Nelson and Israel 1991).

If a child comes to a clinic and is diagnosed with ADHD, about 30-40% of the time the child will also have ODD (Kuhne et al . 1997). Supporting these findings, youth treated in the community at a psychiatric outpatient clinic for ADHD who dropped out of treatment were found, in one study, to have more problems with the law, suggesting a co-morbid diagnosis (Pelkonen et al., 2000).

Over 62% of males and 50% of females exhibit the array of symptoms for a diagnosis of Conduct Disorder (CD) in the year 2000, while 27% of males and 34% of females show symptoms of Oppositional Defiant Disorder (ODD) (Waite, 2000). 18% of children will have ODD if the parents are alcoholic and the father has been in trouble with the law. Children and adolescents with conduct disorder are also likely to show academic deficiencies, as reflected in achievement levels, grades, and specific skill areas, particularly reading (Sturge, 1982). Such children often seen by their teachers as uninterested in school, unenthusiastic toward academic pursuits, and careless in their work.

In a review of the past 10 years' findings of Oppositional defiant and conduct disorder, selected summaries of the literature over the past decade have been presented (Loeber et al.,2000). Evidence supports a distinction between the symptoms of ODD and many symptoms of CD, but there is controversy about whether aggressive symptoms should be considered to be part of ODD or CD. CD is clearly heterogeneous, but further research is needed regarding the most useful subtypes. Some progress has been made in documenting sex differences. Symptoms that are more serious, more atypical for the child's sex, or more age-atypical appear to be prognostic of serious dysfunction.

The prevalence of Conduct Disorder (CD), Oppositional Defiant Disorder (ODD), and various levels of antisocial behaviour and their correlates were studied among the following three major ethnic groups (Bird et al., 2001): 1) Hispanics, subdivided into Island Puerto Ricans and Mainland Hispanics; 2) African Americans; and 3) Mainland Non-Hispanic, Non-African Americans. Correlates considered include stressful life events, birth defects, low birth weight, learning difficulties, teen mothers, family environment, marital adjustment, social competence, parental monitoring, and family relationships. Logistic regression was used to determine the association of outcomes with individual correlates and of interaction terms with ethnicity. Differences between adjusted rates and observed rates of disorders and levels of antisocial behaviours are compared to estimate the extent to which each correlate explains the group differences in rates. Island Puerto Ricans had a lower prevalence of CD, ODD, and various levels of antisocial behaviour than mainland Hispanics, African Americans, and non-Hispanic Whites. The lower prevalence appears to be associated with differences in the extent to which a number of these correlates are found on the island, the most salient being better family relations between the target children and their parents and siblings. Aggressive behaviour measured from ages 6 to 13 consistently predicts later violence among males.

Progress has been made in the methods for assessment of ODD and CD, but some critical issues, such as combined information from different informants, remains to be addressed. A proportion of children with ODD later develop CD, and a proportion of those with CD later meet criteria for antisocial personality disorder. ODD and CD frequently co-occur with other psychiatric conditions. Although major advances in the study of the prevalence and course of ODD and CD have occurred in the past decade, some key issues remain unanswered.

Society is at risk if physical, academic, and behavioural factors predisposing an individual for aggressiveness are not identified and addressed at an early age, because antisocial behaviour is a pattern that originates in early childhood and continues into adulthood (Oregon Social Learning Center, 1990).

Researchers have increasingly recognized that conduct disordered youth are heterogeneous in their behaviour and have pointed out the need to identify distinct subtypes of conduct disorder that arise through different developmental pathways (Hinshaw et al., 1993; Kazdin, 1995; Loeber et al., 1993). If subtypes can be identified through empirical research, interventions can be tailored to meet specific needs, and etiological pathways can be identified.

The aggregate of the research on the developmental pattern of antisocial behaviour seems to indicate two implications for educators. First, children who display antisocial behaviours need to be taught prosocial interpersonal problem-solving skills as early as possible. For example, they must be taught to control their social environment through positive prosocial behaviours rather than through antisocial actions. Second, these students need to develop a sense of belonging and acceptance within the classroom. By developing a sense of community within the classroom, the antisocial students will begin to feel accepted by their prosocial peers, and may be less inclined to search out and join deviant or antisocial peer groups.

SUMMARY

The present chapter described various developmental pathways to antisocial behaviour. This chapter discussed variations in these patterns on the basis of various models. According to Pathways model, acts of Aggression and physical fighting fall under the overt pathway, property damage under covert pathway, and truancy and running away under the authority conflict pathway. According to social development model, children learn patterns of their behaviour from the society in which they live. Economic stress model emphasises the role of economic stress in the parental behaviour towards their children. Parental effectiveness and consistency in parenting play a key role in Parental role model. Lack of social skills puts the child in danger of becoming antisocial, later during the life. As risk factor approach states, the more the risk factors an individual is exposed to, the greater will be the likelihood of exhibiting antisocial behaviour.

Early onset of antisocial behaviour is exhibited as aggression in preschool and kindergarten. These are highly predictive of later antisocial behaviours such as lying, truancy, bullying, fighting, stealing, drug addiction, etc. Life Course Persistant Antisocial behaviour is considered as a form of psychopathology that is related to neuropsychosocial deficiencies but, Adolescent Limited Antisocial behaviour caused by societal and environmental factors is limited to adolescence and is less severe. ADHD, ODD and CD may transform from one another, even though they may co-occur in many cases. Apart from teaching pro-social interpersonal skills to the antisocials, they must be made to develop a feeling of belongingness and acceptance within the society.

REFERENCES

Aguilar, B., Sroufe, A.L., Egeland, B., & Carlson, E. (2000). Distinguishing the Early-onset/Persistent and Adolescent-onset Antisocial Behaviour Types: From Birth to 16 years. *Development and Psychopathology*, 12, 109-132.

American Psychiatric Association. (1994). *Diagnostic and Statistical Manual of Mental Disorders* (4th ed.). Washington, DC: Author.

Biederman Joseph, & Faraone Stephen, et al. (1996). A Prospective 4 Year Follow-up Study of Attention-Deficit Hyperactivity Disorder and Related Disorders. *Archives of General Psychiatry*, 53: 437-446.

Biederman, J., Newcorn, J., & Sprich, S. (1991). Comorbidity of Attention Deficit Hyperactivity Disorder with Conduct, Depressive, Anxiety, and Other Disorders. *American Journal of Psychiatry*, 148(5), 564-577.

Bird, H. R., Gould, M. S., & Staghezza Jaramillo, B. M. (1994). The Comorbidity of ADHD in a Community Sample of Children Aged 6 Through 16 years. *Journal of Child and Family Studies*, 3(4), 365-378.

Bird, H., Canino, G., Davis, M., Zhang, H., Ramirez, R., & Lahey, B. (2001). Prevalence and Correlates of Antisocial Behaviour Among Three Ethnic Groups. *Journal of Abnormal Psychology*, 29:465-478.

Bond, L., Thomas, L., Toumbourou, J., Patton, G. & Catalano, R. (2000). *Improving the Lives of Young Victorians in Our Community: A Survey of Risk and Protective Factor*. Centre for Adolescent Health, Parkville, Australia.

Bor, W., Najman, J.M., O'Callaghan, M., Williams, G.M., & Anstey, K. (2001). Aggression and the Development of Delinquent Behaviour in Children. *Trends and Issues in Crime and Criminal Justice*, May.

Brown, S. A., Gleghom, A., Schuckit, M. A., Myers, M. G., & Mott, M. A. (1996). Conduct Disorder Among Adolescent Alcohol and Drug Abusers. *Journal of Studies on Alcohol*, 57, 314-324.

Caspi, A., Bem, D. J., & Elder, G. H. (1989). Continuities and Consequences of Interactional Styles Across the Life Course. *Journal of Personality*, 57, 375-406.

Caspi, A., Elder, G. H., & Bem, D. J. (1987). Moving Against the World: Life-course Patterns of Explosive Children. *Developmental Psychology*, 23, 308-313.

Catalano, R. & Hawkins, D. (1996). The Social Development Model: A Theory of Antisocial Behaviour", in D. Hawkins (ed.) *Delinquency and Crime: Current Theories*, Cambridge, New York.

Çemkovitch, S. A., & Giordano, P. C. (1992). School Bonding, Race, and Delinquency. *Criminology*, 30, 261-291.

Earls, F. J. (1994). *Violence and Today's Youth*. Critical Health Issues for Children and Youth, 4, 4-23.

Elliot, D.S., Huizinga, D., & Ageton, S.S. (1985). *Explaining Delinquency and Drug Use*. Beverly Hills, CA: Sage.

Elliott, D. S. (1994). *Serious Violent Offenders: Onset, Developmental Course, and Termination—The American Society of Criminology*. Presidential Address. Criminology, 32, 1-21.

Fagan, J. (1996). *Recent Perspectives on Youth Violence*. Keynote Address to Pacific Northwest Conference on Youth Violence, Seattle, May.

Farrington DP. (1994). Early Developmental Prevention of Juvenile Delinquency. *Criminal Behaviour and Mental Health*, 4: 209-27.

Farrington, D. P., Loeber, R., & van Kammen, W. B. (1990). Long-term Criminal Outcomes of Hyperactivity-impulsivity-attention Deficit and Conduct Problems in Childhood. In L. N. Robins & M. Rutter (Eds.), *Straight and Devious Pathways from Childhood to Adulthood* (pp. 62-81). Cambridge: Cambridge University Press.

Farrington, D.P. 1989. Early Predictors of Adolescent Aggression and Adult Violence. *Violence and Victims*, 4, 79-100.

Farrington, D.P. (1991). Childhood Aggression and Adult Violence: Early Precursors and Later-life Outcomes. In (Eds.), D.J. Pepler and K.H. Rubin, *The Development and Treatment of Childhood Aggression*, Hillsdale, NJ: Lawrence Erlbaum, pp. 5-29.

Farrington, D.P. (1995). Key Issues in the Integration of Motivational and Opportunity-reducing Crime Prevention Strategies. In (Eds.), P.O.H. Wikström, R.V. Clarke, and J. McCord. *Integrating Crime Prevention Strategies: Propensity and Opportunity*, Sweden: National Council for Crime Prevention, pp. 333-357.

Goldstein, A. P., Sprafkin, R. P., Gershaw, N. J., & Klein, P. (1980). *Skillstreaming the Adolescent: A Structured Learning Approach to Teaching Prosocial Skills. Champaign*, IL: Research Press.

Griffin, G. (1987). Childhood Predictive Characteristics of Aggressive Adolescents. *Exceptional Children*, 54, 246-252.

Heinrich Hoffman (1865) Quoted in Nikos Myttas Understanding and Recognizing ADHD. *http://www.addiss.co.uk/understandingadhd.htm.*

Hinshaw, S. P., Lahey, B. B., & Hart, E. L. (1993). Issues of Taxonomy and Comorbidity in the Development of Conduct Disorder. Developmental *Psychopathology*, 5, 31-50.

Hinshaw, S.P. (1987). On the Distinction Between Attentional Deficits/ Hyperactivity and Conduct Problems/aggression in Child Psychopathology. *Psychological Bulletin*, 101, 443-63.

Hirschi, T. (1969). *Causes of Delinquency*. Newbury Park, CA: Sage Publications.

Homel, R., Cashmore, J., Gilmore, L., Goodnow, J., Hayes, A., Lawrence, J., Leech, M., O'Connor, I., Vinson, T., Najman, J. & Western, J. (1999). *Pathways to Prevention: Early Intervention and Development Approaches to Crime in Australia*, Attorney-General's Department, National Crime Prevention, Canberra.

Howard, S. & Johnson, B. (2000). Resilient and Non-resilient Behaviour in Adolescents, Trends and Issues in Crime and Criminal Justice, Vol. 183. *http://www.mdx.ac.uk/www/conel/dc2.htm.*

Janardhan Reddy, Y.C., Srinath, S., Prakash, H.M., Girimaji, S.C., Sheshadri, S.P., Khanna., S, & Subbakrishna, D.K. (2003). A Follow-up Study of Juvenile Obsessive-compulsive Disorder from India. *Acta Psychiatr Scand*, 107, 457-464.

Kazdin, A. E. (1995). *Conduct Disorder in Childhood and Adolescence* (2nd ed.). Newbury Park, CA: Sage.

Klinteberg, B.A., Andersson, T., Magnusson, D., & Stattin, H. (1993). Hyperactive Behaviour in Childhood as Related to Subsequent Alcohol Problems and Violent Offending: A Longitudinal Study of Male Subjects. *Personality and Individual Differences*, 15.381-388.

Kratzer, L., & Hodkins, S. (1996). *A Typology of Offenders: A Test of Moffit's Theory Among Males and Females from Childhood to Age 30*. Paper Presented at the Life History Research Society Meeting, London, 3-5 October.

Kuhne, M. et al. (1997). Impact of Comorbid Oppositional or Conduct Problems on Attention-Deficit Hyperactivity Disorder. *Journal of American Academy of Child and Adolescent Psychiatry*, 36(12), 1715-1725.

Lahey, B. B., Goodman, S. H., Waldman, I. D., Bird, H., Canino, G., Jensen, P., Regier, D., Leaf, P. J., Gordon, R., & Applegate, B. (1999). Relation of Age of Onset to the Type and Severity of Child and Adolescent Conduct Problems. *Journal of Abnormal Child Psychology*, 27, 247-260.

Lahey, B. B., Loeber, R., Quay, H., Applegate, B., Shaffer, D., Waldman, I., Hart, E., McBurnett, K., Frick, P. J., Jensen, P. S., Dulcan, M. K., Canino, G., & Bird, H. R. (1998). Validity of the DSM-IV Subtypes of Conduct Disorder Based on Age of Onset. *Journal of the American Academy of Child and Adolescent Psychiatry*, 37, 435-442.

Lipsey, M. W., & Derzon, J. H. (1998). Predictors of Violence or Serious Delinquency in Adolescence and Early Adulthood. In R. Loeber & D. P. Farrington (Eds.), *Serious and Violent Juvenile Offenders* (pp. 86-105). Thousand Oaks, CA: Sage.

Loeber, R. & Farrington, D. P (2000).Young Children who Commit Crime: Epidemiology, Developmental Origins, Risk Factors, Early Interventions, and Policy Implications, *Development and Psychopathology*, 12, 737-762.

Loeber, R. (1982). The Stability of Antisocial and Delinquent Child Behaviour: A Review. *Child Development*, 53, 1431-1446.

Loeber, R. (1988). Natural Histories of Conduct Problems, Delinquency, and Associated Substance Use: Evidence for Developmental Progressions. In B. Lahey & A. Kazdin (Eds.), *Advances in Clinical Psychology*, 11, 73-124. New York: Plenum Press.

Loeber, R. (1990). Development and Risk Factors of Juvenile Antisocial Behaviour and Delinquency. *Clinical Psychology Review*, 10, 1-41.

Loeber, R. (1996). Developmental Continuity, Change, and Pathways in Male Juvenile Problem Behaviours and Delinquency. In (Ed.), D J.D. Hawkins. *Delinquency and Crime: Current Theories*. Cambridge, UK: Cambridge University Press, pp. 1-27.

Loeber, R., & Dishion, T. J. (1983). Early Predictors of Male Delinquency: A Review. *Psychological Bulletin*, 94, 68-99.

Loeber, R., & Stouthamer-Loeber, M. (1987). Prediction. In H. C. Quay (Ed.), *Handbook of Juvenile Delinquency* (pp. 325-382). New York: Wiley.

Loeber, R., and Hay, D.F. (1996). Key Issues in the Development of Aggression and Violence from Childhood to Early Adulthood. *Annual Review of Psychology*, 48:371-410.

Loeber, R., Burke, J.D., Lahey, B,B., Winters. A., & Zera, M .(2000). Oppositional Defiant and Conduct Disorder: A Review of the Past 10 years, Part I: *Journal of American Academy of Child and Adolescent Psychiatry*, 39(12), 1468-84, December.

Loeber, R., Green, S. M., Keenan, K., & Lahey, B. B. (1995). Which Boys Fare Worse? Early Predictors of the Onset of Conduct Disorder in a Six-year Longitudinal Study. *Journal of the American Academy of Child and Adolescent Psychiatry*, 34, 499-509.

Loeber, R., Wung, P., Keenan, K., Giroux, B., Stouthamer-Loeber, M., Van Kammen, W. B., & Maughan, B. (1993). Developmental Pathways in Disruptive Child Behaviour. *Development and Psychopathology*, 5, 101-133.

McCord, J. (1979). Some Child-rearing Antecedents of Criminal Behaviour in Adult Men. *Journal of Personality and Social Psychology*, 37, 1477-1486.

Moffitt, T. E. (1993). Adolescence-limited and Life-course-persistent Antisocial Behaviour: A Developmental Taxonomy. *Psychological Review*, 4, 674-701.

Moffitt, T.E. & Harrington, H.L (1996). Delinquency: The Natural History of Antisocial Behaviour In P.A Silva & W.R. Stanton (Eds.), *From Child to Adult: The Dunedin Multidisciplinary Health and Development Study*, Oxford University Press, Auckland, New Zealand.

Myers, M. G., Brown, S. A., & Mott, M. A. (1995). Preadolescent Conduct Disorder Behaviours Predict Relapse and Progression of Addiction for Adolescent Alcohol and Drug Users. *Alcoholism: Clinical and Experimental Research*, 19, 1528-1536.

Olwens D (1979) Stability of Aggressive Reaction Patterns in Males: A Review. *Psychological Bulletin*, 86, 852-875.

Oregon Social Learning Center. (1990). *Background and Overview Ora Social Interactional Approach to Treatment of Aggression and Violence in Children and Teenagers* (pp. 11-13). Author.

Patterson, G. (1986). Performance Models for Antisocial Boys. American Psychologist, 41, 432-444.

Patterson, G. R., Reid, J. B., & Dishion, T. J. (1992). *Antisocial Boys: A Social Interactional Approach*, 4. Eugene, OR Castalia.

Pelkonen, M., Marttunen, M., Laippala P., & Lonnqvist, J. (2000). Factors Associated with Early Dropout from Adolescent Psychiatric Outpatient Treatment. *Journal of the American Academy of Child and Adolescent Psychiatry*, 39(3), 329-336.

Piper, E. (1985). Violent Recidivism and Chronicity in the 1958 Philadelphia Cohort. *Journal of Quantitative Criminology*, 1: 319-344.

Quinton, D., Rutter, M., & Gulliver, L. (1990). Continuities in Psychiatric Disorders from Childhood to Adulthood in the Children of Psychiatric Patients. In L. N. Robins & M. Rutter (Eds.), Straight and Devious Pathways from Childhood to Adulthood (pp. 259-278). Cambridge: University Press.

Robins, L. (1991). Conduct Disorder. *Journal of Child Psychology and Psychiatry*. 32: 193-212.

Robins, L. N., & Ratcliff, K. S. (1978-9). Risk Factors in the Continuation of Childhood Antisocial Behaviours into Adulthood. *International Journal of Mental Health*, 7(3-4), 96-116.

Robins, L. N., West, P. A., & Herjanic, B. L. (1975). Arrests and Delinquency in Two Generations: A Study of Black Urban Families and Their Children. *Journal of Child Psychology and Psychiatry*, 16, 125-140.

Robins, L.N. (1966). *Deviant Children Grown Up: A Sociological and Psychiatric Study of Sociopathic Personality*, Williams and Wilkins, Baltimore.

Stattin, H., and Magnusson, D. 1989. The Role of Early Aggressive Behaviour in the Frequency, Seriousness, and Types of Later Crime. *Journal of Consulting and Clinical Psychology*, 57,710-718.

Sturge, C. (1982). Reading Retardation and Antisocial Behaviour. *Journal of Child Psychology and Psychiatry*, 23, 21-31.

Thornberry, T.P., Huizinga, D., & Loeber, R. (1995). The Prevention of Serious Delinquency and Violence: Implications from the Programme of Research on the Causes and Correlates of Delinquency. In (Eds.), J.C. Howell, B. Krisberg, J.D. Hawkins, & J.J. Wilson. *Sourcebook on Serious, Violent, and Chronic Juvenile Offenders*, Thousand Oaks, CA: Sage Publications, Inc., pp. 213-237.

Tolan, P. H. (1987). Implications of Age of onset for Delinquency Risk. *Journal of Abnormal Child Psychology*, 15, 47-65.

Tolan, P.H., & Thomas, P. (1995). The Implications of Age of Onset for Delinquency Risk II: Longitudinal Data. *Journal of Abnormal Child Psychology*, 23, 157-181.

Tredgold A.F. (1908). *Mental Deficiency (Amentia)*. W. Wood, New York.

Waite, D. (2000). Mental Health Treatment of Youth in Virginia's Juvenile Correctional Centres. Presented at the Virginia Psychological Society Meeting, Williamsburg, Virginia.

Walker, H. M., Shinn, M. R., O'Neill, R. E., & Ramsey, E. (1987). A Longitudinal Assessment of the Development of Antisocial Behaviour in Boys: Rationale, Methodology, and First Year Results. *Remedial and Special Education*, 8(4), 7-16.

Walker, Hill M., Homer, Robert, Sugai, George, Bullis, Michael, Sprague, Jeffrey R., Bricker, Diane, & Kaufman, Martin J. (1996). Integrated Approaches to Preventing Antisocial Behaviour Patterns Among School-Age Children and Youth. *Journal of Emotional and Behavioural Disorders*, 4.4 ,194-204.

Weatherburn, D., & Lind, B (2001), Delinquent-prone Communities, Cambridge University Press, Cambridge, UK.

Wicks-Nelson, R. and Israel, A.C. (1991). *Behaviour Disorders of Childhood* (p. 191). Englewood Cliffs, NJ: Prentice Hall.

Zhang, Q., Loeber, R., & Stouthamer-Loeber, M. (1997). Developmental Trends of Delinquency Attitudes and Delinquency: Replication and Synthesis Across Time and Samples. *Journal of Quantitative Criminology*, 13, 181-216.

4

IDENTIFICATION AND ASSESSMENT OF ANTISOCIAL BEHAVIOUR

OBJECTIVES

This chapter deals with the methods of identification and assessment of Antisocial behaviour. After reading this chapter, the reader should be able to:

(i) List out the objectives of identification and assessment;

(ii) Specify the sources of information leading to identification of Antisocial behaviour in students;

(iii) Describe the different measures of assessment;

(iv) Understand the importance of proactive screening.

Behavioural problems happen and sometimes, they can affect a child into adulthood. Moreover, the most severe forms of antisocial behaviour are known to emerge early in life and become persistent thereafter, making antisocial behaviour a natural focus for a developmental approach (Moffit, 1993a). The extent of children's early conduct problems is said to be the most important factor in explaining association between peer relationship problems and later adjustments in life (Woodward & Fergusson, 1999). So, if society is concerned about antisocial youth, the easiest and the least expensive way to intervene is to identify and modify such behaviour in children.

If the early risk factors are not prevented or treated children may develop a cascading set of secondary risk factors, including academic failure, social exclusion, school drop out, and membership of deviant peer groups, which in turn accelerate their risk for future antisocial behaviour (Hawkins et al., 1999). To achieve this, we must focus on the identification of early signs of antisocial behaviour.

Antisocial behaviour, by its very nature, leaves its mark on society (e.g., vandalism, firesetting). Where the identification of adolescents with the potential antisocial behaviour is concerned, there are no clear guidelines, and different procedures have been developed depending on the context in which the young persons find themselves. Scott (1977) suggests that to be useful, an assessment of dangerousness must specify the behaviour of concern, the potential damage or harm likely to result from the behaviour and also the probability that the behaviour will occur and under what circumstances.

OBJECTIVES OF IDENTIFICATION AND ASSESSMENT

The major objectives of identification and assessment are:

(i) analyse the student's functional behaviours in various settings and with different people who regularly are a part of her/his environment (functional behaviour assessment);

(ii) integrate information from the different aspects of a student's life;

(iii) focus on strengths as well as needs;

(iv) rule out or address other conditions which may be precipitating or contributing to the behaviour (e.g., hearing loss, learning disabilities, side-effects of medication);

(v) clarify the characteristics of the behaviour disorder or mental illness;

(vi) address the possibility of other medical or health impairments;

(vii) contribute to the process of planning and evaluating the student's educational programme.

The findings of the assessment should be used to plan support, interventions, and services needed by the student.

SOURCES OF INFORMATION

Douglas, Cox and Webster (1999) identified several types of relevant information: Historic and static factors, including aspects of criminal history, previous violent behaviour, previous psychiatric history (including substance abuse, mental illness, and hostile personality disorders), adult adjustment with respect to close relationships and employment, and history of absconding from custody; Dynamic and clinical factors, including impulsivity, antisocial attitudes and beliefs, anger and hostility, and individual symptoms of mental disorders such as delusions'. Risk management factors, reflecting aspects of the situation or environment rather than the person themselves—for example, release plan feasibility, access to professional and informal support, stressors, and idiosyncratic triggers for violence.

Information regarding the frequency and nature of antisocial behaviour among young people is typically obtained from a number of sources: (1) official statistics obtained from the criminal justice agencies (that is, police and courts), or (2) self-reported behaviour, generally obtained during the course of interviews or surveys (Rutter, Giller, & Hagell, 1998). Both types of information have advantages and disadvantages. Official statistics provide a measure of behaviours reported to and recorded by police. However, they provide a conservative assessment, since a high proportion of those committing antisocial acts are not apprehended, and many minor antisocial behaviours may not attract or warrant attention by authorities. Furthermore, particular groups, such as those from disadvantaged families and neighbourhoods, may be more likely to be the focus of official attention and hence have a greater likelihood of being apprehended (Rutter et al., 1998). Thus, official records provide an incomplete picture of the incidence of antisocial behaviours across different sections of the community. Self-report has the potential to provide a more comprehensive picture and can cover a wider array of antisocial acts (not just those that are illegal), but may be affected by social desirability and other biases. It relies on the willingness of individuals to reveal potentially compromising information, and on respondents' veracity and memory. It is also reliant on the representativeness of the sample used, and researchers' ability to reach and engage the young people involved in serious antisocial acts. While recognising the advantages and disadvantages of both approaches, the current report focuses on adolescents' self-reported antisocial behaviour.

MEASURES OF ASSESSMENT

Relatively few measures developed for antisocial behaviour among children and adolescents have been in widespread use. Typically, measures have been devised and used for a specific purpose as part of an ongoing research programme. With few exceptions, little validation work has been conducted, nor have data been provided to indicate the normative levels of antisocial behaviour on the measure over the course of development (Kazdin, 1995). Shamsie and Hluchy (1991) classified four common ways of assessing children with antisocial behaviour as Behaviour checklists, Psychiatric interviews, Interviews based on Diagnostic criteria and Self Reports, Peer Reports and Reports of Significant others. The assessment of antisocial behaviour has relied on a number of measures including interviews, self-report, parent, teacher, and peer ratings, direct observations, and institutional records.

(i) Behavioural Checklists

Many behavioural checklists exist, some designed for teachers to complete such as the Revised Behavioural Problem Checklist and others designed for parents. Child Behaviour Checklist (Achenbach, 1991) is typical of an instrument for parents to rate items conveying characteristics of their children. The measure includes 118 items that refer to behaviour problems, each of which is rated on a 3-point scale. Three sample items include cruelty, bullying, or meanness to others; argues a lot; and sets fires. The scale yields several factors including aggression, delinquency, hyperactivity, anxiety, depression and others. However, many researchers do not use checklists, they are more commonly used in pharmacological and psychological research.

A number of assessment tools are available for measuring need rather than risk status in adolescence. An assessment tool was developed by a team at the Child and Adolescent Mental Health Services, Salford entitled the Salford Needs Assessment Schedule for Adolescents (Kroll et al., 1999). It identifies 21 areas of potential need, and assesses material, familial, social, educational and psychiatric problems, including aggression and self-harm behaviour.

(ii) Psychiatric Interviews

In these interviews, the investigator asks questions on a whole range of subjects but is free to delve into certain areas as they come up (Rutter et al., 1981).

(iii) Interviews based on Diagnostic Criteria

These interviews are tailored to cover diagnostic criteria in official terminologies; for example the Diagnostic Interview for Children and Adolescents (DICA).

(iv) Self-Reports, Peer Reports, Reports of Significant Others

Self-report Measures: Children and adolescents rarely identify themselves as having a "problem" or needing treatment. Although self-report is not usually used as the primary measure to evaluate childhood dysfunction, it can yield important information. Children can report on their symptoms and identify specific problem areas not always evident to their parents. It is to be noted that Self-report may be useful to identify conduct problems often concealed from parents. Information regarding such covert behaviours as vandalism, theft, or drug abuse is more readily reported by children and adolescents than by others, or by institutional records (Elliott, Huizinga, & Ageton, 1985). In general, children can report on their antisocial behaviour readily through self-reports. The validity of self-reported conduct problem behaviours has been attested to in studies showing that they predict subsequent arrest and convictions as well as educational, employment, and marital adjustment (Bachman et al., 1978). The Inventory of Anger self-report was designed with a fourth grade reading level in order to address the reading problems common among children with conduct disorder.

Adolescent Antisocial Self-Report Behaviour Checklist by Kulik, Stein and Sarbib (1968) is a self-report measure that samples a broad range of behaviours from mild misbehaviour to serious antisocial acts. The items load four factors: delinquency, drug usage, parental defiance, and assaultiveness. It consists of 52 items, each of which is rated by the child on a 5-point scale (from never to very often).

Children's Action Tendency Scale (Deluty, 1979), meant for children in the age group of 6 to 15 years, consists of 30 items in forced-choice format. The child selects what he or she would do in interpersonal situations. The Self-Report Delinquency Scale (Elliott, Dunford, & Huizinga, 1987), meant for age range of 11 to 21 years, consists of 47 items that measure frequency with which the individual has performed offences over the last year. This instrument asks the youth directly about the occurrence of delinquent acts at home, at school, and in the community. The items encompass theft, property damage, illegal services (i.e., peddling drugs), public disorder (e.g., making obscene phone calls), status offences (e.g., running away), and index offences (e.g., assault). Items are scored on a 4-point scale with numerical anchors for frequency of occurrence (e.g., 1 = once, 4 = five or more times in the previous year). A total delinquency score reflects delinquent behaviour Subscale scores are available for different types of illegal activity that may be of interest as well. This measure was developed as part of the National Youth Survey, an extensive longitudinal study of delinquent behaviour, alcohol use, and related problems in American youths.

(b) Peer Reports: Peer measures typically reflect an assessment methodology that departs from the rating scales used for parent and teacher assessments. Peer based measures usually consist of different ways of soliciting peer nominations of persons who convince particular characteristics (e.g., aggressiveness).

Reports where children assess the behaviour problems of their peers have been shown to be accurate indicators of peer aggression (Coie & Dodge, 1983). The consensus of the peer group is likely to reflect consistencies in performance and stable characteristics. Elementary school peer evaluations (e.g. measures of dislike or rejection, aggressive behaviour) predict conduct problems years later (Coie, Lochman, Terry, & Hyman, 1992; Huesmann et al., 1984). Peer ratings occasionally are more sensitive as predictors of adjustment than are teacher and clinician ratings (Kazdin, 1995). Peer measures usually consist of sociometric ratings to identify such characteristics as popularity, likeability, acceptance, rejection and social competence. Such characteristics are quite relevant given the difficulties in each of these areas that antisocial children usually evince.

Peer Nomination of Aggression (Lefkowitz et al., 1977) is a measure meant for children of 3rd to 13th grade. It has items that ask children to nominate others who show the characteristics (e.g., "who starts a fight over nothing?") This measure tests the child's reputation among peers regarding overall aggression.

(c) Reports by significant others: Reports by significant others, commonly parents, usually correlate with clinical judgements of child dysfunction (Kazdin, 1987). Given their obviously unique position to comment on their child's functioning and changes over time, parents are the most frequently relied on source of information. Self-reports and reports of others are more influenced by judgements and impressions which are done away with in direct observations. As an assessment modality, measures completed by significant others have major advantages.

In order to gather information on a child, a carefully drawn history based on material gathered from the child, the parents and the child's teacher are used as sources. Many will assess the family to better understand the problems that may exist between the children and their parents. There may be a partial bias in the types of antisocial behaviours that rating scales can assess. Behaviours such as teasing, fighting, yelling, arguing, and other overt acts are likely to be easily detected by parents and teachers.

Eyberg Child Behaviour Inventory (ECBI) (Eyberg & Robinson, 1983; Robinson, Eyberg, & Ross, 1980) is used to assess child behaviour problems that parents report at home. It is meant for the age group 2 to 17 years, designed to measure wide range of conduct problems in the home. It consists of 37 items. Sample items include verbally fighting with one's friends of same age, refusing to do chores when asked for, poor table manners, and yelling or screaming. Except some items that deal with stealing and destroying objects, most of the items reflect refusal and other oppositional behaviours that are annoying to parents, rather than serious antisocial acts. Each item is rated by the parent as to whether the problem exists (yes, no) and how often it occurs (1 = never to 7 = always). The measure yields two scores that reflect the number of problems (i.e., those items scored 'yes') and the intensity of the problems (i.e., a total of the scale scores summed for all items).

Sutter-Eyberg Student Behaviour Inventory (Funderbunk & Eyberg, 1989) meant for the age group of 2 to 127 years, measures a range of conduct problem behaviours at school. It consists of 36 items identical in format but not content to the Eyberg Child Behaviour Inventory.

There are a number of other instruments that are concerned with the assessment of risk of future antisocial behaviour rather than assessments of need. The Psychopathy Screening Device has been developed for children, and is rated by parents and teachers (Frick, 1996; Frick et al., 1994). Another instrument, Early Assessment Risk List for Boys (EARL-20B) is specifically for use with children under the age of 12 (Augimeri et al., 1998). It comprises of three sections—family factors, child factors and amenability factors. EARL-20B may be useful in identifying high-risk children in need of intensive intervention, and also for prioritising the needs of the individual child (Douglas et al., 1999). The rationale behind the intervention offered may also vary across time and context.

(v) Direct Observation

It is considered as yet another way of assessing antisocial behaviour. Specific behaviours at home, at school, or in the community can be observed directly (McMahon & Forehand, 1988). Direct observations involve defining behaviour carefully, identifying the situations in which the behaviour is to be observed, sending observers to record the behaviours, and ensuring that behaviour is observed correctly and reliably. According to Patterson (1982), multiple behaviours are observed while the child interacts with his family at home. Generally, highly trained observers are needed , but at times, parents and teachers can be used in place of trained observes for simple observations. Oservation contributes unique situational information. Direct observations provide samples of the actual frequency or occurrences of particular antisocial or prosocial behaviours.

The Family Interaction Coding System (FICS) has been used to record behaviours of antisocial children as they interact with their parents and siblings at home (Reid et al., 1988). It assesses aggressive behaviours and the antecedents and consequences based on family interactions with which they are associated. Twenty-nine different observations are coded by observers as present or absent in each of the several brief time intervals (e.g., 30 seconds) over a period of approximately one hour. Prosocial and deviant child behaviours (e.g., complying with requests, attacking someone, yelling) and parent behaviours (e.g., providing approval, playing with the child, humiliating the child) are included.

Adolescent Antisocial Behavioural Checklist (Curtiss et al., 1983) is a measure to directly rate the behaviours as having occurred. It consists of 57 items to measure antisocial behaviour during hospitalisation. The items are scored using different sets of subscales; one set focuses on the form of the problem (e.g., physical vs. verbal harm); another set focuses on the objects of aggression (e.g., towards self, others, property).

There are yet other measures like Institutional and Societal Records used to assess antisocial behaviour.

(vi) Institutional and Societal Records

Evaluation of antisocial youths frequently relies on institutional records, such as contacts with people, school attendance, grades, suspensions, and expulsions. Institutional records are critical measures for the evaluation of antisocial behaviour. Institutional records are exceedingly important because they represent socially significant measures of the impact of the problem.

Various agencies at governmental and national level monitor such events as the juvenile arrests or juvenile court cases. At times, most antisocial and delinquent acts are not observed and recorded. Research has suggested that 9 out of 10 illegal acts are not detected or not acted on officially (Empey, 1982). This conclusion has been supported by studies that ask children and adolescents to report on their delinquent and antisocial behaviours (Elliott et al., 1985; Williams & Gold, 1972).

Official records can greatly underestimate the incidence of antisocial behaviours because of slippage between the occurence of antisocial behaviour and the ultimate recording of the act. Those that do not lead to arrest are not always referred to the courts. Those that are referred do not necessarily lead to conviction (Empey, 1982). A particular assessment technique may be suitable for a given situation. At times, more than one type of assessment may be called for.

PROACTIVE SCREENING

Currently, there are a wide range of procedures used to identify students in need of special education and related services, but for the most part they begin with a teacher referral. Studies have shown that teachers are competent judges of student's behavioural characteristics but they tend to be very selective in their referrals. Teacher referrals are also influenced by their idiosyncratic behavioural standards and tolerance of student behaviour. Generally, students are much more likely to be referred for externalising problems (acting out) rather than internalising problems (social avoidance). If students are not disruptive to the classroom setting, but are experiencing emotional or behavioural problems, they are unlikely to get a referral because they do not create problems for the teacher. Children who internalise problems are usually socially withdrawn and teachers assume either that it is not the teacher's responsibility, or that the students' problems cannot be solved in the classroom. For these reasons, many students who need help slip through the cracks.

The importance of proactive mass screening is based on the assumption that early identification and intervention would be much more effective than dealing with a child's antisocial or destructive behaviours later in life. Many times the referral comes after a child's behaviour has already become well established and effective intervention is nearly impossible. For this reason it is important that all students participate in early screening to identify those who are at-risk and manifest their problems either externally or internally. An effective and cost efficient procedure has been developed by Walker and Severson called the Systematic Screening for Behavioural Disorders (SSBD) (Walker, et. al.,1994). This procedure screens all students in an elementary grade classroom and consists of three interrelated stages. *In Stage 1* the teacher evaluates the behavioural characteristics of each student and then ranks them in order according to whether their behaviour is primarily internalizing or externalizing in nature. *In Stage 2* teachers rate the top three ranked externalizes and the top three internalizes on the Critical Event Index (high-intensity-low-frequency behaviours) and Likert scale rating of the frequency of occurrences of adaptive and maladaptive forms of behaviour. Students needing further evaluation are indicated by cutoff points derived from national normative databases. *Stage 3* consists of observations of potentially at-risk students in classroom and playground settings on two occasions. As in Stage 2, normatively derived cut-off points for Stage 3 observations are used to determine if a student needs referral to the school's child study team for further evaluation and possible classification as eligible for special education supports and services. It cannot be stressed enough how crucial this screening process is to the well being of our children and our future. By this, at-risk children can be diverted from an inevitable path of destruction leading to delinquency and adult criminality when identified and helped early enough.

The process of identification and assessment of students with antisocial behaviour sometimes begins at the classroom level, although these students are often identified in the community. To be identified in this category, the behaviours in question should not be transitory but should generalize to different settings and individuals. When teachers first notice a problem, they must consult with the parents and attempt alternate strategies to manage the behaviour or support the student in the classroom. If these prove unsuccessful, the teacher must seek assistance from other school-based services or from the school-based team.

The teacher's observations should be incorporated into an identification and assessment process for educational purposes, as should the assessments of other professionals. The school-based team may access other school or district support services, and/or request additional assessment. It may also be appropriate at this stage to involve the family's physician, child and youth mental health services, or other community agencies in the identification and intervention process.

Assessment should analyse the student's functional behaviours in various settings and with different people who regularly are a part of her/his environment integrate information from the different aspects of a student's life, focus on strengths as well as needs, rule out or address other conditions which may be precipitating or contributing to the behaviour (e.g., hearing loss, learning disabilities, side-effects of medication), clarify the characteristics of the behaviour disorder or mental illness, address the possibility of other medical or health impairments, and contribute to the process of planning and evaluating the student's educational programme.

SUMMARY

In this chapter, the authors have explained the need to identify and assess antisocial behaviour in students. The contextual, or contributory factors must be identified at the earliest. Different types of information such as static (past history, etc.) and dynamic (anger, impulsivity, mental disorders, etc.) must be gathered from different sources of information. A vivid account of various measures of measurements that have been devised and used by many researchers has also been presented. Some of the measures used are behaviour checklists, psychiatric interviews, self-reports, and reports of others. Several characteristics such as inattention, hyperactivity, oppositional defiance, bullying and aggression are measured by behaviour checklists designed for parents and teachers. Interviews help in dealing with all issues related to antisocial behaviour and this helps in early diagnosis. Self-reports bring to light specific conduct problems exhibited by the antisocials by self-expression and self-analysis. Antisocial acts such as thefts, peoperty damage and drug abuse can be identified through self-reports, peer reports, and reports by others. Direct observations help in observing multiple behaviours in any given situation. They also help in observing frequency of occurrence of antisocial behaviour such as attacking, yelling and lying. Institutional and societal records are socially significant measures of the impact of the problem.

Early or proactive screening is essential as an effective and cost efficient procedure to identify those who are at risk and who manifest their problems externally or internally. Teachers and parents serve as first-hand observers of antisocial behaviours exhibited by children and adolescents.

REFERENCES

Achenbach, T.M. (1991). *Manual for the Child Behaviour Checklist /4-18 and 1991 Profile*. Burlington: University of Vermont, Department of Psychiatry.

Augimeri, L.K. Webster C,D., Koegel, C.J., & Levene, K.S. (1998). Early Assessment Risk List for Boys (Version 1): Consultation Edition, Toronto, Ontario: Earlscourt Child and Family Centre.

Bachman, J.G., Johnston, L.D., & O'Malley, P.M. (1978). Delinquent Behaviour Linked to Educational Attainment and Post-high School Experiences. In L. Otten (Ed.), *Colloquium on the Correlates of Crime and the Determinants of Criminal Behaviour* (pp. 1-43). Arlington, VA: The MITRE Corp.

Coie, J. D., & Dodge, K. A. (1983). Continuities and Changes in Children's Social Status: A Five-year Longitudinal Study. *Merrill-Palmer Quarterly*, 29, 261-282.

Coie, J. D., Lochman, J. E., Terry, R., & Hyman, C. (1992). Predicting Early Adolescent Disorder from Childhood Aggression and Peer Rejection. Journal of Consulting and Clinical Psychology, 60: 783-792.

Curtiss, G., Rosenthall, R.H., Marohn, R.C., Ostrov, E., Offer, D., & Trujillo, J. (1983). Measuring Delinquent Behaviour in Inpatient Settings: Revision and Validation of the Adolescent Antisocial Behaviour Ckecklist. *Journal of the American Academy of Child Psychiatry*, 22, 459-466.

Deluty, R.H. (1979). Children's Action Tendency Scale: A Self-report Measure of Aggressiveness, Assertiveness, and Submissiveness in Children. *Journal of Consulting and Clinical Psychology,* 47, 1061-1071.

Douglas, K.S., Cox, & Webster, C.D. (1999). Violence Risk Assessment: Science and Practice, Legal and Criminal Psychology, 4, 149-184.

Elliot, D.S., Dunford, F.W., & Huizinga, D. (1987). The Identification and Prediction of Career Offenders Utilising Self-reported and Official Data. In J.D. Burchard & S.N. Burchard (Eds.), *Preventing Delinquent Behaviour* (pp.90-121). Newbury Park, CA: Sage.

Elliot, D.S., Huizinga, D., & Ageton, S.S. (1985). *Explaining Delinquency and Drug Use.* Beverly Hills, CA: Sage.

Empey, L.T. (1982). *American Delinquency: Its Meaning and Construction*, Dorsey, Homewood, Illinois.

Eyberg, S.M., & Robinson, E.A. (1983). Conduct Problem Behaviour: Standardization of a Behavioural Rating Scale with Adolescents. *Journal of Clinical Child Psychology*, 12, 347-354.

Frick, P.J. (1996). Callous-unemotional Traits and Conduct Problems: A Two-factor Model of Psychopathy in Children. In D.J. Cooke, A.E. Forth, J.P. Newman, & R.D. Hare (Eds.), *International Perspectives on Psychopathy. Issues in Criminological and Legal Psychology*, 24, 47-51, Leicester: British Psychological Society.

Frick, P.J., O'Brien, B.S., Wootton, J.M., & McBurnett, K. (1994). Psychopathy and Conduct Problems in Children. *Journal of Abnormal Psychology*, 103 (4). 700-707.

Funderbunk, B.W., & Eyberg, S.M. (1989). Psychometric Characteristics of the Sutter-Eyberg Student Behaviour Inventory: A School Behaviour Rating Scale for Use with Preschool Children. *Behavioural Assessment*, 11, 297-313.

Hawkins, J..D., Catalano, R.F., Kosterman, R., Abbott, R. and Hill, K.G. (1999). Preventing Adolescent Health-Risk Behaviours by Strengthening Protection During Childhood. *Archives of Paediatric and Adolescent Medicine*, 153: 226-234.

Huesmann, L.R., Eron, L.D., Lefkowitz, M.M., & Walder, L.O. (1984). Stability of Aggression Over Time and Generations. *Developmental Psychology*, 20, 1120-1134.

Kazdin A.E. (1995). *Conduct Disorders in Childhood and Adolescence*. London: Sage.

Kazdin, A.E. (1987). Treatment of Antisocial Behaviour in Children: Current Status and Future Directions. *Psychological Bulletin*, 102(2), 187-203.

Kroll, L., Woodham. A., Rothwell, J., Bailey, S., Tobias, C., Harrington, R., and Marshall, M. (1999). Reliability of the Salford Needs Assessment Schedule for Adolescents. Psychological Medicine, 29, 891-902.

Kulik, J.A., Stein, K.B., & Sarbin, T.R. (1968). Dimensions and Patterns of Adolescent Antisocial Behaviour. *Journal of Consulting and Clinical Psychology*, 32, 375-382.

Lefkowitz, .M., Eron, L.D., Walder, L.O., & Huesmann, L.R. (1977). *Growing Up to Be Violent: A Longitudinal Study of the Development of Aggression*. New York: Pergamon.

McMahon, R.J., & Forehand, R. (1988). Conduct Disorders. In E.J. Mash & L.G. Terdal (Eds.), *Behavioural Assessment of Childhood Disorders* (2nd ed., pp. 105-153). New York: Guilford.

Moffit, T.E. (1993a). Adolescent-limited and Life-course Persistent Antisocial Behaviour: A Developmental Taxonomy. *Psychological Review*, 100, 674-701.

Patterson, G.R. (1982). *Coercive Family Process*. Eugene, OR: Castalia.

Reid, J.B., Baldwin, D.V., Patterson, G.R., & Dishion, T.J. (1988). Observations in the Assessment of Childhood Disorders. In M. Rutter, A.H. Tuma & I.S. Lann (Eds.), *Assessment and Diagnosis in Child Psychopathology* (pp. 156-195). New York: Guilford.

Robinson, E.A., Eyberg, S.M., Ross, A.W. (1980). The Standardization of An Inventory of Child Conduct Problem Behaviours. *Journal of Clinical Child Psychology*, 9, 22-28.

Rutter, M., Cox, A., Egert, S., Holbrook, D. and Everitt, B. (1981). Psychiatric Interviewing Techniques. IV. Experimental Study: Four Contrasting Styles. *The British Journal of Psychiatry*, 138: 456-465.

Rutter, M., Giller, H., & Hagell, A. (1998). *Antisocial Behaviour by Young People*. Cambridge University Press, New York.

Scott, P. (1977). Assessing Dangerousness in Criminals. *British Journal of Psychiatry*, 131, 127-142.

Shamsie, J. and Hluchy, C. (1991). Youth with Conduct Disorder: A Challenge to be Met. (Review). Canadian Journal of Psychiatry, 36 (6):405-414, (Summary). (Online) Available: *http://www.mentalhealth.com/dis/p20-ch02.html.*

Walker, Hill M., Severson, Herbert H., Nicholson, Fulvia, Hehle, Thomas, Jenson, William R., & Clark, Elaine (1994). Replication of the Systematic Screening for Behaviour Disorders (SSBD) Procedure for the Identification of At-Risk Children. *Journal of Emotional and Behavioural Disorders*, 2.2 , 66-77.

Williams, J.R., & Gold, M. (1972). *From Delinquent Behaviour to Official Delinquency. Social Problems*, 20, 209-229.

Woodward, L.J., & Fergusson, D.M. (1999). Early Conduct Problems and Later Risk of Teenage Pregnancy in Girls. *Development and Psychopathology*, 11, 127-141.

5

PREVENTION AND INTERVENTION STRATEGIES

OBJECTIVES

This chapter deals with various prevention and intervention strategies for Antisocial behaviour. After reading this chapter, the reader should be able to:

- *(i)* Identify the need for development of appropriate prevention and intervention strategies;
- *(ii)* Give an account of primary, secondary and tertiary strategies to prevent Antisocial behaviour;
- *(iii)* Describe the various child-focussed, parental, peer, school and community programmes available;
- *(iv)* Appreciate the need for a comprehensive intervention programme.

Risk factors identified with adolescent antisocial behaviour include failure in school, family problems (history of criminal activity, sexual or physical abuse, neglect, abandonment, lack of parental control over a child), substance abuse (alcohol, other drugs), pattern behaviours (running away, stealing) and conduct problems (not outgrowing aggressiveness by early adolescence), gang membership and gun possession (Juvenile Crime-Outlook for California, 1995). It has been shown that children exposed to these risk factors follow a well described and documented path beginning with behavioural manifestations and reactions such as defiance of adults, lack of school readiness and aggression toward peers (Walker & Sprague, 1999). This leads to negative short term outcomes including truancy, peer and teacher rejection, low academic achievement and early involvement in drugs and alcohol. These factors set a child up for school failure and eventual dropout, which leads finally to negative and destructive long term outcomes.In adulthood, these same children will often be involved in alcohol and substance abuse, suffer psychiatric disorder including depression, antisocial adult behaviour, have marital, social and occupational difficulties, social isolation, and perhaps become criminals.

NEED FOR DEVELOPMENT OF APPROPRIATE PREVENTION AND INTERVENTION STRATEGIES TO OVERCOME ANTISOCIAL BEHAVIOUR

The effects of serious behaviour problems are felt across many settings and create direct expenses for families, communities, schools, government agencies and businesses. These effects significantly diminish the life prospects of a substantial proportion of children and contribute to a cycle of inter-generational disadvantage. Today the precise cost of child behaviour problems in terms of wasted lives and social and economic damage-or even the full cost of services-is unknown but the annual figure is known to run into many billions of dollars.

The costs from juvenile and adult crime represents only the extreme end of the list of costs associated with child behavioural problems and their resulting conduct disorders. Behaviour problems of many thousands of children become a burden on the health, welfare and education systems, as well as, put serious strains on their families while becoming problems to themselves.

An increasing number of children are now exposed to these risk factors and then follow this unfortunate path. We know that a child can be diverted from this path, but success depends on early intervention. The farther the child goes down this destructive path, the more likely it is that he or she will reach the end, and adopt an antisocial behaviour pattern throughout life. In the words of Reid (1993), "We have the ability to find these at-risk children and youth early, but we generally prefer to wait, to not do anything, and hope that they grow out of their problems. In far too many cases, in the absence of intervention and appropriate supports for their emerging behaviour problems, they grow into and adopt an antisocial behaviour pattern during their school careers." Thus it is important to nip in the bud the earliest risk factors (Carolyn Webster-Stratton, 2002). Focused activities and strategies are needed to reduce risk factors and increase protective factors to ensure optimal physical, cognitive, language, emotional and social development and to achieve significant and positive life outcomes for our children. There is currently a developing understanding for the need for early intervention and prevention. What we need to do now is build on this, to use the research evidence to guide decisions necessary for the well-being of our families and children.

The Indian Scenario

The Government of India has started schools in every nook and corner of the country with the view to provide universalisation of elementary education. In India, the schools are mostly over-crowded. The Teacher-Student ratio is more than 1:50. The teachers are unable to give individualised attention for all the students. There are inadequate preschools or nursery schools or balwadis for children at pre-primary level. The material and human resources flowing into the school systems are inadequate considering the number of students enrolled at primary and secondary levels.

On the other hand, from the familial side, parents do not seem to care much about the development of the children. Due to rapid increase in cost of living, both parents are forced to work for their livelihood. Due to disintegration of the Joint family system, children are left without proper care. Loneliness, unsociability and unwanted peer group lead to unacceptable social behaviour from early years.

Illiteracy and ignorance are more in rural and tribal areas. In spite of Adult Literacy and Adult Education Programmes, the country is experiencing more-than 40% of illiteracy rate in several states. Even after independence, even though the Government has launched and implemented several welfare and development schemes, the fruits have not reached the doorsteps of the poorest of the poor communities. As a result, poverty is still a common phenomenon one can observe in Indian sub-continent. On one side, rich are becoming richer, and on the other hand, the poor are becoming poorer. Ignorance about parental childbearing and rearing practices is also one of the contributing factors for the poor nurturing of children.

A combination of all these impoverished factors has deprived the children from getting exposed to stimulation programmes for the better growth and development. In fact, the discussion throughout this chapter reveals that in the western context, Individual and Environmental factors are the potential contributors for antisocial behaviour in children. Almost all the factors related to family, society and culture discussed in this chapter are of great relevance to India today. It is not surprising that one can spot antisocial behaviour in every nook and corner of the country.

Even in schools, one can find such children in almost every classroom. Neither the parents nor the teachers pay adequate attention towards these children. While the parents are totally ignorant about the concept, the teachers are not taking effective steps, with the pretext of lack of time. No need to say, they lack knowledge about techniques to tackle these children. This issue has been much talked about by the Central as well as State Governments, but there seems to be no sign of any strategic training programme for teachers in the offing. Various Television channels highlight the issues now and then, but no concrete steps have been taken either at school or at community level. Proper identification and assessment of antisocial behaviour prevailing in students will help to understand the causes and characteristics of antisocial behaviour in students. If one knows this, it is possible to develop appropriate need-based situation-oriented strategies to overcome antisocial behaviour in students. School personnel and parents must play a key role in planning for remedial strategies for children.

Millions children and youth in schools have been identified as antisocial (only some of whom are identified as having an educational disability), and the numbers are increasing. Without treatment, children with antisocial behaviour may experience rejection by classmates and other peers because of their poor social skills, and aggressive and annoying behaviour. Although it may not be possible to prevent antisocial behaviour such as ODD, recognizing and acting on symptoms when they first appear can minimize distress to the child and family, and prevent many of the problems associated with the illness. Family members also can learn steps to take if signs of relapse (return of symptoms) appear. In addition, providing a nurturing, supportive and consistent home environment with a balance of love and discipline may help reduce symptoms and prevent episodes of defiant behaviour. If society is concerned about today's youth, the easiest and the least expensive way to intervene is to identify and modify antisocial behaviour in children.

The outcomes of successful intervention include decreasing the prevalence of child, adolescent and adult mental health disorders—such as conduct problems, substance abuse, depression; lowering academic failure; truancy and bullying; child maltreatment; coercive parenting; teenage parenthood; juvenile offending and adult crime; social isolation; and poor occupational and social relationships. There will be many benefits such as better behaviour and performance at school, self-efficacy, social competence and peer relationships, use of community support services and safer communities.

STRATEGIES TO PREVENT ANTISOCIAL BEHAVIOUR

Young people around the world are increasingly affected by violence, social problems, and a lack of respect for each other and the world around them. Parents, educators and concerned citizens in many countries are asking for help to turn around this alarming trend. Many of them believe that part of the solution is an emphasis on teaching values.

We must not just educate our children and youth 'to know' and 'to do', we must also educate them 'to be' and 'to live together' (Delors et al., 1996). Quality education recognizes the whole person and promotes education that involves the affective domain as well as the cognitive. Values such as peace, love, respect, tolerance, cooperation and freedom, are cherished and aspired for the world over. Such values are the sustaining force of human society and progress. What children and youth learn is later woven into the fabric of society and so education must have positive values at its heart and the resulting expression of them as its aim if we are to seek to create a better world for all.

In a world where negative role models, the glorification of violence, and materialism abound, older children and youth rarely acquire positive social skills or values simply by being told to do so. While 'good' students may adopt values-based behaviours when exposed to 'awareness- level' activities, they gain greater benefit when guided through an exploration of values and their implications for the self, others and the larger society. On the other hand, more 'resistant' students or marginalized youth turn away from a moralizing approach to character education. Educators, and activities, that actively engage and allow students the opportunity to explore and experience their own qualities are therefore of crucial importance. Students benefit by developing skills to cognitively explore and understand values. For students to be motivated to learn and utilize positive and cooperative social skills, the creation of a values-based atmosphere in which they are encouraged, listened to and valued is also essential.

'Human aggression is learned and therefore can be reduced or prevented through learning' (Eron & Slaby, 1994). Frederico and Davis (1996) following a literature review outline a series of protective factors for individual young people which can act to mitigate levels of risk. Factors listed include:

(i) beliefs such as being able to see value and meaning in life, self-esteem and belief in survival and coping;

(ii) fear of suicide and moral objections to suicide;

(iii) skills such as stress management;

(iv) communication and problem solving skills; and

(v) supports such as family responsibilities, community support networks, and a sense of belonging.

There is some empirical support for the potential effectiveness of interventions targeted at early primary school. Prevention programmes implemented during the early primary school years have shown considerable success in reducing behaviour problems and preventing the development of later antisocial behaviour (Farrington, 2002; Greenwood et al., 1998; Homel et al., 1999). These programmes have generally been multi-faceted, involving teacher and parent training in behaviour management skills—monitoring behaviour, using effective discipline, and promoting prosocial behaviours and, child skills training—social, cognitive, and problem solving skills (Homel et al., 1999).

There is also considerable evidence suggesting that preventative interventions are more cost effective than the treatment of antisocial behaviour after it has become an established pattern of behaviour. Ialongo and his colleagues (1999) randomly assigned 678 first-grade children in nine Baltimore City public schools to three intervention conditions: Classroom Centered Intervention, Family-School Partnership Intervention and A control group that received no intervention.

Classroom Centred Intervention (CC) included curriculum enhancement, improved behaviour management practices, and backup strategies for children who failed to respond adequately to the intervention. Family-School Partnership Intervention (FSP) was designed to improve achievement and reduce early aggressive behaviour, shy behaviour, and concentration problems by enhancing parent teacher communication and providing parents with effective teaching and child behaviour management strategies. The interventions were provided over the first-grade year, after pretest assessment in the early Fall. Intervention impact was assessed in the spring of the first and second grades. The results were as follows:

(i) Children who underwent the CC and FSP interventions did better in math and reading than children in the control group. The improvement was most pronounced for those children who were doing poorly before the intervention;

(ii) Children who received the CC intervention demonstrated significantly fewer behaviour problems as rated by teachers both at the end of first and second grade. For children who received the FSP intervention, their behaviour also improved by the end of first grade but the improvement did not reach a statistically significant level until the follow up at the end of the second grade;

(iii) Significantly fewer boys in the CC group were nominated as aggressive by peers in the Spring of first grade than boys in control group. No significant effects were found for CC girls or FSP girls or boys. [Although fewer boys in FSP group were nominated by peers as aggressive compared to the control group, the difference was not statistically significant.]

Primary Prevention Strategies

'Primary prevention is much like putting fluoride in a community's water supply in order to prevent dental cavities' (Walker et al., 1996). Teaching skills for school success decreases the likelihood of dropout and perhaps delinquency. These skills include being prepared, arriving to class on time, completing assignments and asking for assistance when needed.

Primary prevention will be effective for 80-90% of the students (those without serious problem behaviours) and includes violence prevention skills training, instruction in conflict resolution and anger management strategies, effective academic instruction, and school-wide behaviour expectations and disciplinary policies to ensure a smoothly run school environment.

Rae-Grant (1991) has summarised Primary prevention as any intervention designed to reduce the incidence of a particular disorder in a target population. According to him, the aim is protection or competence enhancement. Family and community environments, institutions that influence children, and the interactions of these domains should be considered when planning interventions. Interventions should aim to improve situations at the beginning of causal chain, in which one event leads to another.

Combinations of risk factors in the child and the environment are more likely to produce negative outcomes. Outcomes depend on the following factors: i) number of stressors in the wider environment; ii) number of stressors in the family environment; iii) vulnerability of the child; iv) timing and nature of events; v) resiliency of child (individual protective factors), vi) protective factors in the family environment; and vii) protective factors in the wider environment.

To increase the likelihood of resiliency in a child, it is essential to reduce the number of risk factors of the child and/or environment, and increase the number of protective factors in the child and/or the environment. What is needed is to reduce family dysfunction in the home, and increase academic emphasis and recreation and sports opportunities at school. Primary prevention can target several levels: individual, family, school and community, and government policies and legislation.

Secondary Prevention Strategies

'Secondary prevention is much like increasing one's scheduled visits to the dentist because of an increased susceptibility (e.g., soft or thin enamel) for dental cavities or initiating an orthodontic intervention because of teeth overcrowding' (Walker et al., 1996). Examples of secondary prevention include individual counselling, provision of adult mentors, behaviour management programmes, scheduling changes and additional supports and services.

Tertiary Prevention Strategies

Finally, tertiary prevention is designed for children who usually exhibit life-course-persistent antisocial behaviour usually involving delinquent or violent acts. 'In our dental analogy, individuals at this level would be candidates for significant cavity repairs, root canals, bridges, and other expensive forms of dental care' (Walker et al., 1996).

Generally schools alone cannot provide all the resources and services needed to accommodate these children. It is not only necessary economically but also essential to the child's development to include other services. There is strong evidence that prevention started early in a child's life is very effective and is essential. Interventions that begin in the antenatal period add to the benefits. It is easier to modify risk factors before patterns of behaviour are entrenched. Later prevention and/or treatment attempts are likely to be more difficult, if not impossible. For example, teaching interpersonal problem-solving skills may be more effective in preschoolers than older children.

INTERVENTION STRATEGIES TO OVERCOME ANTISOCIAL BEHAVIOUR

Intervention refers to systematic efforts to reduce, alleviate, or eliminate a problem. The task for interventions for antisocial behaviour is enormous. Antisocial youth are likely to experience a broad range of problems. Their parents and families may also show problems that affect and affected by the children (e.g., parental psychopathology and marital discord). Studies of childhood interventions with socially disruptive behaviour, cognitive deficits, or parenting as an outcome generally have positive effects (Tremblay et al., 1996; Wasserman et al., 2000). In the last two decades, many new and promising approaches have appeared which seem to prove outcome. Some of them are: Child focussed Programmes, Parent Management Programmes, Peer Programmes, School Programmes, Neighbourhood or Community-based Programmes and Comprehensive Intervention Programmes.

I. CHILD FOCUSSED PROGRAMMES

These are oriented towards the individual with antisocial behaviour. Included under this are: A) Cognitive Behaviour Modification; B) Medication; C) Counselling; and D) Continuum of care.

(A) Cognitive Behaviour Modification

Cognitive processes refer to a broad classes of constructs that pertain to how an individual perceives, codes, and experiences the world (Kazdin,1995). Individuals who engage in antisocial behaviour, particularly aggression, have been found to show distortions and deficiencies in various cognitive processes.

The interrelationships among cognitive processes, environmental events, and behaviour are perhaps more clearly conveyed in the context of social behaviour. For example, a person who believes that other people are very friendly may initiate social responses (greetings, conversations) with acquaintances and strangers.

The belief (cognitive process) leads to greeting and chatting with others (behaviour), which in turn generate environmental consequences (attention, praise, and other sources of reinforcement from others). These consequences are likely to affect the person's perceptions and behaviours in future. If a person js led to believe that another person has a particular characteristics (e.g., past serious mental illness, great academic skill, physical handicap), he or she perceives the actions of that person differently from someone without that characteristic and acts differently. Clearly, cognitive process (e.g., perceptions, expectations) and environmental events (e.g., behaviour of others) mutually influence each other.

A variety of cognitive processes have been studied, including the abilities to generate alternate solutions to interpersonal problems (e.g. different ways of handling social situations); to identify the means to obtain particular ends (e.g., making friends) or consequences of actions (e.g., what would happen after a particular behaviour); to make attributions to others of the motivation of their actions; to perceive how others feel; and to formulate expectations of the effects of one's own actions (Shirk,1988; Spivack & Shure, 1982). Deficits and distortions among these processes relate to teacher ratings of disruptive behaviour, peer evaluations, and direct assessment of overt behaviour (Lochman & Dodge, 1994; Rubin, Bream, & Rose-Krasnor, 1991).

Children with ADHD, because of their poor attention span and lack of impulse control, are unable to learn the techniques and monitor their behaviour. Cognitive therapies include verbal self-instructions, problem solving skills, self-monitoring, and other therapies, which aim to help the child to control his or her attention and impulse. Baer and Nietzel (1991) and, Durlak, Fuhrman and Lampman (1991) examined whether Cognitive Behaviour Therapy (CBT) decreased inattentiveness, impulsivity, and hyperactivity in boys with ADHD in the home settings. Their study revealed that CBT was effective for hyperactivity and some improvement was shown in attentiveness and impulsivity. Teacher ratings on attentiveness in class also showed improvement.

Cognitive Behaviour Modification involves:

1. Development of Right Thinking Patterns;
2. Moral Reasoning;
3. Anger Management;
4. Assertiveness Training;
5. Problem Solving Skills Training;
6. Conflict Mediation, and 7) Teaching Social Skills.

1. Development of Right Thinking Patterns

Deficits impinge in a negative way on the demonstration of pro-social behaviour. Interventions must target specific prosocial and antisocial behaviours and the 'thinking skills' that mediate such behaviours. Such a combination provides an atmosphere of warmth, care and necessary support. Zimmerman (1983) maintains that effective interventions with youth should include the simultaneous attainment of a combination of skills drawing from behavioural, affective and cognitive treatment modalities.

Flavell (1976) defines metacognition as the knowledge and awareness of one's own cognitive processes. Thus metacognitive processes 'enable individuals to think better and thereby become more efficient and flexible learners'. Metacognitive thinking explores the procedural strategies, skills, dispositions of thinking well. Improvement in thinking involves generating standards, criteria and norms for better thinking. Being aware of how to learn helps motivation in tackling what to learn.

Learning activities that encourage higher order thinking begin with concrete experience and preparation. Concrete preparation connects the antisocial to prior experience, relevance, authentic and real contexts etc. Learning activities that encourage higher order thinking take the antisocial beyond their thinking comfort zones to higher order thinking processes. Cognitive conflict is set at a level that challenges the minds of the antisocials. Construction zone activity helps the antisocials to make sense of reality for themselves. The conflict is at least partially resolved as the antisocials go beyond this previous thinking capability.

Learning activities that encourage higher order thinking engage the antisocials in thinking about their own thinking in order to improve their learning. Watson, Bruce and Richard Kopnicek (1990) actively promoted new thinking patterns through a variety of methods:

(i) *stressing relevance* (connect new concepts to the student's everyday life);

(ii) *making predictions* (link their new knowledge with what they already know in order to form hypotheses); and

(iii) *stressing consistency* (to be consistent in their thinking).

With the help of such metacognitive strategies, attention of the antisocial adolescents is drawn to the inconsistencies in their thinking and techniques are provided for controlling or changing these habits of thinking. In other words, Metacognition helps the antisocials to consciously reflect on the problem solving process and identify the reasoning patterns developed for future use. It also facilitates bridging or transfer of the reasoning patterns to new contexts in order to generalise them and consolidate their use. This has been of immense help to the students in not only examining their own offence cycles but also in interrupting them to prevent themselves from victimising others in future.

Rational-emotive Therapy

Rational-emotive therapy developed by Robert Ellis, is based on the view that psychological problems arise from faulty or irrational thought patterns (Ellis, 1979, 1999). These patterns are evident in implicit verbalisations that people make, that is, things people say to themselves. The verbalisations arise from assumptions that we make about the world and the events that happen to us. More specifically, some event occurs and in response to that, we have thoughts. These thoughts or self-statements, lead to a series of emotions (e.g., disappointment, anger, disgust, negative views about oneself) and behaviours (e.g., vengeful acts, suicide attempt). The purpose of rational-emotive therapy is to examine the implicit self-verbalisations people make, to challenge them, and point to their irrationality, and most importantly, to substitute more adaptive self-verbalizations. Rational-emotive psychotherapy has been applied to a number clinical problems such as anger control, anxiety disorders, and others (Ellis & Dryden, 1998 ; Lyons & Woods, 1991).

A very useful way to illustrate this technique is by using Ellis' 'ABC' model. In this framework 'A' represents an activating event or experience and the person's inferences or interpretations about the event; 'B' represents their beliefs about the event; 'C' represents the consequence—the emotions and behaviours that follow from those thoughts and beliefs. Here is an example of an 'emotional episode', as experienced by an adolescent whose history indicates a biological proneness to low mood and a tendency to misinterpret how he is viewed by his friends:

(a) Event

My friend Rahul did not acknowledge me when I attended his birthday party.

Inferences about the event:

'He's ignoring me; he doesn't like me.

(b) Beliefs about a:

'I may not have friends at all'.

'I want everyone to like me. Only then, I will be happy'.

'I am not worth being a friend and so I don't qualify being a person also'.

(c) Reaction

Feelings: lonely, depressed

Behaviours: avoiding all my friends generally.

The task of rational-emotive therapy in the above case is to identify and challenge these processes and to substitute more adaptive thoughts in their place as follows:

(d) Disputing (new rational beliefs to help me achieve this new reaction):

'Just because he did not talk with me, it does not mean that I will no longer have friends'.

'Friendship is important and if he does not need me as his friend, I will have still others'.

(e) New Effect (how I would prefer to feel/behave):

Disappointed but not depressed.

(f) Further Action (what I'll do to avoid repeating the same irrational/thoughts)

'Go and see my friend, talk to him and look for the real reason'.

'If he does not want me as a friend, I will turn to other classmate's.

2. Moral Reasoning

Cognitive development theory posits that antisocial behaviour is attributable in part to socio-moral development delay (Gibbs, Potter, & Goldstein, 1995). Goldstein and Glick (1987) state that chronically delinquent youth have been shown to reason at a more self-centred and concrete level of moral reasoning. Moral Reasoning involves at cognitive and metacognitive level:

(i) Resistance to temptation;

(ii) Guilt or acute emotional discomfort that follows transgression leading to confession, or self-blame;

(iii) Altruism, representing various pro-social acts of kindness, helpfulness, sympathy, and service to others;

(iv) Moral belief and insight, covering all aspects of what people think and say about morality, including their willingness to blame others who do wrong.

Moral reasoning is devised by the use of Role taking and Self-control and self-instruction. Role-taking is meant to develop and enhance the ability of the antisocials to see themselves from another perspective and to appreciate the views of other people. In self-control and self-instruction technique, a model performs a task making appropriate overt self-statements, the antisocial performs the same behaviour, gradually moves to whispered self-instruction and moved to covert silent self instruction. The student with Antisocial behaviour is encouraged to self observe, self-evaluate and self-reinforce appropriate overt behaviours. In the case of an aggressive behaviour exhibited by a student, following steps were followed:

- Identify self-statements prior to aggressive episode;
- Explore the consequences of such statements with the students with antisocial behaviour;
- More appropriate, less aggressive verbalisations are modelled, rehearsed and practised;
- New verbalisations—self-monitoring for successful behaviour are used.

Homework are given as assignments to further develop self-monitoring and self-reinforcement skills.

3. Anger Management

Anger is an emotion, which, like anxiety, affects many systems (emotional, cognitive and physiological). It is typically activated when a person believes he or she has been deliberately provoked. In terms of survival, anger can be looked at as a necessary driving force when 'fight' as opposed to 'flight' is required. Cognitively, research has shown that, students when are angry, they show changes in their thinking (Novaco, 1979). Typically one becomes 'single minded,' focusing exclusively on what they believe is provoking them. Most students' anger is isolated to situations in which it is justified, when they have been taken advantage of, lied to, cheated, abused and so forth.

Many researchers have discovered that anger control problems tend to be associated with a number of 'thinking errors' (Dodge & Frame, 1982; Lochman, White, & Wayland, 1991). Students with anger control problems have an insufficient number of adaptive responses to provoking events. Angry students, due to such cognitive deficits, when asked how they would solve provocative situations, have fewer ideas than students without anger problems. Their ideas, not surprisingly, tend to be hostile.

People with anger control problems often tend to see part of the picture, and have false beliefs. They often possess steadfast beliefs like 'People are, for the most part, stupid and need to be dealt with forcefully'. They also tend to respond quickly without much forethought. The impulsive and aggressive behaviour of students with antisocial behaviour speak to an inability to contain their anger.

Anger management training is based on a cognitive-behavioural approach to anger reduction. It is meant to train the students with antisocial behaviour in skills needed to manage anger and other emotions associated with the occurrence of aggression and antisocial behaviour. The objectives of anger management training are to make the antisocials to:

- understand the factors that trigger their anger and aggression;
- learn skills to reduce levels of arousal;

- challenge cognition that creates, escalates, and sustains arousal;
- learn skills to resolve conflict effectively; and
- learn how to deal with relapsing into former patterns of aggression.

The technique of Anger Control involves:

(a) *Cognitive Preparation*– To educate the individual about the causes and effects of anger;

(b) *Skill Acquisition*– self statement and modification, relaxation and assertion skills are trained;

(c) *Application Training*– Newly acquired skills are put to test in supervised in vivo (closed settings) and role play settings.

In the technique of Anger Control, following steps are to be followed:

1. *Develop a Hierarchy:* Start by having the antisocial to list anger situations they are likely to meet in real life;
2. *Exposure via Imagery:* Progressively using each hierarchy scene, expose the client to manageable doses of anger stimuli, via the use of imagery and role-playing. Use cognitive procedures such as Rational-Emotive Imagery (Maultsby & Ellis, 1974; Froggatt, 1997) and Rational Self-Analysis (Froggatt, 1993; 1997) to assist the client to identify and dispute the thoughts that create the anger they feel while carrying out the imagery exercise;
3. *Exposure in Real-life Situations:* When the student with antisocial behaviour is ready, move him on to using exposure with response-prevention: The antisocial students deliberately (in a planned way) confront situations that would normally trigger anger. They inhibit their usual response (eg. argumentativeness, defensiveness, demanding of others, etc.) and instead use the new strategies they

> have learned. The purpose is to give the antisocials, behaviour practice at increasing their frustration-tolerance and coping in a non-hostile way with a variety of situations, where the practice is under their control.

Anger can be thought of as interactive responses that affect cognition, and physiological processes (Geen, 1990). Triggers can be identified as both external or internal sources of anger. An external trigger is a behaviour by one person to make another individual angry, such as an obscene gesture. Internal triggers are statements people say to themselves that influence whether or not they become angry (Goldstein & Glick, 1987). For instance, a student may make the statement, 'This class leader thinks I'm good for nothing. I want to slap him.' Students can be taught to reframe this kind of statement, perhaps eliciting a more acceptable reaction such as 'I shouldn't think of him as my enemy. May be I am in the wrong.' Individuals can also be taught to recognize behaviours that accompany feelings of anger. A second component of anger control is reduction of physical responses to anger. Behaviours in response to anger need to be recognized because everyone has his or her own physical reactions to anger. Physical signs such as clenched fists, sweaty palms, heightened heart rate, and others can indicate anger. Deep breathing exercises or relaxation techniques can assist a person in reducing these physical responses to anger (Goldstein & Glick, 1987).

Finally, self-assessment is a third component of anger control that can be taught to aggressive individuals. According to Goldstein and Glick (1987), self-assessment after exposure to a conflict situation is one way to: (a) monitor progress; (b) provide a reward for handling a difficult situation well; and (c) determine how the situation could have been handled better. Encouraging youths to generate a list of self-statements such as 'I really controlled my temper this time' can be used as a reward or as an evaluative measure. Although anger control techniques have worked successfully with youths, often this training is insufficient alone. Standing up for one's rights without jeopardizing the rights of others, as taught in assertiveness programmes, may also be necessary.

Self-analysis with anger problems will usually involve:

- increasing frustration-tolerance;
- challenging demands directed at other people or the world, especially the idea that other people or the world 'must' conform to one's expectations and, the 'need' to punish others or control their behaviour;
- developing the concept of accepting people, even when their behaviour is rejected.

Shyamala (2004) studied anger management as an extension of self-control measure. Students were made to recognize early arousal signs and were taught how to step back and evaluate the situation thoroughly, so that anger will lose a great deal of its power. Students could do many things to reduce anger: relax, meditate, perform yoga, distract themselves (e.g. the old advice of counting to ten) or talk about it. Due importance was given to yoga and meditation and recreational activities in the daily schedule of the students with antisocial behaviour.

Yoga and Meditation

Yoga and meditation can contribute positively to various cognitive processes, including perception and in turn, on Subjective Well-being, and Quality of Life. Yoga and Meditation have been used in terms of Cognitive skill development such as concentration in work, stress management and anger control. According to Aminabhai (1996) Yoga training leads to highly significant improvement in subject's mental health. Yoga is claimed to endow perfect physical, mental and social well-being of an individual. A series of research investigations have revealed that there are many beneficial effects of yoga, which would help in the stress management (Selvamurthy, 1993).

Jin (1992) has observed the efficacy of Tai chi, a moving meditation, in reducing mood disturbance caused by mental/emotional stressors. Jhansi and Rao (1996) have investigated the role of practicing Transcendental Meditation (TM) in improving the attention regulation capacity. Their study reveals greater attention regulation capacity among TM practitioners compared to their counterparts, due to the regular cognitive exercises involved in meditation practice. The Transcendental Meditation programme represents a scientifically proven, cost-effective approach to eliminate experience-induced imbalance in brain function and antisocial behaviour while developing the full creative potential of the child. Research has shown this programme can be a cost-effective intervention for prevention and rehabilitation to reduce violence across a wide range of applications, including stress-ridden schools, drug and alcohol dependence, and criminal behaviour.

Transcendental Meditation programme offers an effective solution to violence (Arenander, 2000b; Jones et al., 2001). Considerable scientific research indicates that the Transcendental Meditation programme represents a simple solution to the complex problem of violence. This is good news to those who would like to apply simple solutions to complex social problems. Moreover, the TM programme provides a tool to eliminate the underlying root cause-not just diverse symptomatic, surface aspects—of violence and aggression. By providing a powerful coherent influence on the functioning of brain and body, the TM technique is unique in its unified effect on the diverse, complex functioning of the physiology (Alexander et al., 1990; Arenander, 1996; Jevning et al., 1992; Wallace, 1993). The TM technique can 'feed orderliness' to the developing or adult brain and counteract imbalances. In addition, the TM programme is one of the few treatments that has been extensively researched over the last 40 years in diverse populations around the world. Thus, this simple programme is unique because it can help transform the three key concerns of schools—the need for: a) scientific validation; b) prevention-oriented programmes; and c) programmes that impact the underlying cause of violence, imbalances in brain function (Sherman et al., 1997).

Provision of Recreational Activities

Antisocial behaviours can be observed as adolescents become frustrated with the lack of socially acceptable outlets available to them, and they may feel that they have no opportunity to engage in activities that are purposeful. Extracurricular activities provide one means to empower individuals and may offer a sense of accomplishment. An assault on society may emerge when extracurricular school and community activities are cut because of shortage of funds, resulting in children having fewer opportunities to feel a sense of achievement (Lipsitt, 1990).

The provision of a variety of supervised recreational activities for youth in the community is also a key component of an effective crime prevention strategy, especially in high risk communities where they are most likely to be lacking (Steinhauer, 1996).

Objectives for providing Recreation activities:

- A source of skills (potential source of self-esteem) and fun;
- A source of being part of a socialized group (rules: taking turns);
- A group leader can serve as a mentor (common factor to many students who prosper despite disadvantage);
- A socially acceptable avenue for sublimation of aggression;
- An antidote to boredom.

Some of the recreation activities that could be provided are:

(a) Sports and Games; (b) Science, Social, Philatelic and Heritage clubs; (c) Music and Dancel; and (d) Stage play.

For example, for students with conduct disorder, Shyamala (2004) used the traditional game of Kabaddi as a recreational activity to imbibe in them, the spirit of following rules (avoidance of purposive kicking act), discipline (keeping up reporting time in correct uniform, obeying the leader), leadership qualities (to identify the individuality of his team-mates, co-ordinating his team mates and guiding them to perform well, considering the suggestions given by other members of the team), and also to develop mutual understanding and co-operation. It also gave them the opportunity to: i) understand self-identity (their calibre and weakness); ii) reflect (compare and contrast one's own performance); iii) plan (take suggestions into consideration); and iv) execute (put into use during the course of next play). The good cognitive-behavioural skills thus learnt, are put to use later, in the real life-time situations to rectify his conduct disorders.

4. Assertiveness Training

Assertiveness training teaches individuals to do something about problems rather than to just talk about them. Yet, this action approach is frequently not done in an appropriate manner because of confusion surrounding the differences among aggressive, passive, and assertive responses.

According to Baer (1976), aggressiveness is an action that enhances the aggressor while it minimizes and violates the rights of others. The intent of the aggressive behaviour is to humiliate and dominate. This behaviour is in contrast to passive behaviours that are self-denying and inhibiting as a person's own rights are disregarded and he or she gives in to demands of others. Instead, Baer defined assertiveness as 'win-win' behaviour in which an individual can stand up for his or her own rights in such a way that the rights of others are not disregarded.

Various types of assertiveness training programmes have been implemented in the classroom with students of various ages. Disruptive, low achieving eighth- and ninth-grade urban male students, who were referred to the counsellor for objectionable classroom behaviour, were given 8 hours of assertiveness training. They met for 1 hour twice a week for 4 weeks. After the training, these students showed a decrease in aggressive behaviours and an increase in assertive behaviours in the classroom setting (Huey & Rank, 1984).

A four-step model proposed by Alberti (1986) has been used to help individuals recognize and practice assertive responses in various role-play situations. The four steps, paraphrased, are as follows:

Step 1. 'When . . .' (The speaker concretely describes the other individual's behaviour.);

Step 2. 'The effects are...' (The speaker describes objectively how the other individual's actions have affected his or her life.);

Step 3. 'I feel...' (The speaker accurately describes his or her feelings.);

Step 4. 'I prefer...' (The speaker suggests what he or she would like to see happen.).

These steps can be seen in the following situation:

Every morning a friend is chronically late in picking you up for school.

Step 1. 'When you are late picking me up for school in the morning...';

Step 2. 'I am always late for my first period class and I always get a detention...';

Step 3. 'I feel hurt and angry at you...';

Step 4. '... and I was hoping that we could make plans so that I don't have to be late anymore.'

This method allows an individual to identify the situation of concern, the feelings evoked by this situation, and a suggested course of action.

5. Problem-Solving Skills Training

Teaching cognitive-problem solving skills to children is a promising psychosocial approach since maladaptive cognitive processes are related to antisocial behaviour. In this the emphasis is primarily on how children approach situations. The primary focus is on the thought processes rather than the outcome or specific behavioural acts that result. Second, children are taught to engage in a step-by-step approach to solve interpersonal problems. Third, treatment uses structured tasks involving games, academic activities, and stories. Over the course of treatment, the cognitive problem-solving skills are applied to the real-life situations. The researchers use cognitive processes by making verbal self-statements, apply the sequence of statements to particular problems, provide cues to prompt the use of the skills, and deliver feedback and praise to develop correct use of the skills. Finally, treatment usually combines several different procedures, including modelling and practice, role-playing, and reinforcement and mild punishment (loss of points or tokens).

Problem solving skills related to social adjustment in children and adolescents (Spivack, Platt, & Shure, 1976) are:

1. Alternative solution thinking (generate alternatives);
2. Means-end thinking (plan intermediate steps);
3. Consequential thinking (identify likely consequences of choosing a particular course of action);
4. Causal thinking (linking on event to the next over time and understand why one led to another);
5. Sensitivity to interpersonal problems (perceive existence of problem and accurately identify interpersonal issues involved).

Problem-solving skills training has been used extensively in the context of treatment with children and adolescents who show disruptive, aggressive , and delinquent behaviour. The benefits have been evident in behaviour changes at home, at school, and in the community (Durlak et al., 1991). Kazdin, Siegel and Bass (1990) used problem-solving skills training with children (aged 7 to 13) who were aggressive and antisocial (e.g., fighting at school, stealing, lying, truancy, cruelty to animals). Children were seen individually on a weekly basis and trained to engage in problem-solving steps using modelling, shaping and feedback in a variety of interpersonal situations such as interactions with parents, teachers, peers, and siblings. Parents were also involved in the treatment by learning the problem-solving skills and practicing their application to situations at home and at school. Training children in problem-solving skills led to reduction in aggressive and antisocial behaviour at home, at school, and in the community.

In one study, training for the development for interpersonal problem-solving skills was offered both to the offender and the parents resulting in recidivism rate of approximately 24 per cent for the experimental group and 43 per cent for the control group (Collingwood & Genthner, 1980).

Several outcome studies have been completed with impulsive, aggressive, and conduct disorder children and adolescents (Baer & Nietzel, 1991; Durlak, Fuhrman, & Lampman, 1991). The findings in many of these studies has led to significant reductions in aggressive antisocial behaviour at home, at school, and in the community and that these gains are evident up to 1 year later.

6. Conflict Mediation

Conflict mediation is a structured programme in which critical thinking and serf-discipline are part of the dispute resolution process (Lane & McWhirter, 1992). Schrumpt, Crawford, & Usadel (1991) outlined six basic steps in the mediation process. The mediation process is as follows:

Step 1: Open the session. Following introductions, the mediator states the ground rules and the disputants are asked to commit to the ground rules before moving to the next step;

Step 2: Gather information. Each disputant is given uninterrupted time to state his or her perception of what caused the dispute;

Step 3: Focus on common interests. The purpose of this step is to search for commonalities that can serve as the foundation for an agreement. The mediator may have to ask each disputant questions such as 'What would you like to see happen?' to identify mutual goals;

Step 4: Create options. Disputants are encouraged to brainstorm and list options that may solve the problem. Allowing disputants to solve their own problem empowers individuals and provides an opportunity to recognize that many solutions exist in conflict resolution;

Step 5: Evaluate options and choose a solution. Disputants are encouraged to mutually agree on an option from the list of possible solutions;

Step 6: Write an agreement and close. A written contract, furnished to each of the participants, is mutually agreed on and signed. In addition, the mediator encourages both disputants to shake hands to promote cooperation and regard.

Some evidence suggests that older children benefit more from treatment than younger children, perhaps due to their cognitive development (Durlak et al., 1991). Conduct disordered children from families with high levels of impairment (parent psychopathology, stress, and family dysfunction) respond less well to treatment than youths from families with less impairment (Kazdin, 1995).

The most important intervention techniques that target the risk factors of impulsiveness and low empathy are cognitive-behavioural skills training programmes. For example, Ross and Ross (1988) devised a programme that aimed to teach people to stop and think before acting, to consider the consequences of their behaviour, to conceptualise alternative ways of solving interpersonal problems, and to consider the impact of their behaviour on other people, especially the victims. It included social skills training, lateral thinking (to teach creative problem-solving), critical thinking (to teach logical reasoning), values education (to teach non-aggressive, socially appropriate ways to obtain desired outcomes), negotiation skills training, interpersonal cognitive problem-solving (to teach thinking skills for solving interpersonal problems), social perspective training (to teach how to recognise and understand other people's feelings), role-playing and modelling (demonstration and practice of effective and acceptable interpersonal behaviour).

Ross and Ross implemented this 'Reasoning and Rehabilitation' programme in Ottawa, and found (in a randomised experiment) that it led to a large decrease in re-offending for a small sample of adult offenders in a short nine-month follow-up period. Their training was carried out by parents or teachers. This programme has been implemented widely in several different countries, and forms the basis of many accredited cognitive-behavioural programmes used in the UK prison and probation services, including the Pathfinder projects (McGuire, 2001).

Teaching Social Skills

List of eight fundamental social skills that can be taught through direct instruction (Hazel et al., 1981):

1. Giving positive feedback (e.g., thanking and giving compliments);
2. Giving negative feedback (e.g., giving criticism or correction);
3. Accepting negative feedback without hostility or inappropriate reactions;
4. Resisting peer pressure to participate in delinquent behaviour;
5. Solving personal problems;
6. Negotiating mutually acceptable solutions to problems;
7. Following instructions; and
8. Initiating and maintaining a conversation.

They recommended teaching these skills by providing definitions, illustrations with examples, modelling, verbal rehearsal, behavioural rehearsal, and additional practice.

Similarly, Walker, Colvin and Ramsey (1995) recommended a nine-step direct instructional procedure, the ACCEPTS instructional sequence.

The steps include:

1. Definition of the skill with guided discussion of examples;
2. Modelling or video presentation of the skill being correctly applied;
3. Modelling or video presentation of incorrect application (non example);
4. Review;
5. Modelling or video presentation of a second example with debriefing;
6. Modelling a range of examples, coupled with hypothetical practice situations;
7. Modelling or video presentation of another positive example if needed;

8. Role playing; and
9. Informal commitment from student to try the skill in a natural setting.

Cognitive-behavioural programmes that combine skills training gave better impact on severe and chronic antisocial behaviours (Kazdin, 1996). Treatment programmes combining social skills training, anger management, moral reasoning training and problem-solving skills training showed better results (Leeman, Gibbs, & Fuller, 1993). Programmes for children of divorce adapt a variety of clinical techniques to help children deal with the stress of divorce. Opportunities for discussion, ventilation of feelings, and social support are provided, usually in a group context (Alpert-Gillis, Pedro-Carroll, & Cowen, 1989).

Cognitive-behavioural therapy techniques emphasizing self-monitoring and self-control have been used effectively to reduce aggressive behaviour (Camp, Blom, Herbert, & Van Doorninck, 1977; Lochman, Burch, Curry, & Lampron, 1984). La Greca and Santogrossi (1980) used social learning procedures to train social isolates in skills designed to increase their rates of peer acceptance. In a frequently cited study, Oden and Asher (1977) found it was possible to coach socially isolated children on how to improve their peer interactions.

Two groups of studies fit this mould: those involving affective education and those involving interpersonal problem-solving training. Programmes involving affective education represent a diverse set of interventions that share the common goal of emotional and social growth. The general intent of these programmes is to improve children's adjustment by increasing their self-understanding and self-acceptance, and by helping them understand factors that influence their own and others' feelings and behaviours.

Lesson plans and units meant for early and middle elementary students combine puppet play, music, stories, group discussions, and various exercises. Self-monitoring, problem solving, conflict resolution, and communication skills, values such as personal responsibility and respect for self and others, content about health, culture, interpersonal relationships, and careers form the core of their curriculum.

As the implementation of individual cognitive behavioural strategies progress, students become better self- correctors, more thoughtful contributors and more caring of one another's individual contributions. This encourages self-correction without losing face. In this process, they learn to enrich themselves in sharing one another's outlooks with increased openness to the value of exploring their differences. Thus, the antisocial student will be able to

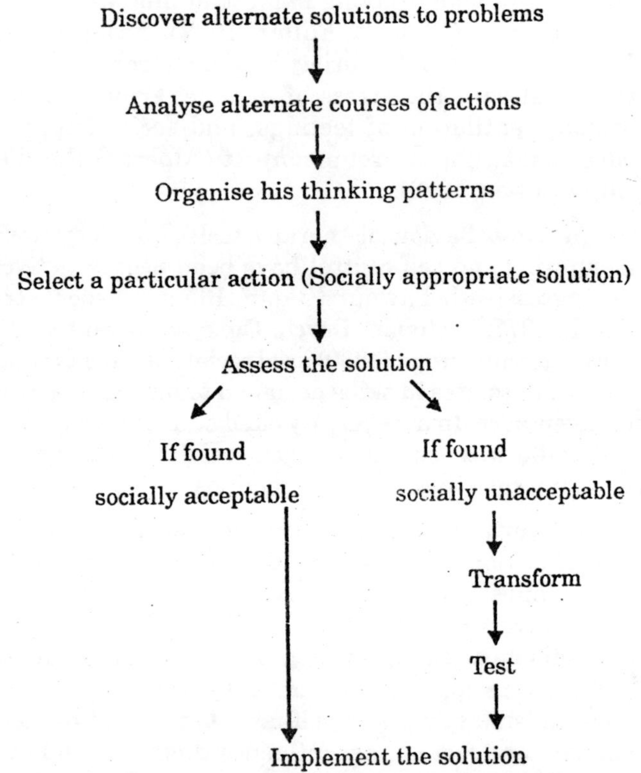

Andrews and Bonta (1994) attempted to lesson serious antisocial and violent behaviours by changing cognitive mechanisms linked with such behaviour. Cognitive behavioural interventions attempt to provide social perspective taking opportunities to address and alter deficits in thinking patterns. These are used to modify the individual's social perspective-taking skills, belief system, or motivational system, and encourage the students to deal assertively with negative peer pressures.

Positive consequences that demonstrate to students the benefits of appropriate behaviour are also designed and incorporated into the treatment plan. Opportunities for power or recognition are a key element of treatment. Continued thinking-errors help students to identify various types of rationalizations used by them regarding their behaviour . This is much in line with the reassurement of Lipman (1994) that such skill development will be a gradual but comprehensive process: '*Gradually the children will come to discover inconsistencies in their own thinking . . . They (will) learn to cooperate by building on one another's ideas, by questioning each others' underlying assumptions, by suggesting alternatives when some find themselves blocked and frustrated, and by listening carefully and respectfully to the ways in which other people express how things appear to them*'.

Becoming educated to think well requires the necessary self-discipline to develop listening and speaking skills to reach goals. Furthermore, these goals are not just personal ones; they are shared and practised in the community of inquiry and, in the short term, will most probably be articulated by the teacher and after a while could be devised by the class.

(B) MEDICATION

Effective and safe use of psychiatric drug therapy in children and adolescents is based on:

- a reliable diagnosis;
- appropriate administration of the drug therapy (monotherapy, starting with low dosage and increasing slowly, and periodic re-evaluation for side effects);
- ongoing training in the skills of assessment and diagnosis of children and adolescents, taking age and developmental status into account;
- ongoing interaction with antisocials and their families throughout treatment.

Medication may be more effective in reducing the main symptoms of ADHD while behavioural therapies may be more effective with other components of ADHD, such as confictual relationships with peers and poor academic performance (Klassen et al., 1999).

(C) COUNSELLING

It is helpful to view the process of working with students with antisocial behaviour as a process of adaptation of thinking rather than the restructuring him into a person whose morals and values match those of the society. It is enough to guide such students to lead lives that follow society's rules. It is an opportunity to point out students' errors in thinking without causing them to feel humiliated in the presence of the whole class. Other issues for individual counselling include continued relapse management and identity of empathy. Parents, family members, and friends should be invited to participate in counselling sessions as a way to provide collateral data.

In confronting students with antisocial behaviour, it is necessary to be direct without being abusive. Antisocial thinking patterns should be clearly pointed out pointing out antisocial thinking patterns thereby enabling the students to understand the consequences of their behaviour. For instance, when violation of rules are to be recorded, students with antisocial behaviour must be encouraged to report behaviour, thus taking responsibility for their own actions.

(D) CONTINUUM OF CARE

There is a remarkable decrease in the antisocial behaviour of adolescents while they are being treated with behavioural techniques. Behavioural techniques aim at changing the behaviour of the individual, but do not alter the environment from which the individual comes. Therefore, when the individual returns to the same environment which was responsible for producing the undesirable behaviours, some of the old behaviours may reappear. So, it is essential that the reatment modalities be continued for a longer duration of time.

When students with antisocial behaviour shed aspects of the behaviour, they may become more dependent. Such a transition often represents a healthy change. Feelings of dependency are easily frustrated at this stage, and disappointment may result in relapse. So it is necessary to continue to play the role of a mentor to such students who wished to come out of the shell of antisocial behaviour by individualised treatment sessions.

II. PARENTING PROGRAMMES

Parenting Programmes refer to procedures in which parents are trained to alter the antisocial child's behaviour in the home. Training is based on the general view that antisocial behaviour is inadvertently developed and sustained in the home by maladaptive parent-child interactions. There are multiple facets of parent-child interaction that promote aggressive and antisocial behaviour. These patterns include directly reinforcing deviant behaviour, frequently and ineffectively using commands and harsh punishment, and failing to attend to appropriate behaviour (Patterson, 1982; Patterson et al., 1992).

It would be misleading to imply that the parent generates and is solely responsible for the child-parent interactions. Influences are bi-directional, so that the child influences the parent as well (Bell & Harper, 1977; Lytton, 1990). The general purpose of Parenting programmes is to alter the pattern of interchanges between parent and child so that prposocial rather than coercive behaviour (deviant behaviour on the part of one person (e.g., the child) that is rewarded by another person (e.g., the parent) is directly reinforced and supported within the family. This requires several different parenting behaviours such as establishinbg rules for the child tpo follow, providing positive reinforcement for appropriate behaviour, negotiating compromises, and other procedures. The inept discipline practices and coercive exchanges have direct implications for intervention.

There have been a number of treatment approaches where the families of the antisocials are involved. A distinction is made between two main approaches involving families. The first approach involves family in the treatment of the individual, the primary objective being to change the behaviour of the individual. The second approach involves the treatment of the family and, disturbed behaviour is perceived as a result of the family system not functioning adequately. The objective of this approach is to change the family interaction. In the first approach, families may be asked to be involved in behavioural contracting which consists of explicitly stating in writing the responsibilities of the adolescent and the parents. The results of this approach reported success at times and return to antisocial behaviour after treatment at some other times. With the second approach, the objective is to change the family interaction, and the results seem to be encouraging. The likelihood of improvement will the depend upon the ability of the family to respond, rather than on the diagnosis of the individual.

Of the interventions that target parenting and family relationships, behavioural family interventions (BFI) based on social learning models have the strongest empirical support and warrant serious consideration for broader population-level application (Patterson, 1982). BFI are the most thoroughly evaluated interventions available to assist children with conduct problems (Breston & Eyberg, 1998; Lochman, 1990; McMahon, 2000; Sanders, 1996; Taylor & Biglan, 1998). Typically, parents are taught to increase positive interactions with children and to reduce coercive and inconsistent parenting practices. BFI produce positive changes in parental perceptions and parenting behaviours, which in turn are associated with changes in child behaviours (Barlow & Stewart-Brown, 2000; Webster-Stratton, & Taylor, 1998).

Many different parenting programmes have been used (Barlow, 1997; Kazdin, 1997), but the behavioural parental management training developed by Patterson (1992) in Oregon is one of the most promising approaches. His careful observations of parent-child interactions showed that parents of antisocial children were deficient in their methods of child rearing. These parents failed to tell their children how they were expected to behave, failed to monitor their behaviour to ensure that it was desirable, and failed to enforce rules promptly and unambiguously with appropriate rewards and penalties. The parents of antisocial children used more punishment (such as scolding, shouting, or threatening), but failed to make it contingent on the child's behaviour. Patterson attempted to train these parents in effective child rearing methods, namely noticing what a child is doing, monitoring behaviour over long periods, clearly stating house rules, making rewards and punishments contingent on behaviour, and negotiating disagreements so that conflicts and crises did not escalate. His treatment was shown to be effective in reducing child stealing and antisocial behaviour over short periods in small-scale studies (Dishion, Patterson, & Kavanagh, 1992; Patterson, Chamberlain, & Reid, 1982; Patterson, Reid, & Dishion, 1992).

Parent training was shown to reduce childhood antisocial behaviour in an experiment conducted in London and Chichester (Scott et al., 2001). About 140 mainly poor, disadvantaged children aged 3 to 8 referred for aggressive and antisocial behaviour were allocated to experimental (parent training) or control (waiting list) groups. The parent training programme, based on videotapes, was given for two hours a week over thirteen-sixteen weeks, covering praise and rewards, setting limits, and handling misbehaviour. Follow-up parent interviews and observations showed that the antisocial behaviour of the experimental children decreased significantly compared to that of controls. Furthermore, after the intervention, experimental parents gave their children far more praise to encourage desirable behaviour, and used more effective commands to obtain compliance.

It has been suggested that parent management training may only be helpful in reducing adolescent antisocial behaviour as an additional component within family therapy models or that parent training in combination with cognitive-behavioural therapy for the child may bring about better results than either treatment alone (Webster-Stratton, & Hummond, 1997). Parent training intervention appeared to be effective in improving the compliant behaviour of ADHD preschoolers but had no effect on the attention span of these children (Pisterman et al., 1992).

Since peer influences peak during early adolescence (Steinberg, 1996), the quality of the parent-child relationship can affect adolescents' susceptibility to antisocial peer pressure. Adolescents whose parents are authoritative—warm, firm, and demanding—are less influenced by negative peer pressure than adolescents whose parents are permissive and indulgent or whose parents are dictatorial and harsh (Collins et al., 2000).

Steinberg and Levine (1997) opine that it is never too late to alter or adapt one's style of parenting. The authors offer the following practical tips for becoming (or continuing to be) an authoritative parent:

Start with love and trust: Adolescents continue to need love and affection just as they did as young children. Spend time together as a family enjoying shared interests (watching TV side by side does not count). Talk about your teenager's interests, feelings, and concerns, and share your own feelings and concerns. Trust your child and treat him or her with respect.

Set clear, reasoned limits: Show respect for your teenager's point of view by discussing rules and regulations. Be clear about which family rules are negotiable and which are not. Balance control with independence and grant freedom in stages. Tie privileges to responsibilities.

Be firm and fair: Try not to overreact when your adolescent breaks a house rule. Listen to his or her side of the story before assuming blame. Express your displeasure and disappointment and use natural consequences in response to irresponsible behaviour when possible—for example, a poor grade as a consequence of inadequate studying. Take action when your adolescent's misbehaviour is repeated or dangerous. Make the penalty fit the crime—for example, refusal to follow car safety rules results in loss of car use privileges. Never use physical punishment or verbal abuse. Research has shown these responses to be counterproductive—they only serve to promote adolescent rebellion and aggression. Be consistent both in enforcing rules and in living by the values and beliefs you espouse.

Accept your adolescent as an individual: Treat your child as your child, not as a stereotypical adolescent. Parents may notice temporary disruptions as their adolescent adjusts to new situations such as a new school or dating, and puberty may contribute to periodic moodiness. These events do not result in personality changes, however. Remember that most of an adolescent's choices are not lifelong commitments. Assuming 'mistakes' are not dangerous or irreversible, let your adolescent learn about life through mistakes on occasion.

Let your child be the teenager he or she wants to be, not the adolescent you were or wish you had been, nor a replica of an older sibling: Adolescents need to be loved for themselves, not for measuring up to an arbitrary standard of worth based on your unfulfilled dreams or the achievements of another sibling.

Parents must be vigilant to protect their children from the potential threats to children's emotional and physical health-threats that seem increasingly complex in our modern culture. Parents should not, however, be distracted from the day-to-day business of parenting, of developing a strong family, and of building healthy relationships with their children. Building relationships based on love, trust, and acceptance combined with firmness, consistency, and high, yet reasonable, levels of expectations is a violence prevention strategy that parents can influence.

Although Parenting Programmes have been effective with adolescents (Bank et al., 1991), evidence suggests that trearment is more effective with younger children (Dishion & Patterson, 1992). Parents of adolescents may less readily change their discipline practices; they may also have higher rates of dropping out of treatment. The influence of parents diminishes as the child enters adolescence. This has been suggested by a number of researchers who highlight the role of peer group as a dominant influence once adolescence has been reached (Allen & Land, 1999). On balance, parenting programmes form one of the most promising treatment modalities suggested by many researchers. A few parenting programmes have been developed specifically for adolescents. No other intervention for antisocial behaviour has been as thoroughly investigated as parenting programmes.

III. PEER PROGRAMMES

There are no outstanding examples of effective intervention programmes for antisocial behaviour on peer risk factors. The most hopeful programmes involve using high-status conventional peers to teach children ways of desisting peer pressure; this has been effective in reducing drug abuse (Tobler et al., 2000).

Feldman, Caplinger and Wodarski (1983) showed that placing antisocial adolescents in activity groups dominated by prosocial adolescents led to their reduction in antisocial behaviour.

The most important interventional programme whose success seems to be based mainly on reducing peer risk factors is the Children at Risk programme (Harrell et al., 1997), which targeted high risk youths (average age 12.4) in poor neighbourhoods of five cities across the United States. Eligible youths were identified in schools, and randomly assigned to experimental or control groups. The programme was a comprehensive community-based prevention strategy targeting risk factors for delinquency, including case management and family counselling, family skills training, tutoring, mentoring, after-school activities and community policing. The programme was different in each neighbourhood. The initial results of the programme were disappointing, but a one-year follow-up showed that (according to self-reports) experimental youths were less likely to have committed violent crimes and used or sold drugs (Harrell, Cavanagh, & Sridharan, 1999). The process evaluation showed that the greatest change was in peer risk factors. Experimental youths associated less often with delinquent peers, felt less peer pressure to engage in delinquency, and had more positive peer support.

In contrast, there were few changes in the individual, family or community risk factors, possibly linked to the low participation of parents in parent training and of youths in mentoring and tutoring (Harrell et al. 1997). In other words, there were problems of implementation of the programme, linked to the serious and multiple needs and problems of the families.

A longitudinal investigation was conducted (Ladd & Wendy, 2003) to explicate how the confluence of early behavioural dispositions, relational histories, and cognitive representations of the self and others contributes to internalizing problems, externalizing problems, and loneliness. One-hundred and ninety three girls, and 206 boys were assessed annually from age 5 (kindergarten) to age 10 (Grade 4). Early aggressive behaviour was related to Grade 4 maladjustment directly and indirectly through subsequent relational stressors. Significant associations emerged between chronic friendlessness and rejection and later adaptation not accounted for by concurrent relational difficulties. Self- and peer beliefs partially mediated the relation between peer difficulties and internalizing problems and loneliness. The results highlight the utility of child-by-environment models as a guide for the investigation of processes that antecede psychosocial maladjustment. School personnel using peer mediation report an improvement in behaviours, in listening skills among students, and in school climate (Lane & McWhirter, 1992).

IV. SCHOOL PROGRAMMES

Instead of asking, 'Who can I blame?' we need to be asking, 'What can I do?' To help prevent or remediate punitive school climates, an emphasis must be placed on positive, preventive interventions using functional assessments. School and classroom rules and policies need to be clear, with a positive focus. Support must be provided for staff, and allowances made for individual student differences in terms of provided consequences, social skills training, and the selection of academic materials and instructional methodology.

Academic programmes that show the most promise of preventing antisocial behaviours are those that adjust to the student's functional level, programme frequent success, and assume the responsibility for teaching without relying on out-of-school resources. Some programmes, such as the Morningside Model (Johnson & Layng, 1994), not only use well designed and sequenced instructional material matched to students' performance levels, but also build skills to fluency by using peer coaching and testing to provide multiple opportunities for fluency practice, recognition of progress, and correction of errors within the school. Such an approach maximizes success and recognizes that the home environment for antisocial youth often tends not to be very supportive (i.e., these students are not likely to receive home tutoring, nor assistance or encouragement with homework).

Students also need to become more skilled in self-management and aware of the individual factors that contribute to their antisocial behaviour. Psychologists can teach them to monitor their own behaviour, to recognize its communicative purpose and the possible chain of events that leads to the escalation of their antisocial behaviour (Watson & Tharp, 1993). They also can be taught more adaptive ways of achieving the function served by the antisocial behaviour.

Until contextual factors such as these are addressed early in the lives of our students, we will continue only temporarily to suppress violence and related behaviour problems. Quick fixes that rely on security and punitive measures appear to aggravate, not reduce, antisocial behaviour over time. Security arrangements and punitive measures, when necessary, must be viewed as temporary expedients to help gain control in the situation while contextual factors are addressed.

Punitive measures are not the solution. We will not be able to durably prevent violence and other antisocial behaviour until we address the identified contextual factors. Psychologists, because of their related training, are ideally suited to take a leadership role in helping other educators to remediate the contextual factors causing antisocial behaviour and school dropouts. We cannot afford to fail a large percentage of our human resources by continuing to place the emphasis in discipline on security arrangements, punishment, and incarceration.

School bullying is a risk-factor for offending (Farrington, 1993). Several school-based programmes have been effective in reducing bullying. The most famous of these programmes was implemented by Olweus (1994). The programme involved 42 schools that received feedback information from the questionnaire, about the prevalence of bullies and victims, in a specially arranged school conference day. Also, teachers were encouraged to develop explicit rules about bullying (e.g., do not bully, tell someone when bullying happens, bullying will not be tolerated, try to help victims, try to include children who are being left out) and to discuss bullying in class, using the video and role-playing exercises. Also, actions were taken to improve monitoring and supervision of children, especially in the playground. The programme was successful in reducing the prevalence of bullying by half.

A similar programme was implemented in 23 Sheffield schools by Smith and Sharp (1994). The core programme involved establishing a 'whole school' anti-bullying policy, raising awareness of bullying and clearly defining roles and responsibilities of teachers and students, so that everyone know what bullying was and what they should do about it. In addition, there were optional interventions tailored to particular schools (e.g., reading books, watching videos), direct work with students (e.g. assertiveness training for those who were bullied) and playground work (e.g. training lunchtime supervisors). This programme was successful in reducing bullying (by 15 per cent) in primary schools but had a relatively small effect (a 5 per cent reduction) in secondary schools. The effects of these anti-bullying programmes on later antisocial behaviour need to be investigated.

Until recently, schools have typically responded to antisocial behaviour with the traditional punitive methods: school suspensions, expulsions, referrals to Principal and detention. These methods are never adequate. They do not produce long-term change because they do not address the roots of the problem. In fact, research has shown that punishment based interventions with these youth result in an increase in antisocial and violent activities (Mayer & Sulzer-Azaroff, 1990).

Walker and his colleagues (1996) have devised a model for prevention of antisocial behaviour in the school involving primary, secondary and tertiary strategies. According to them,

Primary prevention is 'much like putting fluoride in a community's water supply in order to prevent dental cavities'. It involves Violence Prevention Skills Training, Effective Academic Instruction and School-wide Behaviour Expectations. Secondary Prevention is like 'increasing one's scheduled visits to the dentist because of orthodontic susceptibility (e.g., soft or thin enamel) for dental cavities or initiating an orthodontic intervention because of teeth overcrowding'. Examples of secondary prevention include individual counselling, provision of adult mentors, behaviour management programmes, and additional supports and services. Tertiary prevention is for students with life-course persistent antisocial behaviour. In our dental analogy, 'individuals at this level would be candidates for significant cavity repairs, root canals, bridges, and other expensive forms of dental care'. Interventions at the tertiary level must be comprehensive, involving parents, teachers and peers, apart from school counsellors. The school should establish a programme of peer and teacher mentors who take an active interest in the antisocial, at-risk student's school success.

Interaction Skills of the Staff

In order to effectively implement a programme for high-risk adolescents, staff need the following critical interaction skills:

1. *Relationship-building components*— The ability to develop warm, caring relationships with youth-relationships that emphasize a partnership in the youth's treatment, rather than relationships built on power and the exercise of authority;
2. *Praise and differential reinforcement*—The ability to recognize appropriate youth behaviours when they occur and to offer immediate verbal reinforcement (praise) of them;
3. *Behavioural specificity*— The ability to specifically observe, describe and target behaviours that the youth demonstrates;
4. *Meaningful rationales*— The ability to provide youth with personalized, meaningful reasons for the

behaviour changes requested of them. For example, telling a youth, 'Following directions right away is important for keeping a job and earning money' rather than saying, 'Do it because I say so';

5. *Effective consequences*— The ability to develop an effective system of consequences that will, over time, motivate high-risk youth to decrease the use of antisocial behaviour and increase the use of prosocial skills;
6. *Role-play and rehearsal*— The ability to find or create opportunities for youth to practice the new prosocial skills that they are being taught;
7. *Non-aversive crisis intervention*— The ability to respond appropriate to youth who are defiant or have lost self-control. Responding appropriately means maintaining a calm, positive manner even when the youth is verbally abusive and to praise any approximations of appropriate behaviour that might occur (Tierney et al., 1993).

An Intervention Strategy to Address Antisocial Behaviour in the Schools

There are multiple determinants of antisocial behaviour, and the school appears to be a major contributor. In addition, similar factors to those identified in the school have been identified in the home: a coercive and punitive environment, and inconsistencies in setting rules and applying consequences. Three major factors within schools were identified that appear to promote a context in which punishment conditions are likely to occur: lack of clarity of both rules and policies; weak or inconsistent staff support; and, few or no allowances made for individual differences. The resultant specific occurrences of punishment and extinction (e.g.., disapproving comments, academic task errors, and a lack of recognition for either student or staff effort) appear to evoke aggression, attendance problems (escape) and other antisocial behaviours.

Contextual factors have not been given sufficient emphasis in research or practice. Because of their remoteness in time to antisocial acts, contextual factors can be hard to identify or associate with antisocial behaviour. Many decision makers therefore find themselves unable to support a given programme of prevention because it does not make sense to them. Thus, care should be taken by school psychologists to educate school staff and parents as to the relevance of contextual factors.

A major strategy for creating safe, constructive school environments would be to address the contextual factors within our schools that promote antisocial behaviour. This approach implies that our efforts should no longer emphasize 'treating' students as the source of the problem. Rather, our focus must be on identifying and correcting the factors that promote antisocial behaviour. To assist in the identification of the specific factors, the School Discipline Survey (Mayer & Sulzer-Azaroff, 1991; Mayer, et al., 1987) can be administered to teachers. It is designed to measure how punitive the total school climate is, particularly the discipline environment.

To address these contextual factors the Constructive Discipline approach was developed. A brief description of this approach is provided to illustrate how psychologists might use Constructive Discipline to address such contextual factors within the school. These contextual factors are grouped under three main categories: Clarity, support, and individual differences.

A 'behavioural vaccine' provides an inoculation against morbidity or mortality, impacting physical, mental, or behaviour disorders. An historical example of a behavioural vaccine is antiseptic hand washing to reduce childbed fever. In current society, issues with high levels of morbidity, such as substance abuse, delinquency, youth violence, and behavioural disorders (multi-problems), cry out for a low-cost, widespread strategy as simple as antiseptic hand washing.' The behavioural vaccine offered in this case is a behavioural strategy that can be developed at schools called the Good Behaviour Game (Embry, 2002).

Every mother knows the feeling. As she struggles to complete the washing/dinner/cleaning, a small child is clamouring for attention. Here the tantrum of a young child is raised as a problem. However, 'problems' such as these are not simply looked at in their own terms but are either explicitly or implicitly understood as part of a host of wider social problems that are collated under the banner of ASB.

Establish Clear-Cut Rules and Policies of School (Clarity)

As illustrated by Mayer (1995), unclear rules of school result in more misbehaviour and rule violations. These violations prompt teacher punishment which in turn results in an increase in student antisocial behaviour.

UNCLEAR RULES → STUDENT RULE BREAKING → PUNISHMENT → ANTISOCIAL BEHAVIOUR

To address clarity, school-wide rules can be developed jointly by the administration and staff with both student and parent input. Similarly, classroom rules are jointly established by the teacher and students, integrated with school-wide rules, posted in the class where all can view them easily, and reviewed by the teacher and class periodically. Students receive reinforcement for adhering to the rules, because rules will only be followed when differential consequences are applied for compliance and non-compliance (Mayer & Sulzer-Azaroff, 1991). Rules also need to be stated positively to stress how to behave, rather than how not to behave (e.g., 'Be in your seat by the time the tardy bell rings,' rather than 'Don't be late'), and the list kept short to promote recall, usually not more than 5-7 rules.

Provide Support for Staff

Absent or inconsistent support for staff promotes an aversive environment, with staff tending to respond with higher rates of absenteeism, a greater reliance on punitive methods of classroom control, and inconsistent follow-through or support of the school discipline policy (Manlove & Elliott, 1979; Mayer, 1995). This results in more student misbehaviour that evokes more punishment from the teacher. The outcome: an increase in antisocial student behaviour.

LOW SUPPORT FOR STAFF → STAFF RESPONDS INCONSISTENTLY, GIVES AVERSIVES AND/OR ESCAPES → STUDENT MISBEHAVIOUR → PUNISHMENT → ANTISOCIAL BEHAVIOUR

To address this aversive environment that has been created for staff, and subsequently for students, support must be developed for staff. To develop support, Constructive Discipline uses programmes designed to improve staff morale, communication and cohesiveness. Many of these programmes—such as 'secret pals' for staff members, 'extra thanks board,' and 'hot messages' to teachers—have been illustrated (Mayer, et al., 1983c, Sulzer-Azaroff & Mayer, 1991; 1994). Briefly, their purpose is to decrease the aversives and increase the reinforcement for teachers and administrators. For example, administrators, psychologists, and other support staff are asked to positively comment on the constructive programmes that teachers are implementing in their classes. Similarly, other teachers and parents can be encouraged to make positive comments and demonstrate their appreciation for what others in the school do to assist students and one another. For example, teachers can be encouraged to write one another positive notes on a 'Fuzzy Gram' or 'Thank-U-Board' located in the faculty lounge. Individual staff might also be assigned 'secret pals' to whom they are responsible for writing positive notes. A principal or counsellor may send 'hot messages' to teachers congratulating them for the successful programmes implemented in their classroom. Of course, it is important to note that these affirmations must be in response to real programmes and efforts, not gratuitous or mindless thank-you's. Part of the rationale for implementing such activities is to help the school environment become more positively reinforcing and to serve as a prompt for implementing Constructive Discipline programmes.

Provide for Individual Differences

When individual student differences are not taken into sufficient account, student misbehaviour, teacher punishment, and antisocial behaviour all increase (Mayer, 1995).

LACK OF ALLOWANCE FOR INDIVIDUAL DIFFERENCES → STUDENT MISBEHAVIOUR → PUNISHMENT → ANTISOCIAL BEHAVIOUR

To address individual differences, students' existing performance levels are matched with appropriate academic materials and instructional methodology to minimize failure and maximize learning. Frequent success is programmed into the academic experiences by interspersing tasks that have a high probability of resulting in success for the student (Munk & Repp, 1994). Staff are taught how to select and apply various behavioural strategies (Mayer, et. al., 1983a; Mayer, et al., 1983b), such as: (a) increasing rates of teacher delivered praise and other forms of positive recognition for constructive classroom behaviour; (b) identifying and maximizing reinforcers; (c) emphasizing differential reinforcement strategies, modelling, and social skills training over the use of aversives; and, (d) using various group contingencies. Some youngsters also might be helped to discriminate among their peers' prosocial and antisocial behaviours. Most importantly, though, educational programmes must address individual differences in students' academic and social skills, rather than respond with punishment when a student lacks critical academic or social skills.

Individual differences also are addressed by using functional assessments (Mayer, 1996). Functional assessments are used to determine what might be causing or contributing to the individual's behaviour. Treatment approaches based on behavioural function can result in major reductions in (a) the misuse of behaviour procedures, and (b) the use of punishment by educators, which in turn can provide a more reinforcing environment conducive to learning.

For dealing with low school involvement and integration, a concerted effort must be made to provide, and involve these youngsters in, after school activities. In addition, peer tutoring has been shown to be helpful for promoting both involvement and integration (Carta, Greenwood, Dinwiddie, Kohler, & Delquadri, 1987; Maheady & Sainato, 1985; Polirstok & Greer,

1986). Many of the strategies are described in detail by Sulzer-Azaroff and Mayer (1991; 1994). These have been presented to school personnel through a series of workshops with follow-up consultation and support by both project and school personnel for programme implementation (Mayer et al., 1983b; 1983c).

Some guidelines to negate thinking errors are:

1. Give the student reading (if they have adequate reading skills) to educate them about self-defeating thinking and how it can be changed;
2. Help the child develop empathic abilities, using techniques like role-reversal;
3. Help the child develop a task-orientated attitude to dealing with problems-that is, changing circumstances (where possible) rather than upsetting themselves;
4. Assist the child to increase their motivation to change by listing and weighting the advantages and disadvantages of their anger.

Constructive Discipline, then, is an approach that addresses contextual factors within the school environment that promote antisocial behaviour, rather than 'treating' students as though they are the source of the problem. It focuses on how to behave rather than on how not to behave. It builds repertoires by teaching appropriate, effective ways to behave through a supportive, reinforcing environment for both students and staff, an environment that recognizes individual differences.

Future studies in this area could examine what types of support teachers would find helpful in dealing with students with emotional and behavioural disturbances and how we can effectively assist them as the struggle to be accommodated within regular school programmes. Similarly, a trial of a collaborative intervention programme similar to those described within the literature could be carried out, with quantitative measures of change within a classroom situation as a determinant of success. Case studies following the progress of individual children could also provide valuable reference and data as teachers work to overcome the difficulties expressed in this study.

R.E. Kefford (1997) states that there is a need for us to conceive of schools as families as we enter the new millennium. He outlines ways in which a school can adopt such a model within the aspects of the teaching learning process, in pastoral care, in leadership and in community involvement. Schools conceived of as a family emphasises patterns of collaborative learning which are non-competitive and goal oriented. Order and discipline remain important dimensions of the school's activity, recognising that the exercise of consistent control limits the child's behaviour and gradually allows the exercise of independence within socially accepted guidelines. The changing patterns of family relationships mean that many children miss out on a traditional family subculture, and on learning norms and values that are essential to a just and humane society. The difficulty society is encountering today in raising strong children stems from the deterioration of family life, drug abuse, materialism and what Kefford terms, spiritual emptiness. If schools can conceive of themselves as families, they have some chance of providing what children need to become healthy, empathetic and productive adults. We live in a time that conspires to disconnect us from one another, from institutions and from ideals, so that the individual family is precariously alone. Schools can provide a means by which we can affiliate with one another, to enter into mutual relationships, and to take strength and grow through cooperative endeavour and thus cope with some of the problems that children experience.

V. COMMUNITY-BASED OR NEIGHBOURHOOD TRAINING PROGRAMMES

Programmes need to be offered in communities to reduce isolation, to strengthen social support networks and improve community collaboration. Attempts are needed to protect the autonomy and rights of both children and families, and the need to involve the families and communities in the decision-making structure.

Community-based interventions use existing facilities in the community (e.g., recreational centres, parks) or bring intervention to youth in the contexts of their every day lives.

These interventions take advantage of the resources in the every day environment that can support prosocial behaviour. Thus, community-based programmes are often conducted in local recreational or youth centrtes in which activity programmes are already underway. Integration of programmes in the community also helps to promote the carry over of pro-social behaviour to every day situations because the intervention is conducted in these situations rather than in special and more restricted settings (e.g., psychiatric hospitals, juvenile correctional facilities).

There is no single intervention that will ensure all young children avoid developing serious behaviour problems. There is good evidence that effective strategies provide comprehensive and multiple component intervention programmes that focus on a range of risk and protective factors. Multiple diverse outcomes may be addressed in a single programme. A mix of interventions is needed to address a range of risk factors and developmental stresses of families and children. pecific risk and protective factors need to be addressed. The impact of programmes is akened if general strategies are used rather than specific attention to particular risks and protective factors.

As parents and people within the schools and community agencies work within a network, the strategies of anger control, assertiveness training, problem-solving practice, and conflict mediation can be taught to our children. Safer schools and a safer society will be the result of our efforts (Studer, 1996). While the individual must be held responsible for his or her behaviour, membership of the major social institutions and participation in the major arenas of community life, are a group responsibility.

The three protective processes that lead to bonding are: opportunities or active involvement in the group,the skills that permit successful involvement recognition, and reinforcement for skillful performance.

Opportunities for Involvement

Young people want to be involved. They want to participate in a group. Without the opportunity for meaningful, active involvement in group endeavours, young people become disaffected and alienated, and all too often drift away. But given the opportunity to become involved and to make a contribution, they become invested in achieving the group's goals and furthering its success.

In school, children can work in small learning groups to master the material together. They can participate in group projects and take part in school activities. At home, children can play a role in managing family life: doing chores, helping to plan vacations, having input into decisions about family goals and finances. And in the community at large, children and young people can make valuable contributions to a variety of causes and events.

Skills that Permit Successful Involvement

It's not enough to create opportunities for young people to become involved, however. Opportunity without skill leads to frustration and failure. The second protective factor that needs to be present is the development of appropriate skills.

Researchers know what skills must be cultivated throughout a child's life to ensure healthy development into adulthood—from the early stages of social and interpersonal skills development to the mastery of cognitive skills in problem solving, decision making, refusal skills... and including specific functional skills such as reading, writing, math, and artistic or athletic competence.

Individual characteristics and abilities will certainly determine what skills are mastered and to what degree—but it's also true that schools, communities, and families can take concrete steps to foster a child's competence. The benefit to the group is significant. The more skills a young person is able to acquire, the more he or she will be able to take advantage of opportunities to participate and succeed.

Recognition and Reinforcement for Skillful Performance

Everyone likes to be recognized for their achievements. Young people are no different. Yet all too often, adults focus on their children's shortcomings and setbacks, and fail to adequately acknowledge their efforts, improvements, and successes.

Positive reinforcement is the critical third element that creates the bond between young people and their communities. It says to a child, 'We see you. We value your contribution. We are proud to have you as a member of our family, our community.' Recognition tells young people that there is value in acquiring skills and becoming involved—in short, it's the psychological and emotional payoff for their commitment to positive attitudes and behaviours.

Opportunities provide a chance to develop skills and gain group recognition. Mastery of skills leads to recognition and more opportunities for involvement. Positive reinforcement cements the bond between young people and the group, and encourages further involvement and skill development.

Opportunities without skills leads to frustration and feelings of incompetence. Skills without opportunities leads to boredom and disaffection, and prevents recognition. Lack of reinforcement discourages further involvement, devalues skills, and weakens bonding between young people and the group.

OPPORTUNITIES, SKILLS, AND RECOGNITION → ATTACHMENT AND COMMITMENT → BONDING: STRIKING THE RIGHT BALANCE

The Social Development Strategy begins with the goal of achieving healthy behaviours among young people—people who reach adolescence with the skills, attitudes, and behaviours necessary to function as positive, successful members of their community... and who are free from the destructive influences of substance abuse, delinquency, school dropout, teen pregnancy, and violence. Human beings are hard-wired for group involvement, and interaction. It doesn't matter whether that group is the school drama club or the local gang—young people will affiliate with and adopt the standards of the group that offers the strongest incentives and the greatest psychic rewards. It's called bonding—and it's a vital element in healthy development.

NEED FOR A COMPREHENSIVE INTERVENTION PROGRAMME

Until recently, schools have typically responded to antisocial behaviour with the traditional punitive methods: school suspensions, referrals to Principals and detentions. These methods are very inadequate. They do not produce long-term change because they do not address the roots of the problem. In fact, research has shown that punishment based interventions with these youth result in an increase of antisocial and violent behaviour (Mayer & Sulzer-Azaroff, 1990). These methods may make schools safer at the expense of other communities, but these out of school youth are increasingly found on the streets engaging in socially inappropriate destructive behaviours (Bostic, 1994).

Threats, bullying, and classroom disruptions—are common. Thus, early responses to warning signs are most effective in preventing problems from escalating (Walker, Colvin, & Ramsey, 1995). Intervention programmes that reduce behaviour problems and related school violence typically need to be multifaceted, long-term, and broad reaching (Kazdin, 1991). They must also be rigorously implemented. Effective early intervention efforts include working with small groups or individual students to provide direct support, as well as linking children and their families to necessary community services and/or providing these services in the school (Kazdin, 1993; Reid, 1993).

It is generally true that a combination of interventions is more effective than a single technique (Wasserman & Miller, 1998), although combining interventions makes it harder to identify which was the 'active ingredient'. A group of scientists (Klassen et al., 1999) studied some of the current strategies for managing ADHD and searched for What Works Best for ADHD Children. Some of the current strategies used are: Medicating the child to reduce the frequency and intensity of problematic behaviours and to allow the child to achieve better self control and better regulation of attention to tasks, Educating the parents and teachers about the nature of ADHD, thereby allowing them to have realistic expectations of the child, providing simple strategies to modify the child's environment to reduce behaviour problems, and training them to acquire effective behaviour-management skills and using psychological therapy to teach the child self- control and self-monitoring skills. Three treatment strategies for ADHD were examined to determine their relative effectiveness. Diagnoses of ADHD were based on parents' and teachers' completed questionnaires on the child's behaviour (the Hyperactivity Index of Conners' Teacher Rating Scale and Conners' Parent Rating Scale are two widely used measures). The three treatment conditions were tested against either a no treatment condition or a placebo condition. In the majority of the studies (22 of 26), children were randomly assigned to these conditions. The results brought forth by this study are that Medication—only therapy was effective in reducing ADHD. Behavioural therapies used alone appeared not to be effective. Combination therapy was more effective than placebo or no treatment (for parent but not for teacher ratings), not more effective than drug therapy alone and more effective than behavioural treatments alone (based on parent but not teacher ratings).

Comprehensive Intervention Programme is a family and home-based approach that has been viewed as a highly promising treatment for antisocial youth. This approach is based on the concept that, as many factors contribute to the development of antisocial factors, any approach which is to produce good results has to provide interventions aimed at all systems which may contribute to the development of antisocial behaviour. CIS provides interventions aimed at the antisocial as well as their family, peers and school. As different adolescents and students have different needs and involvements, the interventions are individualised and flexible. As the main thrust of the approach is to effect a change in the family, the cooperation of the family is vital to success. To encourage cooperation by the family, the sessions can be held in the home at a time convenient to the family. The goal of the family intervention is to preserve and empower the family. It provides skills and resources to the parents so that they can address the problems of their difficult adolescents. Sessions are also held at community locations (schools, recreation centres).

ELEMENTS OF A COMPREHENSIVE INTERVENTION PROGRAMME

A relatively strong consensus is emerging among experts that a successful, comprehensive intervention programme for antisocial behaviour (Loraine Thompson, 1994) should contain the following elements:

1. Schools should take the lead in setting up and coordinating a home, school, and community agency intervention programme;
2. The school should monitor student behaviour carefully so that it can begin the intervention process as soon as a student's antisocial behaviour indicators merge;
3. A brief parent training programme should focus on five basic parenting practices:
   - How to closely monitor a child's whereabouts, activities, and friends;
   - How to participate actively in a child's life;
   - How to use such positive techniques as encouragement, Praise, and approval to manage a child's home behaviour;
   - How to ensure that discipline is fair, timely, and appropriate to the Offence; and
   - How to use effective conflict-resolution and problem-solving strategies.

The programme should assist parents in setting up reward systems—in the home that provide incentives for the child to achieve academic success and to behave appropriately at school, and it also should help parents to encourage their child to develop a positive attitude toward school.

A tracking-monitoring system for school and home should provide daily, two-way communication about the student's performance at school and parental acknowledgement of that performance.

The school programme should teach the personal, academic, and social skills that the at-risk student needs for school success. This instructional programme should be accompanied by unobtrusive but sensitive school monitoring systems that measure progress.

EFFECTIVENESS OF COMPREHENSIVE INTERVENTION PROGRAMMES

This approach focuses on the many systems which may affect the child (i.e. school, peers, neighbourhood) but the primary focus is on the family. It uses a variety of techniques such as joining, reframing, and enactments. The main goal of this approach is to build cohesion and emotional warmth among family members. Multisystemic therapy uses other approaches such as problem solving, skills training, parent management training, and marital therapy (if and when needed). This therapy is effective with delinquent youth in reducing the rate of recidivism.

Treatment is determined based on many factors, including the child's age, the severity of symptoms, and the child's ability to participate in and tolerate specific therapies. Treatment usually consists of a combination of counselling aimed at helping the child develop more effective ways to express and control anger and cognitive-behavioural therapy to reshape the child's thinking (cognition) to improve behaviour. Family therapy may be used to help to improve family interactions and communication among family members, parent management training (PMT) teaches parents ways to positively alter their child's behaviour. While there is no medication formally approved to treat ODD, various medications may be used to treat some of its distressing symptoms, as well as any other mental illnesses that may be present, such as ADHD or depression.

If positive results are to endure, evidence suggests that treatment should affect the total environment of the antisocial, including the family, school, and the peers. A combination of interventions may be more effective than a single method. For example, in Montreal about 250 disruptive (aggressive/

hyperactive) boys were identified at age 6 for a prevention experiment (Tremblay et al., 1995). The experimental group received training to foster social skills and self-control. Coaching, peer modelling, role playing and reinforcement contingencies were used in small group sessions on such topics as 'how to help', 'what to do when you are angry' and 'how to react to teasing'. Also their parents received training using the parent management training techniques developed by Patterson (1982). This prevention programme was quite successful. At every age from 10 to 15, the experimental boys had lower self-reported delinquency scores than the control boys (Tremblay et al., 1996). Interestingly, the differences in antisocial behaviour between experimental and control boys increased as the follow-up progressed.

Medication (Pharmacological approach), and working with the family, teachers and with the child (Psychological approaches) help in treating ADHD children. Carlson and his colleagues (1992) examined the effects of methylphenidate, behaviour therapy, and a combination of the two treatments on the classroom performance of children with ADHD. The participants for this study were 24 boys, aged 6-12 years, who participated in an eight-week summer treatment programme for children with ADHD. The results indicated that although both treatments improved classroom behaviour, the effect of the two treatments combined was superior to that of individual treatments observed that children with ADHD are best helped with a combination of social skills training (for themselves and their parents) and stimulant medication.

Methylphenidate (Ritalin) plays an integral role in the treatment of ADHD. Pelham, Wheeler, and Chronis (1998). In their critical review of treatments for ADHD children conclude that medications such as Ritalin (methylphenidate) have significant benefits in many areas, including classroom performance, have not proven effective in improving long term academic achievement' do not make these children any more liked by their peers and have not proven to improve long term prognosis. Results of this study indicate that training parents in behavioural methods (rewarding good behaviour and ignoring or punishing difficult behaviour) seems to produce good results. Behavioural interventions in classroom settings have proven effective. Cognitive behaviour therapies do not lead to positive results in the behaviour or in the academic performance of children with ADHD.

IMPACT OF INTERVENTIONS: RESPONSE TO TREATMENT

Antisocial behaviour is caused by many factors. Various systems such as the family, peers and the school affect the child's life. Therefore, strategies designed to overcome antisocial behaviour will not be effective unless they have an impact on these systems.

However, the long-term impact of prevention interventions is not well studied. Relatively few studies focus directly on antisocial behaviour as an outcome. Little is known about the critical components that produce change. Little is known about the optimal time to intervene. The response to treatment is poor if the age of onset of behaviour is early, if the child has more than one disorder, if the child is from a poor family, if the child is from a single-parent family and if parents have had a history of antisocial behaviour in their childhood.

If treatments are given in groups, at times, there is every chance for the antisocials to learn more tricks of the trade from other antisocials. By separating them from the family, school, neighbourhood and community contexts, they are deprived of the normative developmental experiences which help them to adapt to these contexts (Kazdin, 1997b).

Preventive programmes do reduce the onset of antisocial behaviour (McCord & Tremblay, 1992; Yoshikawa, 1994; Zigler et al., 1992). The outcomes have included reductions in aggression towards peers, parents and siblings, truancy, cruelty, school suspensions and expulsions, substance abuse, and delinquency. The strategies used should be individualised and need-specific.

In the words of Kazdin (1995), "we know that early intervention with families (e.g., prenatal care, parenting instruction, and direct assistance) can have marked impact when it is continued for a few years (e.g., into the early preschool years of the child's life or longer); focussed on multiple domains and risk factors (e.g., nutrition, parent-child interaction, cognitive development of the child); done in different settings (e.g., at home, and school); and done among high-risk samples (e.g., socioeconomically disadvantaged)"

MAINTAINING IMPROVEMENT

Many antisocial youth show improvement during implementation of intervention strategies. However, once the intervention is stopped, and the youth is back to school, antisocial behaviour returns, Therefore studies determining the effectiveness of interventions without follow-up report much higher success rate than studies with long-term follow up (Basta & Davidson, 1988)

Those youth who have taken to chronic antisocial behaviour tend to return to antisocial behaviour after a lapse of time. Therefore, those involved in implementing the comprehensive intervention strategy should continue to keep in touch with the family even after the active phase of intervention is over. If necessary, the youth may once again be put in active treatment group rather than follow-up.

Until society is willing to adequately support schools in this effort, educators will continue to be challenged by barriers that make successful outcomes for antisocial students less likely. Policies, standards and processes that enable practitioners to make informed decisions about the adoption of practices that are trustworthy, accessible, and useable need to be established. Behavioural support systems that are proactive, instructional, sustained and comprehensive must be implemented. A team based approach for development, implementation, management, and evaluation of a school wide response to enhancing the whole school climate is also possible with such a model. Problems must be addressed and solutions developed on a school-wide perspective, establishing long term plans with commitment from people from all walks of life to work towards comprehensive solutions to individual's behaviour. Policies, structures, opportunities and contingencies must be in place for positive outcomes for students in the contexts that define their difficulties. Success has the potential to impact on all society.

SUMMARY

In this chapter, the authors have highlighted use of appropriate prevention and intervention strategies to overcome antisocial behaviour in students. The need for early intervention calls for co-ordinated efforts by school personnel and parents in order to develop need-based, situation-oriented strategies to identify and modify antisocial behaviour in students. What is needed is a supportive and consistent home environment and a concerned society.

'Prevention is better than cure'. It is cost-effective to prevent the occurrence of of antisocial behaviour rather than to treat it after escalation. Prevention strategies can be primary (skills training, anger manangement training, etc), secondary (individual counselling, behavioural management programmes, etc.) or tertiary (interpersonal problem solving skills taught at schools).

Once firmly established, interventions for antisocial behaviour have to be properly implemented. Child focussed programmes such cognitive behaviour modification help in generating alternate solutions to interpersonal problems. Self-instruction, self-monitoring and problem-solving skills help the antisocial to check his behaviour patterns. Development of right thinking patterns involves stressing relevance, making predictions and stressing consistency in student behaviours. Rational emotive therapy checks irrational thought processes. Moral reasoning helps to eliminate self-centredness through role-taking and self-control. Anger management training uses self-assessment techniques such as yoga and meditation that lead to right perception and subjective well-being of the individual. Participation in recreational and extra curricular activities help in self-identity, relection of one's own performance, planning and execution of prosocial acts, etc. Alternative solution thinking, means-end thinking, causal thinking and sensitivity to interpersonal problems help in decreasing aggressive feelings in the young. In conflict mediation, critical thinking and self-discipline are given due importance. Social skills such as right feedback, resisting negative peer pressure and initiation of friendly conversatioon are taught through modelling and practice. Thus, cognitive and metacognitive aspects are given due importance. Medication may prove to be useful with ADHD in combination with other therapies. Counselling and continuum of care require working with the antisocials for a fairly longer duration of period.

Parenting programmes include setting clear limits and accepting the child as an individual. Peer mediation leads to better skills among the antisocials and improves school climate. The school staff should have the interaction skills that will help them to modify the behavioural aspects of the antisocial students. The community or the neighbourhood must work to provide comprehensive and multiple intervention strategies that focus on a range of risk or protective factors. Opportunities for active involvement in group activities, development of skills that permit successful involvement and recognition and reinforcement for skilful performance are the three forces that lead to bonding in community.

In most cases, a combination of interventions works better than any single one. Comprehensive Intervention is situation-based, need-based and individualistic involving the schools, the parents, the peers and the individual himself. The response to treatment is dependent on the age of onset and co-occurence of more than one disorder in the individual, family involvement in the treatment and parental psychopathology. It is necessary that proper follow-up is done to ensure eradication of antisocial behaviour in students.

This book has focussed on antisocial behaviour among children and adolescents. The range of factors that influence the emergence of antisocial behaviour is broad. The breadth raised not only suggests the complexity of the problem but also points to possible areas of intervention to produce change.

REFERENCES

Alberti, R. E. (Speaker). (1986). *Making Yourself Heard: A Guide to Assertive Relationships* (Cassette Recording No. 29532 29533) New York: BMA Audio Cassettes.

Alexander, C.N., J.L. Davies et al. (1990). *Higher Stages of Human Development: Perspectives on Adult Growth*, (Eds.), C.N. Alexander and E.J. Langer. New York: Oxford University Press.

Allen, J.P., & Land, D. (1999). Attachment in Adolescence. In J. Cassidy & P.P. Shaver (Eds). *Handbook of Attachment: Theory, Research and Clinical Applications*, 319-335. New York; Guilford Press.

Alpert-Gillis, L., Pedro-Carroll, J., & Cowen, E. (1989). The Children of Divorce Intervention Programme Development: Implementation and Evaluation of a Programme for Young Urban Children. *Journal of Consulting and Clinical Psychology*, 57(5), 583-589.

Aminabhi, Vijayalaxmi A. (1996). Effect of Yogic Practice on Attitudes Toward Yoga and Mental Health of Adults. *Praachi Journal of Psycho-Cultural Dimensions*, 12 (2), 117-120.

Andrews, D. A. and Bonta, J. (1994). *Psychology of Criminal Conduct*. Anderson Publishing.

Arenander, A.T .(2000). *Can you Inoculate Your School Against Violence?* Learning and the Brain-Conference III. Boston, MA: Public Information Resources, Inc.

Arenander, A.T. (1996). Global Neural Ground State: *Coherent Brain Mechanisms Associated with Transcendental Consciousness. Toward a Science of Consciousness*. Tucson, AZ.

Baer, J. (1976). *How to Be An Assertive (Not Aggressive) Woman in Life, in Love, and on the Job: A Total Guide to Self-assertiveness*. New York: New American Library.

Baer, R.A., & Nietzel, M.T. (1991). Cognitive and Behavioural Treatment of Impulsivity in Children: A Meta-analytic review of the outcome Literature. *Journal of Clinical Child Psychology*, 20, 400-412.

Bank, L., Marlowe, J.H., Reid, J.B., Patterson, G.R., & Weinrott, M.R. (1991). A Comparative Evaluation of Parent-training in Interventions for Families of Chronic Delinquents. *Journal of Abnormal Child Psychology*, 19, 15-33.

Barlow J., & Stewart-Brown. S. (2000). Behaviour Problems and Group-based Parent Education Programmes. *J Dev Behav Paediatr* 2000; 21: 356-370. <PubMed>

Barlow, D.H. (1997). Cognitive-behaviour Therapy for Panic Disorder: Current Status. *Journal of Clinical Psychiatry*, 58(suppl. 2), 32-37.

Basta J.M., & Davidson, W.S. (1988) Treatment of Juvenile Offenders: Study Outcome Since 1980. *Behavioural Science and Law*, 6(3): 355-384.

Bostic, M. (1994). *Juvenile Crime Prevention Strategies: A Law Enforcement Perspective*. Paper Presented at the Council of State Governments Conference on School Violence. Westlake Village, CA.

Brestan, E.V., & Eyberg, S.M. (1998). Effective Psychosocial Treatments of Conduct-disordered Children and Adolescents: 29 years, 82 Studies, and 5,272 kids. *Journal of Clinical Child Psychology*, 27, 180-189.

Camp, B.W., Blom, G.E., Herbert, F., & Van Doorninck, W.J. (1977). 'Think Aloud': A Programme for Developing Self- control in Young Aggressive Boys. *Journal of Abnormal Child Psychology*, 5, 157-169.

Carlson, C.L., Pelham, W.E. Jr., Milich, R., & Dixon, J. (1992). Single and Combined Effects of Methylphenidate and Behaviour Therapy on the Classroom Performance of Children with Attention-deficit Hyperactivity Disorder. *Journal of Abnormal Child Psychology*, 20, 213-232.

Carolyn Webster-Stratton, Commentary: Nipping Conduct Problems in the Bud. *Bmj.com Scott et al. 323 (7306)*: 194. Retrieved 24th of July 2002.

Carta, J. J., Greenwood, C. R., Dinwiddie, G., Kohler, F., & Delquadri, J. (1987). *The Juniper Gardens Classwide Peer Tutoring Programmes for Spelling, Reading, and Math: Teacher's Manual*. The Juniper Gardens Children's Project, Bureau of Child Research, University of Kansas.

Collingwood, T. R. & Genthner, R. W. (1980). Skills Training as a Treatment for Juvenile Delinquents. *Professional Psychology*, 11, 591-598.

Collins, Andrew W., Maccoby, Eleanor, E., Steinberg, Laurence., Hetherington, Mavis E., & Bornstein, Marc H. (2000). Contemporary Research on Parenting. *American Psychologist*, 55(2), 218-232.

Delors, Jacques, et al. (1996). *Learning: The Treasure Within, Report to UNESCO of the International Commission on Education for the Twenty-first Century*. UNESCO Publishing.

Dishion, T.J., & Patterson, G.R. (1992). Age Effects in Parent Training Outcomes. *Behaviour Therapy*, 23, 719-729.

Dishion, T.J., Patterson, G.R., & Kavanagh, K.A. (1992). An Experimental Test of the Coercion Model: Linking Theory, Measurement, and Intervention. In J. McCord & R.E. Tremblay (Eds.), *Preventing Antisocial Behaviour* (pp. 235-282). New York: Guilford.

Dodge, K.A., & Frame, C.L. (1982). Social Cognitive Biases and Deficits in Aggressive Boys. *Child Developmant*, 53:620-635.

Durlak, J.A., Fuhrman, T. & Lampman, C. (1991). Effectiveness of Cognitive-behavioural Therapy for Maladapting Children: A Meta-Analysis. *Psychological Bulletin*, 110, 204-214.

Ellis, A. (1979). *New Developments in Rational Emotive Therapy*. Pacific Grove, CA: Brooks/Cole.

Ellis, A. (1999). *Reason and Emotion in Psychotherapy: A Comprehensive Method for Treating Human Disturbances* (Revised Edition). Secaucus, NJ: Citadel.

Ellis, A., & Dryden, W. (1998). *The Price of Rational Emotive Behaviour Therapy*. New York: Free Association.

Embry DD. (2002). The Good Behaviour Game: A Best Practice Candidate as a Universal Behavioural Vaccine. (Review). *Clinical Child and Family Psychology Review*, 5(4): 273-297.

Eron, L. D., & Slaby, R. G. (1994). Introduction. In L. D. Eron, J. H. Gentry, & P. Schlegel (Eds.), *Reason to Hope: A Psychosocial Perspective on Violence and Youth* (pp. 1-22). Washington.

Farrington, D.P. (1993). Understanding and Preventing Bullying. In M. Tonry & N. Morris (Eds.), *Crime and Justice*, 17, 381-458. Chicago: University of Chicago Press.

Farrington, D.P. (2002), Developmental Criminology and Risk-focussed Prevention', in M.Maguire, R. Morgan, & R. Reiner (Eds.), *The Oxford Handbook of Criminology* (3rd Edn), Clarendon Press, Oxford.

Feldman, R.A., Caplinger, T.E., & Wodarski, J.S. (1983). The St. Louis Conundrum: The Effective Treatment of Antisocial Youths. Engglwood Cliffs, NJ; Prentice Hall.

Flavell, J. (1976). Metacognitive Aspects of Problem-solving. In L. Resnick (Ed.), *The Nature of Intelligence*. Hillsdale, NJ: Erlbaum Assoc.

Frederico, M., & Davis, C. (1996). Gatekeeper Training and Youth Suicide Prevention. Report to the Commonwealth Department of Health and Family Services, p 42.

Froggatt, Wayne. (1993). *Choose to be Happy: Your Step-by-step Guide*. HarperCollins, Auckland, 1993.

Froggatt, Wayne. (1997). *GoodStress: The Life That Can Be Yours*. HarperCollins, Auckland.

Geen, R. G. (1990). *Human Aggression*. Pacific Grove, CA: Brooks/Cole.

Gibbs, J. C., Potter, G. B, & Goldstein, A. P. (1995). *The EQUIP Programme: Teaching Youth How to Think and Act Responsibly Through a Peer-Helping Approach*. Champaign, IL: Research Press.

Goldstein, A. P., & Glick, B. (1987). *Aggression Replacement Training: A Comprehensive Intervention for Aggressive Youth*. Champaign, IL: Research Press.

Greenwood, P.W., Model., K.E., Rydell, C.P., & Chiesa, J.R. (1998). Diverting Children from a Life of Crime: Measuring Costs and Benefits, Online *http://www.rand.org/publications/MR/MR699/*

Harrell, A., Cavanagh, S., & Sridharan, S. (1999). *Evaluation of the Children at Risk Programme: Results 1 Year After the End of the Programme*. Washington, DC: National Institute of Justice.

Harrell, J.S., Gansky, S.A. et al. (1997). Leisure Time Activities of Elementary School Children. *Nursing Research,* Sep-Oct; 46(5): 246-53.

Hazel, J. S., Schumaker, J. B., Sherman, J. A., & Sheldon-Wildgen, J. (1981). *ASSET: A Social Skills Programme for Adolescents*. Champaign, Il: Research Press.

Homel, R., Cashmore, J., Gilmore, L., Goodnow, J., Hayes, A., Lawrence, J., Leech, M., O'Connor, I., Vinson, T., Najman, J., & Western, J. (1999). *Pathways to Prevention: Early Intervention and Development Approaches to Crime in Australia*, Attorney-General's Department, National Crime Prevention, Canberra.

Huey, W. C., & Rank, R. C. (1984). Effects of Counsellor and Peer-led Groups' Assertive Training on Black Adolescent Aggression. *Journal of Counselling Psychology*, 31, 95-98.

Ialongo, N.S., Werthamer, L., Kellam, S.G. Brown, C.H., Wang, S., & Lin, Y. (1999). Proximal Impact of Two First-grade Preventive Interventions on the Early Risk Behaviours for Later Substance Abuse, Depression, and Antisocial Behaviour. *American Journal of Community Psychology*, 27, 599-641.

Jevning, R., R.K. Wallace, & M. Biedebach. (1992). The Physiology of Meditation: A Review. A Wakeful Hypometabolic Integrated Response. *Neuroscience and Biobehavioural Reviews*, 16:. 415-424.

Jhansi, Rani N., & Krishna Rao, P. V. (1996). Meditation and Attention Regulation. *Journal of Indian Psychology*, 14(1&2), 26-30.

Jin, Putia. (1992). Efficacy of Tai Chi, Brisk Walking, Meditation, and Reading in Reducing Mental and Emotional Stress. *Journal of Psychosomatic Research*, 36(4), 361-370.

Johnson, K. R., & Layng, T. V. (1994). The Morning Side Model of Generative Instruction. In R. Gardner III, D. M. Sainato, J. O. Cooper, T. E. Heron, W. L. Heward, J. W. Eshelman, & T. A. Grassi (Eds.). *Behaviour Analysis in Education: Focus on Measurably Superior Instruction* (pp. 173-197). Pacific Grove, CA: Brooks/Cole.

Jones, C.H., et al. (2001). Attacking Crime at its Source: Consciousness-Based Education in the Prevention of Violence and Antisocial Behaviour. *Journal of Offender Rehabilitation*.

Juvenile Crime-Outlook for California. (1995). Legislative Analyst's Office, State of California, May.

Kazdin, A. E. (1991). Effectiveness of Psychotherapy with Children and Adolescents. *Journal of Consulting and Clinical Psychology*, 59, 785-798.

Kazdin, A.E. (1993). Treatment of Conduct Disorder: Progress and Directions in Psychotherapy Research. *Development and Psychotherapy*, 5, 277-310.

Kazdin A.E. (1995). *Conduct Disorders in Childhood and Adolescence*. London: Sage.

Kazdin, A.E. (1996). Combined and Multimodal Treatments in Child and Adolescent Psychotherapy: Issues, Challenges and Research Directions. *Clinical Psychology: Science and Practice*, 3 (1), 69-100.

Kazdin A.E. (1997). Parent Management Training: Evidence, Outcomes, and Issues. *Journal of American Academy of Child and Adolescent Psychiatry*, 36: 10-18

Kazdin, A.E. (1997b) Practioner Review: Psychosocial Treatments for Conduct Disorder in Children. *Journal of Child Psychology and Psychiatry*, 38(2), 161-187.

Kazdin, A.E., Siegel, T.C., & Bass, D. (1990). Drawing Upon Clinical Practice to Inform Research on Child and Adolescent Psychotherapy: A Survey of Practitioners. *Professional Psychology; Research and Practice*, 21, 189-198.

Kefford, R.E. (1997) The School as Family. A New Metaphor for the New Millennium. *The Practising Administrator*, 4, 31-44.

Klassen, A., Miller, A., Raina, P., Lee, S.K., & Olsen, L. (1999). Attention-deficit Hyperactivity Disorder in Children and Youth: A Quantitative Systematic Review of the Efficacy of Different Management Strategies. *Canadian Journal of Psychiatry*, 44, 1007-1016.

La Greca, A. M., & Santogrossi, D. A. (1980). Social Skills Training with Elementary School Students: A Behavioural Group Approach. *Journal of Consulting and Clinical Psychology*, 48, 220-227.

Ladd, Gary W., & Troop-Gordon, Wendy (2003). The Role of Chronic Peer Difficulties in the Development of Children's Psychological Adjustment Problems. *Child Development*, 74 (5), 1344-1367.

Lane, P. S., & McWhirter, J. J. (1992). A Peer Mediation Model: Conflict Resolution for Elementary and Middle School Children. *Elementary School Guidance & Counselling*, 27, 15-21.

Leeman, L.W., Gibbs, J.C., & Fuller, D. (1993) Evaluation of Multicomponent Group Treatment Programme for Juvenile Delinquents. *Aggressive Behaviour*, 19, 281-292.

Lipman, M. (1994). *Caring Thinking.* Paper Presented to the Sixth International Conference on Thinking, Massachusetts Int. of Tech., Boston MA.

Lipsitt, L. P. (Ed.). (1990). Violence and Aggression in Adolescence. *The Brown University Child Behaviour and Development Letter*, 1-6 January.

Lochman, J.E. (1990).. Modification of Childhood Aggression. In: Hersen M, Eisler RM, Miller, P.M. (Eds.), *Progress in Behaviour Modification*, 25, 47-85. Thousand Oaks, CA: Sage Publications.

Lochman, J. E., White, K. J., & Wayland, K. K. (1991). Cognitive-Behavioural Assessment and Treatment with Aggressive Children. In P. C. Kendall (Ed.), *Child and Adolescent Therapy: Cognitive-Behavioural Procedures.* New York: Guilford Press.

Lochman, J.E., & Dodge, K.A. (1994). Social-cognitive Processes of Severely Violent, Moderately Aggressive, and Non-aggressive Boys. *Journal of Consulting and Clinical Psychology*, 62, 366-374.

Lochman, J.E., Burch, P.R., Curry, J.F., & Lampron, L.B. (1984). Treatment and Generalization Effects of Cognitive behavioural and Goal Setting Interventions with Aggressive Boys. *Journal of Consulting and Clinical Psychology,* 52(5), 915-916.

Loraine Thompson. (1994). One Incident if Too Many: Policy Guidelines for Safe Schools, SSTA Research Report # 94-05: 64 Pages Available Online: *http://www.ssts.sk.ca/research/school_im...94-05.ht.* Retrieved 27th July, 2002.

Lyons, L.C., & Woods, P.J. (1991). The Efficacy of Rational-emotive Therapy: A Quantitative Review of the Outcome Research. *Clinical Psychology Review*, 11, 357-369.

Maheady, L., & Sainato, D. (1985). The Effects of Peer Tutoring upon the Social Status and Social Interaction Patterns of High and Low Status Elementary Students. *Education and Treatment of Children*, 8, 51-65.

Manlove, D. C., & Elliott, P. (1979). Absent Teachers. Another Handicap for Students? *The Practitioner*, 5, 2-3.

Maultsby, M.C., & Ellis, A. (1974). *Technique For Using Rational-Emotive Imagery*. Institute For Rational Living, New York,.

Mayer, G. R. (1995). Preventing Antisocial Behaviour in the Schools. *Journal of Applied Behaviour Analysis*, 28, 467-478.

Mayer, G. R., & Sulzer-Azaroff, B. (1991). Interventions for Vandalism. In G. Stoner, M. K. Shinn, & H. M. Walker (Eds.), *Interventions for Achievement and Behaviour Problems*. Washington, DC: National Association of School Psychologists Monograph.

Mayer, G. R., (1996). Conducting a Functional Assessment and Its Relevance to Intervention. *California School Psychologist*, 1, 29-34.

Mayer, G. R., Butterworth, T., Komoto, T., & Benoit, R. (1983a). The Influence of the School Principal on the Consultant's Effectiveness. *Elementary School Guidance & Counselling*, 17, 274-279.

Mayer, G. R., Butterworth, T., Nafpaktitis, M., & Sulzer-Azaroff, B. (1983b). Preventing School Vandalism and Improving Discipline: A Three-year Study. *Journal of Applied Behaviour Analysis*, 16, 355-369.

Mayer, G. R., Butterworth, T., Spaulding, H. L., Hollingsworth, P., Amorim, M., Caldwell-McElroy, C., Nafpaktitis, M., & Perez-Osorio, X. (1983c). *Constructive Discipline: Building a Climate for Learning. A Resource Manual of Programmes and Strategies*. Downey, CA: Office of the Los Angeles County Superintendent of Schools.

Mayer, G. R., Nafpaktitis, M., Butterworth, T., & Hollingsworth, P. (1987). A Search for the Elusive Setting Events of School Vandalism: A Correlational Study. *Education and Treatment of Children*, 10, 259-270.

Mayer, G.R., & Sulzer-Azaroff, B. (1990). Interventions for Vandalism. In G. Stoner, M. R. Shinn, & H. M. Walker (Eds.), *Interventions for Achievement and Behaviour Problems* (pp.559-580) [Monograph]. Washington, DC: National Association of School Psychologists.

McGuire, J. (2001). Property Offenders. In C.R. Hollin (Ed.), *Handbook of Offender Assessment and Treatment*. Chichester: John Wiley & Sons.

McMahon, R.J. (2000). Parent Training. In: Russ SW, Ollendick TH, (Eds.), *Handbook of Psychotherapies with Children and Families*. New York: Plenum Publishers.

Munk, D. D., & Repp, A. C. (1994). The Relationship Between Instructional Variables and Problem Behaviour: A Review. *Exceptional Children*, 60, 390-401.

Novaco, R.W. (1979). The Cognitive Regulation of Anger and Stress. In P.C. Kendall & S./D. Hollon (Eds.), *Cognitive-behavioural Interventions: Theory, Research and Procedures* (pp.241-285). New York: Academic Press.

Oden, S., & Asher, S. R. (1977). Coaching Children in Social Skills for Friendship Making. *Child Development*, 48, 495-506.

Olweus D. (1994). Bullying at School: Basic Facts and Effects of a School Based Intervention Programme. *Journal of Child Psychology and Psychiatry*, 7, 1171-90.

Patterson, G.R. (1982). Coercive Family Process. In: Patterson, G.R., & Reid, J.B. (Eds.), *A Social Learning Approach to Family Intervention*. Vol 3. Eugene, Oregon: Castalia Publishing.

Patterson, G., Reid, J., & Dishion T. (1992). *Antisocial Boys: A Social Interactional Approach*. Eugene, OR; Castalia Publishing.

Patterson, G.R. (1992). Development Changes in Antisocial Behavioural. In R.D. Peters, R.J. McMahon, & V.L. Quinsey (Eds.), *Aggression and Violence Throughout the Life Span*. Newbury Park, CA: Sage.

Patterson, G.R., Chamberlain, P., & Reid, J.B. (1982). A Comparative Evaluation of a Parent Training Programme. *Behaviour Therapy*, 13, 638-650.

Pelham Jr., W.E., Wheeler, T. and Chronis, A. (1998). Empirically Supported Psychosocial Treatments for Attention Deficit Hyperactivity Disorder. *Journal of Clinical Child Psychology*, 27, 190-205.

Pisterman, S., Firestone, P., Mc Grath, P. et al. (1992). Outcome of Parent Training in the Therapy of Preschooler with ADHD. *American. Journal of Orthopsychiatry*, 62: 397-408

Polirstok, S. R., & Greer, R. D. (1986). A Replication of Collateral Effects and a Component Analysis of a Successful Tutoring Package for Inner-city Adolescents. *Education and Treatment of Children*, 9, 101-121.

Rae-Grant, N. (1991). Primary Prevention. In M. Lewis (Ed.), Child and Adolescent Psychiatry: *A Comprehensive Textbook*,918-929. Baltimore: Williams & Wilkins.

Reid, J. (1993). Prevention of Conduct Disorder Before and After School Entry: Relating Interventions to Developmental Findings. *Development and Psychopathology*, 5 (1/2): 243-262.

Ross, R.R., & Ross, B.D. (1988). *Delinquency Prevention Through Cognitive Training*. New Education, 10, 70-75.

Rubin, K.H., Bream, L.A., & Rose-Krasnor, L. (1991). Social Problem Solving and Aggression in Childhood. In D.J. Pepler & K.H. Rubin (Eds.), *The Development and Treatment of Childhood Aggression*, (219-248). Hillsdale, NJ: Lawrence Erlbaum.

Sanders M. (1996). New Directions in Behavioural Family Intervention with Children. In: Ollendick T, Prinz, R, (Eds.), *Advances in Clinical Child Psychology*, 283-330. New York: Plenum Press.

Schrumpt, F., Crawford, D., & Usadel, H. C. (1991). *Peer Mediation: Conflict Resolution in Schools*. Champaign, IL: Research Press.

Scott, S., Spender, Q,, Doolan, M., Jacobs, B., & Aspland, H.(2001). Multicentre Controlled Trial of Parenting Groups for Childhood Antisocial Behaviour in Clinical Practice. *BMJ*, 323: 194-198.

Selvamurthy, W. (1993). *Yoga and Stress Management: Physiological Perspectives. Proceedings of the Indian Science Congress*, Part IV, 169.

Sherman, D.K., Iacono, W.G., & McGue, M.K. (1997). Attention-deficit Hyperactivity Dimensions: A Twin Study of Inattention and Impulsivity-hyperactivity. *Journal of the American Academy of Child and Adolescent Psychiatry*, 36, 745-53.

Shirk, S.R. (Ed). (1988). *Cognitive Development and Child Psychotherapy*. New York: Plenum.

Shyamala, V. (2004). *Effectiveness of Certain Strategies to Overcome Antisocial Behaviour Among High School Students*. Ph.D Thesis, Alagappa University, Karaikudi.

Smith, P.K., & Sharp, S. (1994). *School Bullying; Insights and Perspectives*. London: Routledge.

Spivack, G., & Shure, M.B. (1982). The Cognition of Social Adjustment: Interpersonal Problem Solving Thinking. In B.B. Lahey & A.E. Kazdin (Eds.). *Advances in Clinical Child Psychology*, 5, 323-372, New York: Plenum

Spivack, G., Platt, J.J., & Shure, M.B. (1976). *The Problem-solving Approach to Adjustment*. San Francisco: Jossey-Bass.

Steinberg, Laurence, & Levine, Ann. (1997). *You and Your Adolescent: A Parent's Guide for Ages 10-20*. New York: HarperCollins. (ERIC Document No. ED408108).

Steinberg, Laurence. (1996). *Beyond the Classroom: Why School Reform has Failed and What Parents Need to Do*. New York: Simon & Schuster. (ERIC Document No. ED398346)

Steinhauer, P.D. (1996). *Developing Resiliency in Children from Disadvantaged Populations, What Determines Health*? Ottawa: National Forum on Health.

Studer, J. (1996). Understanding and Preventing Aggressive Responses in Youth. *Elementary School Guidance & Counselling*, 30 (3), 194-203.

Sulzer-Azaroff, B., & Mayer, G. R. (1994). *Achieving Educational Excellence*. San Marcos, CA: Western Image.

Sulzer-Azaroff, B., & Mayer, G.R. (1991). *Behaviour Analysis for Lasting Change*. Fort Worth: Harcourt, Brace & Javanovich.

Taylor TK, Biglan A.(1998). Behavioural Family Interventions for Improving Child-rearing: A Review of the Literature for Clinicians and Policy Makers. *Clinical Child and Family Psychological Review*, 1 41-60. <PubMed>

Tierney, J., Dowd, T., & O'Kane, S. (1993). Empowering Aggressive Youth to Change. *Journal of Emotional Behavioural Problems*, 2(1), 41-45.

Tobler, N. et al. (2000). School-based Adolescent Drug Prevention Programmes: A 1998 Meta-Analysis , *Journal of Primary Prevention*, 20, 4.

Tremblay, R. E., Masse, L. C., Pagani, L., & Vitaro, F. (1996). From Childhood Aggression to Adolescent Maladjustment: The Montreal Prevention Experiment. In. R. Dev. Peters & R. J. McMahon (Eds.). *Preventing Childhood Disorders, Substance Abuse and Delinquency*, 268-298. Thousand Oaks, CA: Sage.

Tremblay, R.E.& Craig, W.M. (1995). Developmental Crime Prevention, in Tremblay, R.E., Masse, L.C., Vitaro, F., & Dobkin, P.L. The Impact of Friends' Deviant Behaviour on Early Onset of Delinquency: Longitudinal Data from 6 to 13 years of Age. *Development and Psychopathology*, 7, 649-67.

Walker, H., Colvin, G., & Ramsey, E. (1995). *Antisocial Behaviour in School: Strategies and Best Practices*. Pacific Grove, CA: Brooks/ Cole.

Walker, H.M., Horner, R.H., Sugai, G., Bullis, M., Sprague, J.R., Bricker, D., & Kaufman, M.J. (1996) Integrated Approaches to Preventing Antisocial Behaviour Patterns Among School Age Children and Youth. *Journal of Emotional and Behavioural Disorders*, 4(4), 194-209.

Walker, Hill M., & Sprague, J. (1999). The Path to School Failure, Delinquency and Violence: Casual Factors and Some Potential Solutions. *Intervention in School and Clinic*, January.

Walker, Hill M., Homer, Robert, Sugai, George, Bullis, Michael, Sprague, Jeffrey R., Bricker, Diane, & Kaufman, Martin J. (1996). Integrated Approaches to Preventing Antisocial Behaviour Patterns Among School-Age Children and Youth. *Journal of Emotional and Behavioural Disorders*, 4.4 ;194-204, October.

Wallace, R.K. (1993). *The Physiology of Consciousness*. Fairfield, Iowa: Maharishi International University Press.

Wasserman, A., Miller, S., & Cothern, L. (2000.) Prevention of Sericus and Violent Juvenile Offending. *Juvenile Justice Bulletin*, April.

Wasserman, G.A., & Miller, L.S. (1998). The Prevention of Serious and Violent Juvenile Offending. In R. Loeber and D.P. Farrington (Eds.), *Serious and Violent Juvenile Offenders: Risk Factors and Successful Interventions*. Thousand Oaks, CA: Sage Publications, Inc., pp. 197-247.

Watson, Bruce, & Richard Kopnicek. (1990). Teaching for Conceptual Change: Confronting Children's Experience, Phi Delta Kappan, 680-684, May. Retrieved March 13, 2002 from *http://www.astc.org/resource/educator/teachcon.htm*.

Watson, D. L., & Tharp, R. G., (1993). *Self-directed Behaviour: Self Modification for Personal Adjustment* (6th Ed.). Pacific Grove, CA: Brooks/Cole.

Webster-Stratton, C.,& Taylor, T.K. (1998). Adopting and Implementing Empirically Supported Interventions: A Recipe for Success. In: Buchanan, A., & Hudson, B.L., (Eds.), *Parenting, Schooling and Children's Behaviour*. Aldershot, UK: Ashgate.

Webster-Stratton, C., & Hummond, M. (1997). Treating Children with Early-onset Conduct Problems: A Comparison of Child and Parent Training Interventions. *Journal of Consulting and Clinical Psychology*, 65, 93-109.

Zimmerman, J. D. (1983). Psychologists' Multiple Roles in Television Broadcasting. *Professional Psychology Research and Practice*, 14(2), 256-269, April.

Index

F

N

O

P